Fighting Scholars

Key Issues in Modern Sociology

Anthem's **Key Issues in Modern Sociology** series publishes scholarly texts by leading social theorists that give an accessible exposition of the major structural changes in modern societies. These volumes address an academic audience through their relevance and scholarly quality, and connect sociological thought to public issues. The series covers both substantive and theoretical topics, as well as addressing the works of major modern sociologists. The series emphasis is on modern developments in sociology with relevance to contemporary issues such as globalization, warfare, citizenship, human rights, environmental crises, demographic change, religion, postsecularism and civil conflict.

Series Editor

Bryan S. Turner – City University of New York, USA
& Australian Catholic University, Australia

Editorial Board

Thomas Cushman – Wellesley College, USA
Rob Stones – University of Western Sydney, Australia
Richard Swedberg – Cornell University, USA
Stephen Turner – University of South Florida, USA
Darin Weinberg – University of Cambridge, UK

Fighting Scholars

Habitus and Ethnographies of Martial Arts and Combat Sports

Edited by
Raúl Sánchez García
and Dale C. Spencer

ANTHEM PRESS
LONDON · NEW YORK · DELHI

Anthem Press
An imprint of Wimbledon Publishing Company
www.anthempress.com

This edition first published in UK and USA 2014
by ANTHEM PRESS
75–76 Blackfriars Road, London SE1 8HA, UK
or PO Box 9779, London SW19 7ZG, UK
and
244 Madison Ave #116, New York, NY 10016, USA

First published in hardback by Anthem Press in 2013

© 2014 Raúl Sánchez García and Dale C. Spencer editorial matter and selection;
individual chapters © individual contributors

The moral right of the authors has been asserted.

All rights reserved. Without limiting the rights under copyright reserved above,
no part of this publication may be reproduced, stored or introduced into
a retrieval system, or transmitted, in any form or by any means
(electronic, mechanical, photocopying, recording or otherwise),
without the prior written permission of both the copyright
owner and the above publisher of this book.

British Library Cataloguing-in-Publication Data
A catalogue record for this book is available from the British Library.

Library of Congress Cataloging-in-Publication Data
The Library of Congress has catalogued the hardcover edition as follows:
Fighting scholars : habitus and ethnographies of martial arts and
combat sports / edited by Raúl Sánchez García and Dale C. Spencer.
 pages cm. – (Key issues in modern sociology)
 Includes bibliographical references.
 ISBN 978-0-85728-332-0 (hardcover : alk. paper)
 1. Martial arts–Anthropological aspects. I. Sánchez García, Raúl,
editor of compilation. II. Spencer, Dale C., editor of compilation.
 GV1102.7.A56F54 2013
 796.815–dc23
 2013021056

ISBN-13: 978 1 78308 346 6 (Pbk)
ISBN-10: 1 78308 346 8 (Pbk)

Cover image idea by Néstor Revuelta Zarzosa

This title is also available as an ebook.

Dedicated to a lost fighter,
Michael D. Manson

Practical knowledge is very unequally demanded and necessary, but also very unequally adequate and adapted, depending in the situation and the realm of activity. In contrast to the scholastic universes, some universes, such as those of sport, music or dance, demand a practical engagement of the body and therefore a mobilization of the corporeal 'intelligence' capable of transforming, even inverting, the ordinary hierarchies. And one would need to collect methodically all the notes and observations which, dispersed here and there, especially in the didactics of these physical skills – sports, obviously, and more especially the martial arts, but also theatrical activities and the playing of musical instruments – would provide precious contributions to a science of this form of knowledge.

—Pierre Bourdieu, *Pascalian Meditations*

CONTENTS

Contributors   ix

Glossary   xiii

Chapter 1. Introduction: Carnal Ethnography as Path to Embodied Knowledge
Raúl Sánchez García and Dale C. Spencer   1

Chapter 2. Habitus as Topic and Tool: Reflections on Becoming a Prizefighter
Loïc Wacquant   19

Chapter 3. In Search of a Martial Habitus: Identifying Core Dispositions in Wing Chun and Taijiquan
David Brown and George Jennings   33

Chapter 4. Each More Agile Than the Other: Mental and Physical Enculturation in *Capoeira Regional*
Sara Delamont and Neil Stephens   49

Chapter 5. 'There Is No Try in Tae Kwon Do': Reflexive Body Techniques in Action
Elizabeth Graham   63

Chapter 6. 'It Is About Your Body Recognizing the Move and Automatically Doing It': Merleau-Ponty, Habit and Brazilian Jiu-Jitsu
Bryan Hogeveen   79

Chapter 7. 'Do You Hit Girls?': Some Striking Moments in the Career of a Male Martial Artist
Alex Channon   95

Chapter 8. The Teacher's Blessing and the Withheld Hand: Two Vignettes of Somatic Learning in South India's Indigenous Martial Art Kalarippayattu
Sara K. Schneider   111

Chapter 9.	White Men Don't Flow: Embodied Aesthetics of the Fifty-Two Hand Blocks *Thomas Green*	125
Chapter 10.	Japanese Religions and Kyudo (Japanese Archery): An Anthropological Perspective *Einat Bar-On Cohen*	141
Chapter 11.	Taming the Habitus: The Gym and the Dojo as 'Civilizing Workshops' *Raúl Sánchez García*	155
Chapter 12.	'Authenticity', Muay Thai and Habitus *Dale C. Spencer*	171
Chapter 13.	Conclusion: Present and Future Lines of Research *Raúl Sánchez García and Dale C. Spencer*	185
Epilogue	*Homines in Extremis*: What Fighting Scholars Teach Us about Habitus *Loïc Wacquant*	193
References		201

CONTRIBUTORS

Einat Bar-On Cohen is an anthropologist at the Hebrew University of Jerusalem. She studied the cosmology of Japanese martial arts and their globalization, and conducted a comprehensive study on the instruction of Israeli close-combat (krav maga) in private schools and in the Israeli Defense Forces, as sites where the social somatic understanding of nationality, bureaucracy and violence are formed. She has published articles concerning the intensely somatic practice of martial arts and its capability to form social realities dealing with the potentialities of violence, undoing or reiterating social categories, while drawing heavily on the work of Deleuze and Guattari. Currently she is writing a book about kyudo, Japanese archery.

David Brown is a senior lecturer in sociocultural studies with the School of Sport, UWIC, Cardiff. His research interests include exploring embodied sociological theory through the empirical qualitative study of physical culture, including Eastern movement forms, surfing and physical education.

Alex Channon is lecturer of physical education and sport in the Department of Secondary Education at the University of Greenwich. His research project is concerned with mixed-sex martial arts and the subversion of gender, and has been conducted over the past three years using qualitative methods among several different martial arts clubs drawn from around the English East Midlands. As a martial artist, Alex has trained in freestyle kick-boxing (two years) and Shaolin kung fu (five years), in which he holds a first-degree black belt.

Sara Delamont graduated from Girton College Cambridge in 1968 with a first in social anthropology. She did a PhD at Edinburgh. Dr Delamont lectured at the School of Education at Leicester from 1973–76. She came to Cardiff in 1976, was promoted to Senior Lecturer in 1979 and Reader in 1989. She has been Dean of Social Sciences, and served on Senate, Council and Court. Her research on 'The Habitus of Diasporic Capoeira: An Ethnography' began in 2003 and focuses on how the Brazilian dance–fight–game is taught and learnt in the UK. It is affiliated to Qualiti, and is being conducted with Dr Neil Stephens of Cesagen. It contains classic ethnography with a theoretical focus on the area of habits and empirical interests in teaching, enculturation, learning, Brazil and embodiment. Her other current project is 'Teaching Savate: An Exploratory Ethnography', which began in 2009. Savate is a French martial art, and contrasts in sociologically interesting ways with capoeira.

Elizabeth Graham is assistant professor of sociology and gender and women's studies at Brandon University. She received her PhD from McMaster University.

Her background is in the areas of women's health, feminism, symbolic interactionism, and qualitative research methods. In recent years, Elizabeth's substantive interest has moved into the area of the individual's sense of self and experience. Related to this area, she has an ongoing research project on adult participation in tae kwon do. In addition, she is a co-investigator for a project examining students' expectations and experiences of graduate supervision.

Thomas A. Green is associate professor in the Department of Anthropology, Texas A&M University. He has practised martial arts for over 35 years, primarily focusing on Chinese, Japanese and Southeast Asian systems. His books include *Martial Arts of the World: An Encyclopedia* (2001), *Martial Arts in the Modern World* (2003) and *Martial Arts of the World: An Encyclopedia of History and Innovation* (2010). Recent publications explore African, African American and Chinese vernacular martial arts. His research focuses on traditional games and sports, expressive culture and symbolic anthropology.

Bryan Hogeveen is associate professor of sociology at the University of Alberta. He is co-author (along with Joanne Minaker) of *Youth, Crime and Society: Issues of Power and Justice* (2009). He has published widely on his academic interests, which include: continental philosophy, violence, martial arts in society, the sociology of sport, and justice. His SSHRC-funded research project examines neo-liberalism's impact on the marginalized inner-city residents of Edmonton and Winnipeg. Dr Hogeveen teaches Brazilian jiu-jitsu and submission grappling at the University of Alberta. He is a member of the Edmonton Combative Sport Commission.

George Jennings is a lecturer and researcher at the Universidad YMCA in Mexico City, where he teaches classes on social theory and research methods in physical culture. His research interests lie in the qualitative sociological study of traditionalist physical cultures including non-competitive martial arts, folkloric dance and regional games, and these interests have been integrated with an ongoing project examining an emerging Mexican martial art. George's doctorate followed his long-term training in Chinese martial arts, and he continues to blend the lessons in embodied dispositions from his ethnographic studies with his core martial art, wing chun.

Raúl Sánchez García is associate professor in sociology of sport at the Universidad Europea de Madrid. He has published several papers in international journals, such as the *International Review for the Sociology of Sport*; the *International Journal of the History of Sport*; *Sport, Education and Society*; and the *Journal of Motor Behavior*. His PhD research was based on a four-year ethnographic study of boxing and aikido. He has continued to practise aikido since, currently holding a shodan (1st) rank. He is a research member of the International Society of Eastern Sports and Physical Education, contributing editor of the *Electronic Journal of Martial Arts* and member of the scientific committee of the *Journal of Asian Martial Arts* (Spanish edition). His latest research tries to boost a generative dialogue between social and cognitive sciences, enhancing the concept of habitus through the enactive paradigm.

Sara K. Schneider is a performance anthropologist, professor and author. She directs the Centre for Body Lore and Learning in Chicago, linking public education about global cultures with the professional development of educators, health-care professionals and clergy. She has travelled and conducted field research in Vietnam, Thailand, Indonesia, with the Tibetan exile community in northern India, as well as with practitioners of kalarippayattu, an indigenous martial art in South India. She practises and teaches yoga and meditation in Chicago.

Dale C. Spencer is assistant professor at the University of Manitoba in the Department of Sociology. Prior to his current position, he was a Banting Postdoctoral Fellow at the University of Alberta, Edmonton, Alberta, Canada. He specializes in criminology, violence (in its manifold forms), sociology of sport, gender and body studies. His work can be found in such journals as *Body and Society*, *Criminal Law and Philosophy*, and *Qualitative Research in Sport, Exercise and Health*. He recently published *Ultimate Fighting and Embodiment: Violence, Gender and Mixed Martial Arts* (2011), *Emotions Matter: A Relational Approach to Emotions* (co-edited with K. Walby and A. Hunt, 2012), and *Reimagining Intervention in Young Lives: Work, Social Assistance and Marginalization* (co-authored with K. Foster, 2012). In terms of martial arts experience, he trained muay thai for over four years and has trained Brazilian jiu-jitsu for the last six years.

Neil Stephens is a research associate in the School of Social Sciences at Cardiff University. Primarily a sociologist interested in science and technology studies, he has conducted research on social aspects of stem cell science, biobanking and in-vitro meat at the ESRC Centre for the Economic and Social Aspects of Genomics (Cesagen). This work is published in journals including *Social Studies of Science*, *Social Theory and Health* and *Sociology of Health and Illness*. He practiced Shotokan karate for ten years, attaining a second dan black belt, Capoeira for six years attaining the blue and brown corda, and Nam Pai Chuan Kung Fu attaining a yellow belt. With Sara Delamont, he has published on Capoeira in journals including *Qualitative Inquiry*, *Sociological Review* and *Cultural Sociology*.

Loïc Wacquant is professor of sociology at the University of California, Berkeley, and researcher at the Centre européen de sociologie et de science politique, Paris. A MacArthur Foundation Fellow and recipient of the 2008 Lewis Coser Award of the American Sociological Association, his research spans urban relegation, ethnoracial domination, the penal state, embodiment, and social theory and the politics of reason. His books are translated into 20 languages and include the trilogy *Urban Outcasts: A Comparative Sociology of Advanced Marginality* (2008), *Punishing the Poor: The Neoliberal Government of Social Insecurity* (2009), and *Deadly Symbiosis: Race and the Rise of the Penal State* (2013). His 'carnal anthropology' of prizefighting in the black ghetto of Chicago, reported in *Body and Soul: Notebooks of an Apprentice Boxer* (2004), is the germinal work that has inspired practice-based ethnographic studies of combat sports and martial arts ethnographies since, some of which appear in this volume. For more information, see loicwacquant.net.

GLOSSARY*

Aikido is a modern martial system of Japanese derivation, developed by founder Ueshiba Morihei (1883–1969) over the course of his lifetime. Aikido employs the redirection of an attacker's energy (or *ki*) into a variety of holds, locks and projections, and is probably best known for an exclusive focus on defensive manoeuvres and for its unique martial philosophy. Known as *O sensei*, Morihei was considered a martial genius who developed a personal synthesis of martial traditions (Takeda's daito ryu being his main influence) into what he dubbed aikijutsu, aikibudo and, later on, aikido. The task of his son Kisshomaru was crucial to organize and institutionalize the activity during the second half of the twentieth century. The foundation of the Aikikai in Tokyo acting as international aikido's headquarters was paramount for the expansion of the art worldwide.

Boxing is an ancient martial art combining hand strikes, controlled aggression, evasiveness and bone-crushing force. The term *boxing* derives from the box shape of the closed hand, or fist, which in Latin is *pugnus* (hence the alternative terms *pugilism* and *fisticuffs*). Evolved and systematized into a modern sport in nineteenth-century England from the former pastime known as prizefighting (Queensberry rules dating from 1867), it expanded worldwide, becoming part of the Olympic programme and also a giant professional combat sport.

Brazilian jiu-jitsu is a grappling system that maintains both sport and combat forms. The art was derived from Japanese antecedents in twentieth-century Brazil. The Gracie family has been credited as the main agent in the systematization and expansion of the art. Bounded to *valetudo* bouts in Brazil since the 1930s, it played a paramount part in the development of mixed martial arts (MMA) worldwide during the 1990s – especially in the USA (Ultimate Fighting Championship) and Japan (Pride) – with some of the Gracie members (e.g. Royler and Rickson Gracie) outstanding key players in such process.

Capoeira is a Brazilian martial art that relies primarily on striking techniques, although some grappling manoeuvres, especially takedowns utilizing the legs in either tripping or scissoring motions, and weapon techniques complete the repertoire of the capoeirista (practitioner or 'player' of capoeira). Originally based on African slave dance/martial techniques, it was mainly systematized in twentieth-century Brazil, where Mestre Bimba's Capoeira Regional and Mestre Pastinha's Capoeria Angola were set as the two capoeria main lines. An increasing and fast international expansion has been helped by its dance-like and fitness components, helping to open and popularize the art among the general public.

---

* The definitions appearing in this glossary come primarily from Green (2001).

Fifty-two hand blocks is an African American vernacular martial art (VMA) also known as jailhouse, jailhouse boxing, jailhouse rock, or the 52s. It developed as an underground cluster of fighting techniques in places such as prisons and rough urban areas. At the beginning of the twenty-first century, it became more accessible and public, instruction in the art becoming codified and taught on regular bases even though still not in big numbers.

Kalarippayattu (*kalari*, place of training; *payattu*, exercise) is a compound term first used in the twentieth century to identify the traditional martial art of Kerala State, on the southwest coast of India, dating from at least the twelfth century. The kalari for the training of local fighters is under the guidance of the *gurukkal* (honorific, respectful plural of *guru*) or *asan* (teacher) who also administer a variety of traditional Ayurvedic physical/massage therapies for humorous, muscular and bone problems.

Kickboxing is a modern combination of techniques coming from boxing strikes and kicking techniques – mostly – from karate. The term is related to two different but converging martial art disciplines during the 1970s: full-contact karate in the USA and the blend of kyokushin karate and muay thai in Japan, taking a later development also in Europe (the Netherlands and France being two strongholds). Nowadays kickboxing is closely linked to K-1 phenomenon even though the disciplines still remain differentiated.

Kung fu was originally a Cantonese phrase meaning 'hard work', 'human effort', 'exertion' or 'skill' (*gong* carrying the meaning of 'inner power' in the context of the martial arts), and the term kung fu has been used in the West as a generic term for Chinese martial arts ranging from what have been labelled the 'soft' or 'internal' arts of taijiquan (t'ai chi ch'uan), baguazhang (pa kua ch'uan) and xingyiquan (hsing i ch'uan) to the so-called hard or external arts of northern and southern Shaolin. Nonetheless, the Western usage is still linked to Shaolin Temple arts in a stronger sense and with these forms of Chinese martial arts that are presumed to emphasize striking over grappling techniques.

Kyudo refers to Japanese archery. It is traced to two roots: ceremonial archery associated with Shinto, and combative archery developing from warfare and hunting. Formally organized in a ryuha (school or style) by Henmi Kiyomitsi during the twelfth century, kyudo has been called the earliest martial sport of Japan, as the warrior and noble classes used it for recreational hunting. Kyudo was considered as one of the primary arts of a warrior on the battlefield, highly esteemed and preferred by samurai to the use of firearms in the seventeenth century.

Muay thai or thai boxing is a style of kicking and boxing techniques that comes from Thailand, formerly known as Siam. Known as 'the science of eight weapons', muay thai is a striking art for ring fighting that uses the fists, elbows, knees and feet. Developed in the South East during centuries, it became attached to sport format in the twentieth century, the use of a boxing ring and gloves being normal in current bouts. Ritualized practices such as pre-fight ritual dance (*ram muay*) or fight music (*si muay*) display the traditional and religious content still attached to the activity.

Tae kwon do (Korean: hand-foot way) is a Korean unarmed combat system whose traditional history traces its ancestry back 2,000 years. It is a native Korean fighting art, although in the latter part of the twentieth century it has been influenced by other fighting systems. An Olympic sport since Sydney 2000, tae kwon do has undergone a rapid and solid international expansion usually based upon the sport's competitive format. In its current sport version, tae kwon do techniques are strongly focused on kicking actions, differentiating the activity from other striking martial arts (e.g. karate).

Taijiquan (t'ai chi ch'uan) is a profound and varied Chinese martial art and health regimen with a set of core principles, movements and exercises. From the martial point of view, it can be included within the *neijia* (internal) schools, with smooth and fluid movements based not on muscular strength but internal energy or *qi*. Taijiquan is normally practised as forms or sets performed in a series of connected postures. Also, a certain sparring technique known as push-hands is used, applying the principles learnt in the solo practice. Some schools maintain the traditional approach to the activity, including weapons as part of the curriculum.

Wing chun (*yongchun*, perhaps better known outside Asia by its Cantonese name wing chun) is a Chinese martial art that originated and is still currently centred in southern China, mainly the Hong Kong area. Considered as an external martial art, focused mainly on closer fighting distances, it is classified as a boxing system because of its reliance on striking techniques. It favours the use of direct, economical punching techniques over kicking and its approach is based upon practical self-defence.

Chapter 1

INTRODUCTION: CARNAL ETHNOGRAPHY AS PATH TO EMBODIED KNOWLEDGE*

Raúl Sánchez García and Dale C. Spencer

Within Japanese budo lies the pre-modern concept of *bunbu ryodo*. It refers to the ideal of a double path of development regarding the literary (*bun*) and martial (*bu*) skills of the samurai. Far from being uncontroversial, this kind of ideal was not lived up to in a balanced (or symmetrical) way by very many samurai. Normally, either *bun* ran over *bu* or conversely the *bu* dominated the *bun*. *Fighting Scholars* tries to catch, in a simple expression, the tension involved in this ostensible opposition between practice and ethos. Contributors to this volume emanate from the academe (*bun*) but, for varied reasons, they are also interested in the study of combat activities (*bu*). They are interested not only in the philosophical underpinnings of martial arts, but also in a hands-on, embodied analysis of the craft. They have all been seduced into the practice of martial arts or combat sports and concomitantly apply a social-scientific lens to such practices. This conjoining of thought and practice has been achieved through ethnography. That is also why habitus, best understood through ethnography (see Bourdieu 1977; Crossley 1995; Spencer 2009), is conceptually paramount, as it opens the gates to the promises and perils of what Wacquant calls 'carnal sociology' (Wacquant 2004a xiii; 2005a). The French sociologist defines such an approach as one that:

> seeks to situate itself not outside or above practice but at its 'point of production' [and] requires that we immerse ourselves as deeply and as durably as possible into the cosmos under examination; that we submit ourselves to its specific temporality and contingencies; that we acquire the embodied dispositions it demands and nurtures, so that we may grasp it via the prethetic understanding that defines the native relation to that world – not as one world among many but as 'home'. (Wacquant 2005a, 466)

We think this is one of the main reasons why social scientists should be interested in martial arts and combat sports. Martial arts and combat sports are perspicuous settings to study and develop the project of a carnal sociology with 'habitus', 'body techniques' and 'technologies

---

* The authors thank Ron Langlois and Loïc Wacquant for comments on earlier drafts of this chapter.

of the self' as key points of research. Studying subject matter that is as essential, deep and personal as physical assault (despite the ritualization or codification that one might have suffered) is especially suitable for understanding the social nature of epistemic, affective and moral dimensions of embodied practice. The concept of 'habitus' also serves as an advantageous epistemic point in two different layers. The first is as a point through which to (re)gain an embodied and situated sociological gaze into the social phenomena. Avoiding the supposed superior objectivity of the academic distance, habitus raises an epistemic claim about the greater adequacy of a carnal sociology generating knowledge from within the phenomena under study. The second is as a point through which to explore the relationship between the social and cognitive sciences, establishing a more robust and comprehensive understanding of embodied social practices.

Social sciences will benefit from the study of martial arts and combat sport at least for three more reasons. First, martial arts and combat sports imply an acute sense of the management of violence. This issue is important as a research topic in itself, but also violence remains considered a differential factor in gender terms. Thus, such activities offer a vantage point for observations regarding gender relations and construction. Second, these activities are preferential sites to study ethnicity and 'race' issues as the development of martial arts and combat sports is sociohistorically linked to migration and cultural interchanges. In such cases, the art is considered as a mark of authenticity in diasporic communities or is re-elaborated by the receptive culture on the other side of the globe. Third, martial arts and combat sports can be understood as certain kind of 'secular religion'. Not only the whole ritualistic aspect of the craft, but also the ascetic regimes surrounding some of these practices and even the potential for self-transformation of the individuals should be taken into account from a religious perspective.

Ethnographic research on martial arts has been conducted at least since the 1970s but remains an underdeveloped area receiving only scattered attention. *Fighting Scholars* is the first book-length overview of the ethnographic study of combat sports and martial arts. It is interdisciplinary in scope and contains contributions from leading international figures on martial arts and combat sports. The most innovative features of *Fighting Scholars* are its empirical focus and theoretical orientation. While ethnographic research is a widespread and popular approach within the social sciences, combat sports and martial arts have yet to be sufficiently investigated from an ethnographic standpoint. In addition, the present volume shows how the discussion of different theoretical traditions regarding the 'habitus as a tool to conduct research' is best analysed in combat sports and martial arts in a corporeal fashion: that is, through flesh-and-blood observation within social-carnal activities. *Fighting Scholars* is aligned with the project of developing a carnal sociology motivated and inspired by Loïc Wacquant's ethnographic account of boxing as a body trade in the ghetto of Chicago, reported in *Body and Soul* (2004) and a string of related publications tying together 'the body, the ghetto, and the penal state' (see Wacquant 2009b for an overview). *Body and Soul* is a milestone and model for the study of martial arts and combat sports, not only because of its conceptual precision and empirical depth, but because its author apprenticed as a means of elucidating the production of pugilistic competency. Thus Wacquant deploys and elaborates Bourdieu's pivotal concept twice, first as an object of inquiry and second a means of investigation. Many of the contributions in the present volume spring from, extend, as well as challenge Wacquant's analytic strategy.

As a way of depicting the existing literature on martial arts and combat sports, we have chosen two different lines of development – *bu* over *bun* and *bun* over *bu* – each of them representing a predominant element of the *bun–bu* dichotomy. More attention is paid to *bun* over *bu*, as it is embedded in the scholarly tradition of analysis and offers a more fecund basis for the present volume. We offer the following overview as a way of showing how *Fighting Scholars* fits into and contributes to the extant literature on martial arts and combat sports.

Bu Over *Bun*

Ethnographic research of fighting activities is not a novel endeavour in itself. In fact, there is a long tradition of field studies of the fighting arts. Linked to the field of anthropology, such studies of fighting arts became an academic subfield through the work of Sir Richard Burton, a nineteenth-century English explorer-soldier-academic who travelled throughout Asia and Africa, spoke more than 25 languages and co-founded the Anthropological Society of London. He was also the developer of *hoplology*: the science of human combative behaviour and performance (deriving from the Greek root *hopl*, meaning armed and armoured). Embedded in his travel notebooks and studies of the cultures in which he was living, hoplological field notes were collected but were not translated into a coherent systematic study.

The systematic study of combat behaviour and performance would have to wait until the 1960s, when Donn F. Draeger resumed the task of hoplology. His research centred on the study of Asian fighting arts, specifically Japanese martial-art styles. A former major in the US Marine Corps and class judo contender, Draeger placed the old Japanese martial traditions (*koryu*) under scholarly analysis. Being part of the tradition (for example, *katori shinto ryu*), he engaged in ethnographic field research, encouraging his colleagues to do the same in other martial arts, in order to study and preserve as many traditions as they could. He also expanded his research in several hoplological-oriented trips to countries such as Burma, Cambodia, Thailand and Indonesia.

Draeger founded the International Hoplology Society and started the publication of the journal *Hoplos*. He also tried, with not much success, to establish hoplology as an academic field in its own right.[1] While Draeger's hoplological project never progressed to the point of being an academic subdiscipline, his work has continued outside of academia. The International Hoplology Society remains active, through the work of Hunter B. Armstrong and a group of collaborators who keep alive the analysis of *koryu* and other fighting traditions. A remarkable work that sums up the different characters around and within the field of hoplology can be found in three volumes edited by Diane Skoss: *Koryu Bujutsu* (1997), *Sword and Spirit* (1999) and *Keiko Shokon* (2002). Apart from this kind of scholarly approach to the fighting disciplines, there are also myriad autobiographical works by practitioners recounting their personal journeys into the world of martial arts (for example, Powell 2006; Polly 2007; Lowry 1995, 2005).

Bun Over *Bu*

The second tradition of ethnographic research into the martial arts emerged within academia. Historically parallel to the previous line of literary writing are forms of writing that mirror informal ethnographic traditions. One of the most famous literary antecedents was Jack London. A writer and a boxing aficionado with an adventurous passion for travelling – Burton's twin image – he produced extremely beautiful and interesting descriptions of boxing that, in a certain sense, could be understood as works of ethnographic literature. London's *The Game* (1905), *A Piece of Steak* (1909), *The Mexican* (1911a) and *The Abysmal Brute* (1911b) are fours outstanding examples of such a work.[2] Another acclaimed writer interested in martial arts was the Nobel Prize winner Yukio Mishima. As a process of late awakening to his corporeal self, Mishima eagerly took part in bodybuilding and martial arts (especially kendo) during his forties. In his essay *Sun and Steel* ([1968] 1970), Mishima offers a first-person description of this experience; he also wrote a fictional short story called *Ken* ([1968] 1998) on the practice and ethos of kendo. More recent iterations of the literary form include first-person journalistic accounts of the world of boxing (Matthews 2002; Anasi 2002), mixed martial arts (Sheridan 2007), judo (Law 2008) and aikido (Twigger 1999), which offer insights and qualitative material to understand these martial arts and combat sports.

Beginning in the 1980s, ethnographic research on martial arts and combat sports can be found scattered across social science disciplines. For example, George Girton's (1986) analysis of kung fu from an ethnomethodological perspective serves as a groundbreaking work in this respect. From the point of view of a participant, he offers a basic understanding of the craft embedded in the different 'animal styles' (tiger, crane, monkey etc.) that are part of the kung-fu curriculum. Girton's analysis avoids the disembodied study where values, ideas and structures rule out any chance of reporting the naturally occurring activity between flesh-and-blood human beings. Drawing from the ethnomethodological tradition, he delves into the building of 'members' competency'. As a practitioner of kung fu, Girton acquired a command of the art in order to understand the activities going on around him. Nevertheless, his analysis remains at the level of praxeological analysis of the ethnomethods used by the practitioners and remains silent on the morality embedded in kung fu.

During the late 1980s an ethnographic study on boxing was being carried out that would change and energize the study of martial arts and combat sports, as well as exert a more lasting effect on the general practice of ethnography. The embodied, practical know-how of the craft that Girton utilized was applied in another sociological tradition, with fruitful results and consequences. Here we are referring to Loïc Wacquant's (1995a, 1995b, 1995c, 2004d, 2005c) pioneering work on boxing, reported in a string of essays leading to the book *Body and Soul* (2004a). Wacquant's work revolutionized urban ethnography and, in particular, the way to approach field studies of physical activities (such as sports) as privileged points for understanding not only that activity itself, but the lives and social milieu of its practitioners, in their full sensuous, moral and aesthetic aspects. Wacquant's approach to ethnography builds on and extends Pierre Bourdieu's concept of 'habitus' (see Wacquant 2004a), a set of 'durable and transposable disposition' that is structured by the social conditions of the subjects and that, in turn, structures the perception and action of these subjects.[3]

In Wacquant's chapter included in this volume, he recalls how he took up boxing in order to get a vantage point to study the everyday life of young men in the black ghetto of Chicago. As he progressed in the craft, acquiring the skills, wits and sense of the art – the boxing habitus – he became more immersed in the lives of boxers and made the craft itself a second focus of his research, along with the structural transformation of the black ghetto and the rise of the penal state (Wacquant 2009b, 2013). Thus, the habitus became a potent tool with which to pry into the boxing world, a privileged concept to decipher action and meaning from the body and with the body. It also became a topic of investigation in itself: how do pugilists acquire the boxing habitus; what are the social and moral forces, the pedagogical practices, and the cultural constructs that enter into its fabrication; and what does this acquisition entail in terms of the boxers' relation to self and society?

Wacquant documents the ordinary routines and technical learning of which the gym is the site, but more importantly he captures the suffering and joy, the pain and ecstasy that intermingle in the mutual- and self-production of boxers. With a unique mix of social theory, close-up observation and experiential detection, he illuminates all that constitutes the boxing universe and that is customarily undetected or opaque to a distant observer. This is the main lesson embedded in the concept of habitus as a research tool. Rejecting the false dichotomy between distant observation and 'going native', Wacquant proposes that we 'go native but armed' with the theory of habitus in order to capture the production of the skilled, sensitive and desiring body by *undergoing* the process studied. This position is grounded in the fundamental and indissoluble fact of human existence taught by phenomenology (see Merleau-Ponty [1962] 2002, 1968): we live and learn about reality through our embodied condition. That is why 'observant participation' offers a methodological launching pad and habitus is the touchstone for access to the promises of 'carnal sociology' (Wacquant 1995a, 2005a; see also Crossley 1995), which Wacquant characterizes as 'a sociology not only *of* the body, in the sense of object, but also *from* the body, that is, 'deploying the body as tool of inquiry and vector of knowledge' (Wacquant 2004a, xiii). For the French sociologist, such an approach is can help us take 'full epistemic advantage of the visceral nature of social life' (Wacquant 2005a, 446).[4]

Wacquant proposes that

> *carnal sociology* fully recounts the fact that the social agent is a suffering animal, a being of flesh and blood, nerves and viscera, inhabited by passions and endowed with embodied knowledges and skills – by opposition to the *animal symbolicum* of the neo-Kantian tradition, refurbished by Clifford Geertz and the followers of interpretive anthropology, on the one hand, and by Herbert Blumer and the symbolic interactionists, on the other – and that *this is just as true of the sociologist*. This implies that we must bring the body of the sociologist back into play and treat her intelligent organism, not as an obstacle to understanding, as the intellectualism drilled into our folk conception of intellectual practice would have it, but as a vector of knowledge of the social world. (Wacquant 2009b, 120–21; emphasis in the original)

Wacquant's work is pivotal to the present volume because his ethnographic research demonstrates the full potential of studying combat sports, not just for their own sake, but as a fruitful field of contribution to core issues in the social sciences. In fact,

Wacquant's project on boxing cannot be separated from a constant and cautious effort to specify the conditions and rules of construction of the ethnographic object, warning us about the possible perils and pitfalls of urban ethnography (Wacquant 2002b). Wacquant's dissection of boxing in Chicago has drawn attention and created empirical and theoretical ripples in sociology, anthropology, psychology and literary studies, and contributed to the emerging field of body studies (Eliasoph 2005; Farquhar 2005; Henderikus 2009; Lizardo 2009; Hilgers 2009; Manning 2009), with *Body and Soul* (Wacquant 2004a) becoming something of a 'cult book' in several countries.[5] Special issues in journals and academic symposiums were organized around this book, based on the epistemological and methodological implications of Wacquant's research. *Qualitative Sociology* (2005)[6] and *Theory & Psychology* (2009)[7] developed special issues dedicated to the achievements and promise of Wacquant's reworking of habitus among boxers, offering diverse and interesting points of discussion, including: (i) the positioning of the inquirer and the question of membership in the development of ethnographic research; (ii) the dynamics of embodiment; (iii) the gendering and civilizing influences developed within boxing; (iv) the question of apprenticeship as a technique for social inquiry and the scope and possibility of a carnal sociology;[8] (v) issues of writing and representation, or how to reconnect narration and analysis in the reporting of deep ethnographic analysis.

Differing ethnographies of the martial arts and combat sports have been conducted since Wacquant's groundbreaking work. All of them encompass a range of issues, with the degree of attention given to habitus varying from one study to another. In the following subsections we divided approaches to the ethnographic study of martial arts and combat sports into five thematic nodes: body techniques, gender, ethnicity/race, religion/self-transformation and violence/pain. Nonetheless, among almost all of them, the concept of habitus is either explicitly included, or remains implicit, to their analysis.

Body techniques

Body techniques continues to be an extraordinarily influential concept within body studies and the social sciences more broadly. Coined by the French anthropologist Marcel Mauss ([1934] 1973), the notion of 'body techniques' – corporeal schemas that are learned through initiation and repetition and passed on through tradition – remains an influential concept and is utilized by many of the ethnographies included in this volume. Wacquant draws explicitly on Mauss's concept from his first essay on life and labour in the boxing gym (Wacquant 1989) to depict the series of drills and regulated exercises, at once physical and moral, that fighters undertake to mould their 'bodily capital' into specifically 'pugilistic capital' (Wacquant 1995b, 1998c). He also draws on Mauss's key writings on primitive religion and 'total man' to grasp the 'gearing' of 'body, mind, and society' in the production of pugilistic competency as aesthetic, practical and moral achievement (Wacquant 1998d, 1998b). In this section we refer not only to ethnographic research discussing this concept but also to ethnographic research focused on the embodied acquisition of a specific martial art or combat sport as its main concern (see Jones 2002). Here we find a wide range of analysed modalities, from capoeira to taijiquan (t'ai chi), to karate or silat – even to mixed martial arts.

INTRODUCTION 7

One hallmark of this approach to body techniques is the ethnographic work of Greg Downey (2005a) and his immersion into the world of capoeira. His field research in this Afro-Brazilian martial art/acrobatic dance-game spans close to a decade and ended with his enrolment in Mestre João Grande's Academy of Capoeira Angola in New York from 1998 to 2000. Downey's work on capoeira critically tackles the Bourdieuian concept of habitus. He concedes that 'capoeira apprenticeship presents players with the chance to learn diverse skills and change their perceptual habits. Trained adepts accumulate an array of dispositions, habits and sensitivities that make up their way of being in the world' (Downey 2005a, 154). Capoeiristas, for Downey, interiorized a kind of 'structuring structure' (the habitus) that marks their 'sense of the game' (another Bourdieuian conceptualization). But as Downey (2005a, 230) states: 'Instead of a unified "structuring structure" [...] capoeira resembles a loose assemblage of "miscellaneous" techniques, as described by Marcel Mauss.' Downey's dialogue with the neurosciences (developing what he dubs as 'neuroanthropology') is crucial to understanding possible future lines of research in a productive discussion of the concept of habitus.

Capoeira has been one of the most popular ethnographically analysed martial art disciplines in academia. Diverse examples centred on the 'body techniques' of capoeira include: Delamont and Stephens (2007) on the acquisition of the 'embodied habitus of capoeira'; Luna (2005), introducing an interesting characterization of capoeira angola using Laban Movement Notation; Teixeira Reis (2005) and Stephens and Delamont (2010a), both centred on the teaching relations and ways of acquiring the abilities and skills of capoeira.

Pencak silat (also known as silek) has also received considerable attention within the social sciences. Kirstin Pauka (1998) analysed, through personal immersion in silek, the close relation between the martial discipline of silek and the dance of randai in the Minangkabau of West Sumatra. Jean-Marc de Grave's (2011) ethnography of the perceptual training used in silat challenges traditional Western assumptions on the classification and development of sensory modalities. Starting from a broader conception and classification of the senses, silat relies heavily on the refinement of 'touch, tact and proprioception in a very active way' (de Grave 2001, 123). Using breathing exercises and concentration, the practitioners develop extraordinary sensory awareness of such sensory modalities and are able to achieve some remarkable feats such as moving along space blindfolded, guided by the acute feeling of what the Javanese call *getaran* (waves, vibrations). Douglas Farrer (2007) analysed the potential advantages and perils of 'performance ethnography' in studying silek. He suggests that 'embodied practice' is necessary for conducting anthropological analysis of physical activities (e.g. martial arts), in order to avoid relying solely on dialogical, textual and representational techniques. Jaida Samudra's (2008) study makes similar claims. Her ethnography involves her 'thick participation' within the white crane style. She urges the researchers to attempt to do 'an ethnography from the body' (Samudra 2008, 666) in order to render appropriate accounts of the kinesthetic experience of the art.[9]

Lee Wilson (2009) compared the pedagogy of Sundanese pencak silat styles with recent national standardized instruction of the art developed by the Indonesian Pencak Silat Association. Wilson relies on David Sudnow's (2001) ethnomethodological analysis of improvisation in piano jazz playing in order to analyse the acquisition of *jurus* (skills) required by the silek. According to Wilson (2009, 102), in 'the pedagogy of both Pencak and jazz improvisation there is, it strikes me, a recognition and tacit understanding of the ways in which we learn through the acquisition of repertoires and of the critical importance of learning through doing'.

Techniques associated with karate (Bar-On Cohen 2006), tae kwon do (Martínez Guirao 2011), and aikido (Hamilton 1994) have also been studied through embodied ethnography. Einat Bar-On Cohen (2006) analysed how karate's somatic codes become embodied with long-term involvement, acquiring kinesthetically complex sensitivities, such as the sense of *kime*, the inner source of energy in the technique. Not only the external forms, but there is more to the expert feeling and this is precisely expressed in such concepts as *kime*, which allows the possibility of 'rendering somatic interiorities social' (75) and generating a coherent dialogue between participants in the activity.

The most formal utilization of the concept of body techniques and habitus in relation to martial arts and combat sports is found in the work of Dale Spencer (2009, 2011, 2012). Through a four-year ethnographic study of mixed martial arts, he offers a way to understand the production of a mixed martial arts habitus as a lived-in-structure-in-process. He utilizes Crossley's concept of 'reflexive body techniques' to show how mixed martial art fighters produce bodies capable of giving and taking pain. What his work shows, *inter alia*, is how strategy is embodied in the habitus of fighters, how every fighter's body is a veritable invention, and how the group is the locus of emergence.

Gender

Gender issues have been paramount in the ethnographic work on martial arts and combat sports, and they run through Wacquant's ethnography of boxing. In 'From Charisma to Persona', (1996a) he places boxing in the gamut of 'bodily trades' prevalent in the black American ghetto, and among them entertainers, such as bluesmen, for whom developing a masculine style is paramount. In 'The Pugilistic Point of View', (1995a) Wacquant points out that, as a 'true blood sport' with a 'high premium on physical toughness and the ability to withstand – as well as dish out – pain and bodily harm', boxing embodies a 'hypermasculine ethos' that amplifies and dramatizes the conception of manly honour prevalent among the black lower class.

> Prizefighting is tailor made for the personalized construction and public validation of a heroic manly self because it is a distinctively individualistic form of masculine endeavor whose rules are unequivocal and seemingly place contestants in a transparent situation of radical self-determination. (Wacquant 1995a, 514)

The occupational ethic of 'sacrifice' which suffuses the gym and organizes the everyday conduct of the prizefighter affects a distinctive 'civilizing' of the body which is 'most crucially a masculinizing of the body, designed to accentuate, nay demonstrate, the "manly" properties of the organism and thereby the virility of its owner' (Wacquant 1998b, 345). It is effective because it is also the vector of 'masculine communion' between the boxer and his trainer, between gym mates, between run-of-the-mill fighters and gloried champions, and between the boxer and his opponent who has similarly denied himself contact with women and their world during the weeks leading to the bout to achieve a higher grade of masculinity because it is exclusive and agonistic:

> The Manly art purports to provide access to a higher grade of masculinity that can be achieved via an exclusive confrontation between men who have sublimated their heterosexual desire into a homoerotic desire for the martial, belligerent body of another man who similarly followed this ascetic course. (Wacquant 2005a, 463)

Issues of gender relations are similarly central to field studies of combat sports and martial arts. A case in point is Christine Menesson's (2000, 2004; Guérandel and Menesson 2007) ethnographies of boxing and kickboxing. While Bourdieu (2002) tied his iteration of habitus to masculine domination, Menesson turns away from Bourdieu's conceptualization and turns towards Goffman's frame analysis and his characterization of the interaction order. Menesson, in both her ethnographic studies, stresses the influence of previous socializing experience (family, friends, etc.) in order to understand the female entry in the male-dominated world of boxing disciplines, and also the differences in the construction of sexual dispositions of women inside boxing disciplines. She asserts that gender identities are mediated, not only by primary socialization, but also in the interactions between women and men in the gyms. Women classified as 'soft' were those who accepted and reproduced the stereotypical image of women. Those who produced a fighter habitus, engaging in competition (even professional careers), built an alternative, active role deviant from the societal expectations surrounding femininity.

Sara K. Schneider (2010) conducted two months of fieldwork in India studying kalarippayattu. She explored the teacher–student relationship and how the different ways of acquiring the art are mediated by cultural, ethnic and gender categories. The traditional kalarippayattu pedagogy implies touch and body contact, as the masters correct with students' hands and their postures with bamboo poles. As a 'fair skinned, Euro-American female, single and childless, but of childbearing age', Schneider (2010, 61) discovered in the course of her ethnography that she was not receiving a 'real' apprenticeship. The touch of the master was always withheld. Due to her gender, she was just playing a shallow form of the art, not really being accepted into the transmission of this Indian tradition.

In a contrary experience to Schneider, Paula Lökman (2011) conducted ethnographic research on female beginners' experiences in learning tomiki aikido – a sport-related style of aikido – in a London dojo in 2003. Lökman's interest centred on the way the martial art could help women gain consciousness over their bodies and thus challenge gendered characterization of the female body. According to Lökman, 'a breakthrough realization' occurred when the women in her class realized that body power does not necessarily equal strong muscles, insofar as aikido techniques place an emphasis on balance, rhythm and flexibility, which are seen as particularly important for the effective delivery of technique. The tomiki aikido female practitioners obtain a greater sense of power and security as they acquire new bodily dispositions that challenge the social image of the 'weak female body'.

Ethnicity/race

Issues related to ethnicity and race have focused on how the identities of ethnic groups are enacted and embodied through the practices of martial arts and combat sports. Wacquant's (2004a) research reveals the thick and dense imbrications between boxing and racialized masculinity in the ghetto of Chicago, but also the counterintuitive ways in which the Sweet Science reworks ethnoracial hierarchy.[10] While he stresses that 'the boxing universe is no "racial paradise"', Wacquant insists that we 'distinguish between the fabrication of boxers as skilled performers and prizefighting as commercial spectacle and manly fantasy' to discover 'one of the paradoxes of the Sweet science': that 'while its public consumption remains deeply affected by the politics of racial representation, its production side tends in manifold ways to deracialize bodies and social relations' (Wacquant 2005a, 451). Wacquant shows that the gym is the hub of a web of bodily corporeality, patterns of sociability, and moral forces that converge to blunt racial division as they stipulate commitment to the Sweet Science and its specific rules. This leads him to stress, counterintuitively and against the facile projection of racial common sense onto the ring as well as onto scholarship on race and sport, 'the relative autonomy of bodily capital from the symbolic capital of "race"' (Wacquant 2005a, 452).

This finding is validated by Wyrod. Based in the black community of Chicago's South Side, Robert Wyrod (1999/2000) carried out a one-year ethnographic study in two karate dojos. Through involvement in martial arts, the black community members gained a new perspective and image about themselves, challenging the racialized view inherited by the broader, hegemonic white society. Wyrod's research showed how physical activities were a powerful aspect of embodied agency, both on the individual and collective levels.

Investigating similar issues, but far from the United States in the north of India, Joseph Alter (1992) conducted a one-year ethnography of Indian wrestling. According to Alter, Indian wrestling displays an ideology as 'one of many forms of nationalism today' (1992, 261) and its practice is paramount to anchoring personal identity to the national image. The demanding participant observation in the *akharas* (gyms) in the early mornings (5 or 5:30 a.m. until 9 a.m.) helped Alter gain insight into the kinds of practices that influence the participant, literally transforming the bodies of the seasoned participants. Similarly, Einat Bar-On Cohen (2009c) observed the construction of a 'utopian Israeliness' in the largest Israeli School of Ju Jutsu, the 'Survival School'. This idealized national image was progressively embodied in the education of the participants engaged in the dynamics of 'becoming warriors'. This large, influential school not only focused on the acquisition of skills or ethics embedded in traditional martial arts, it aimed at instilling specific connections between bodily violence and national duty through realistic training (using modern weapons) and different rituals that link the students to a glorified national destiny.[11] Stéphane Rennesson's (2011) ethnographic account of muay thai shows the relation between fighters' public image and local and national identities. The dynamic and polymorphous characterization of professional fighters in Thailand either as 'attackers' or 'artists' (with different degrees of amalgamation) is built progressively from the interaction of several agents, including fighters, promoters, managers and journalists. Such characterizations act as a means of conveying local identities when competing among Thai fighters. The more dark-skinned fighters from the north-east Isan region are considered 'attackers' and the lighter-skinned fighters of the south as 'artists'. This also applies at an international level, as Thai identity is expressed in the bodies and abilities of Thai fighters, this time expressing a combination of both attacker and artist as a distinctive mark against foreign competitors.

Other research has focused on arts involving migrating populations, bringing corporeal crafts with them as part of their cultural heritage. In part as a way of enacting their own culture abroad, and in part as a way of living, these practices have been sometimes widely accepted and practised (inducing some regional differences). Perhaps the case of capoeira is the clearest example. Outstanding ethnographic work on capoeira can be found in Sara Delamont and Neil Stephens (Delamont 2006; Delamont and Stephens 2008; Stephens and Delamont 2010a, 2010b; Claudio de Campos, Stephens and Delamont 2010), who studied the Brazilian martial art/dance game as it is performed in different cities around Britain. Of particular relevance is their discussion of the embodied habitus that Brazilian capoeira teachers help to develop in their students in Britain. Stressing differences and similarities between habitus in both national traditions, the teachers help British capoeira students to acquire and sustain a specific kind of embodiment linked to capoeira. Adam Frank (2003) in his study of taijiquan (t'ai chi) in China and the United States, focuses on the precise differences in identities engendered by participation in taijiquan in these respective nations.[12] He argues that 'race' is not static, but must be understood as a dynamic construction, mediated by people's implication in activities. Corporeal activities such as taijiquan can be understood as a privileged point for shaping and anchoring racial images and meanings to people's embodied everyday life. This is achieved in a greater sense due to a process of 'ritualization', a formal exchange of knowledge – something crucial in the world of martial arts. 'Ritualization' in Frank's specific study was heavily influenced by categories such as 'Chinese', 'foreigner', 'white American' and also by the place where practices are performed (either China or the USA).

Religion/transformation of the self

In numerous places, Wacquant makes parallels between boxing and religion. For instance, in *Body and Soul* he opens his description of the boxing gym by comparing it to a church (Wacquant 2004a, 13); he invokes Hubert and Mauss's classic study of 'Sacrifice' (1964) as template through which to study the occupational ethic of prizefighters (Wacquant 1998d); and he insists that Durkheim's *Elementary Forms of Religious Life* ([1912] 1995) was the one book most useful to him to pry into the social making of pugilists.[13] He proposes that we see boxing as a 'secular religion of the skilled, violence, masculine body'. To give but one illustration, in 'The Prizefighter's Three Bodies' (an echo of Kantorowicz's ([1957]1997) classic study of the theology of kingship), Wacquant (1998b, 343) writes:

> By willfully adhering to the dictates of the ethic of sacrifice, boxers tear themselves from the everyday world and create a moral and sensual universe sui generis that

'elevate the individual above himself' and 'affords [them] a life very different, more exalted and more intense' than that to which their mundane circumstances would consign them – which is Émile Durkheim's ([1913] 1975, 23) definition of religion. By embracing the fistic faith, prizefighters make themselves over into living embodiments of professional morality.

Clearly, embodied ethnography provides a conduit for understanding some of the deeper religious and transformative elements of the martial arts and combat sports. Philip Zarrilli (2000 and 2005) conducted an embodied ethnography of the martial art discipline of kalarippayattu on the Indian south-west coast of Kerala. This martial art tradition evinces the distinctive interrelationship between body, mind and practice, which stands in contradistinction to the dualistic Western ontology of mind and body. The practitioners of kalarippayattu are urged by masters to see practice as a serious and rigorous way of life and not as a leisure activity. Zarrilli's insightful ethnography, gained through his implication as a student in the kalari (the site where training takes place), showed how students evolved from an external transformation of the body, rendering its form flexible (*meivalakkam*) and making it flow (*olukku*) like a river, towards a whole transformation of the self. During the most intensive period of training (during the monsoon period), practitioners are to refrain from bad habits (drugs, etc.) and devote their lives to the discipline. From the first day, kalari students are to lead a devotional life honouring the kalari deities and the master. The intent of arduous training is to lead to the progressive purification of the students, that is, to a pure transformation of the self.

In George Jennings's (2010) ethnography he participated as a student and teacher of taijiquan and wing chun in two British traditional Chinese martial arts schools. One of the primary concerns of his research was to analyse the effects of practice in these disciplines upon long-term practitioners. He reveals that a natural development occurred as an effect of collective, shared experience, from a more technique-orientated approach towards a more spiritual/holistic one. He observed changes in body, self and societal relations in a flexible continuum of ideal types, ranging from fighters to martial artists to thinkers. Overall, Jennings's findings support the thesis that martial art participation leads to transformations of the individual on relational and institutional levels for long-term participants.

Jennings, Brown and Sparkes (2010) reach similar conclusions in their study on wing chun.[14] Their ethnography consisted of six years of participant observation within two of the principal training halls (*kwoons*) of the Wing Chun Association in England. As a general pattern, practitioners evolved jointly (as the activity is embodied as a 'shared experience') from a secular/technique/efficacy perspective towards a religious/sacralized view of their practice. They suggest that practitioners can conceive of wing chun as a kind of secular religion. Committed trainee's religious metaphors (for example, monastic devotion) are irremediably linked to the secular physical practice and the practitioners progressively move towards the philosophical side of the craft. This shift of interest affected not only their behaviour inside the training hall but also in their everyday lives.

Violence/pain

For Wacquant (1995a, 1995b), boxing is a *paradoxical violence*: in the ring, the fighter gradually destroys that which he values most, his skilled body; yet immersion in the gym effects a 'civilizing' of violence and serves as a shield from the violence of everyday life (through its disciplining and integrative effect). Boxers learn to tame pain and to give it meaning and purpose; yet that very taming leads them to collude with the exploitative relations that can turn them into 'whores, slaves, and stallions', human fodder to the 'show business with blood' that is professional fightings (Wacquant 1995b, 2001).

Again, following Wacquant, several of the aforementioned studies treated, in varying degrees, the question of violence or pain. This is not surprising, insofar as martial arts and combat sports activities involve intense violent contact between practitioners, where control over fear and rage varies along the apprenticeship. Wacquant's analysis of the 'sweet science' revealed the pain and suffering of bruises and blood, and food and sex deprivations of professional boxers in the gym. He even recounted the personal toll he had to pay, ending up with a broken nose.

Since Wacquant, very few studies have focused specifically on violence and pain issues in relation to martial arts and combat sports. An exception to this can be found in the work of Raúl Sánchez García (2006, 2008) and Dale Spencer (2011, 2012). Sánchez García's four-year ethnography of aikido and boxing elucidates the acquisition of specific habitus attached to these respective fighting styles. Drawing on the Eliasian conception of habitus, the paramount concern was to understand the specific corporeal relation to violence.[15] In both aikido and boxing, dynamic negotiations of violence take place between instructor and participants, and between the participants themselves. The group established an upper and lower threshold of violence, embodied in specific actions. Those actions between the thresholds of violence were considered a normal part of the activity. Those actions out of the zone demarked by the two thresholds were reprehended, considered as weak or non-real (if they fall out of the lower level) or as violent (if they fall over the upper level). Differences between such negotiations in aikido and boxing were strongly mediated by the kind of methodology implied in each fighting art. Boxing included free-sparring that allowed a direct negotiation of the thresholds of violence. On the other hand, aikido included just *kata* (prearranged forms) and allowed an indirect negotiation of the thresholds of violence, strongly affected by the high degree of ritualization attached to the practice. Yet, at another level, Sánchez García converges with Wacquant's argument that the 'the gym constitutes a small-scale civilizing machine in Elias's sense of the term: it simultaneously imposes strict taboos on certain forms of violence, lowers one's threshold of acceptance of disorderly behavior, and promotes the internalization of controls and obedience to authority' (Wacquant 1995a, 499). Being embedded in the social relations of the gym and broader boxing fraternity tends to deflect violence and channel the very aggression that boxing feeds on between the ropes.[16]

In Tan's (2008) ethnography of aikido, complementary results can be found with regards to violence. He concludes that aikido served as a major embodied and contextual ground in the production of 'corporeal mythologies': body techniques were not only acquired in a mere physical form but were shaped and boosted by the alleged development of inner energy (*ki*). During this process, violence was progressively transformed into symbolic violence, not being recognized by participants. Kyle Green's (2011) ethnography, focused on the world of mixed martial arts, analyses the centrality of violence to this sport. Based in a three-year participant observation in a gym in Minnesota, Green states that 'pain' is constituted as a shared experience among members of the community, reinforcing the sense of belonging. Pain also enables participants to get the impression that their activity is 'real' and to install a stronger embodied self-identity, as participants experience the clear limits and boundaries of their bodies. In his ethnographic study of mixed martial arts, Dale Spencer (2012) analyses the narratives of despair and loss of fighters during and after their careers. He documents the specific ways that, on the one hand, athletes conform to masculine ideals through attempts to assume ideal states of embodiment and withstanding pain associated with participation in sport, while on the other hand, through debilitating bodily injury, athletes actually fail to materialize masculine ideals associated with participation in sport.

Overview of the Volume

All of the chapters included in *Fighting Scholars* contribute to the discussion of the habitus as a topic and as a tool of research, and are based on ethnographic studies of martial arts. Chapter 2 is the formative work of Loïc Wacquant on the possibility of studying habitus as a topic within ethnographic research while also deploying it as a methodological tool for more refined accounts of the activity considered. Wacquant recounts how he stumbled upon the boxing gym that was to become to main scene and character of his ethnography of prizefighting in the ghetto; how he developed his double focus on habitus as topic of investigation and technique of inquiry; and how he crafted *Body and Soul* as an empirical extension and methodological radicalization of Bourdieu's theory of action: 'The apprenticeship of the sociologist is a methodological mirror of the apprenticeship undergone by the empirical subjects of the study; the former is mined to dig deeper into the latter and unearth its inner logic and subterranean properties; and both in turn test the robustness and fruitfulness of habitus as guide for probing the springs of social conduct.' Moreover, Wacquant contends that 'observant participation', whereby the researcher resolves to 'go native but *go native armed*', that is, equipped with the tools of social science to objectivize this experience of conversion, brings the possibility of a real embodied dialogue between researcher and participant and constitutes one of the cornerstones for a 'carnal sociology', that is, a sociology not *of* the body but *from* the body.

In Chapter 3, David Brown and George Jennings critically reflect on conceptions of a universal 'martial habitus' and also the possibility of a more specific form, what they view as a 'wing chun kung fu habitus'. The authors argue that different core schemata of dispositions are observable within the habitus of any single martial art and they distinguish ideal types of 'fighters', 'martial artists' and 'thinkers'. In Chapter 4, Sara Delamont and Neil Stephens reflect on the implications of acquiring a 'capoeirista agility'. This concept implies not only the acquisition of a new way of embodiment – a new set of physical skills (*jogo de cintura*), but also a certain sense of the game (*malicia*) that is linked to the former. In Chapter 5, Elizabeth Graham employs Crossley's concept of reflexive body techniques to analyse the complex process of becoming a tae kwon do technician. Tae kwon do 'technician habitus' reveals the dependent and independent nature of the relationship between doing with the body and thinking about what the body is doing in order to gain an expert disposition of the activity.

In Chapter 6, Bryan Hogeveen examines the corporeal experience of Brazilian jiu-jitsu practitioners as they forge a body that is equipped to receive and deliver pain, and where emotions, aches and discomfort intertwine in the process of developing grappling competency. Hogeveen addresses the question of a participant's personal style by examining the variations of a common habitus, which depends on the practitioner's distinct physical and mental attributes (flexibility, height, weight, strength, wit) that are brought to this martial art, rather than being acquired from it. In Chapter 7, Alex Channon deals with the settings of mixed-sex martial arts training, attending to the problematic nature of physically engaging with the opposite sex in combative roles. Gendered relations dictate that it is not appropriate to 'hit girls' as they are considered weaker than males and not prepared for combat. Channon argues that subversive gender discourse asserted within mixed-sexed martial arts settings implies equality in relation to pain and endurance. This is acquired in a conflictive manner (especially for men) through embodied participation in the activity and recognition of female combative prowess. In Chapter 8, Sara K. Schneider elucidates the complex guru–student relationship in learning the South Indian indigenous martial art kalarippayattu, explored across gender, cultural, ethnic and class lines. One paramount line of this relation was mediated by corporal teaching methods involving direct touch as tools of transmission of practice and of master–apprentice communication. This kind of embodied instructional/communicational technique was differently applied depending on the social categorization of the practitioner, giving birth to a myriad of different habitus linked to the practice.

In Chapter 9, Thomas Green examines the acquisition of '52 hand blocks' (or 52s), an African American vernacular martial art, and its relationship to other non-martial activities belonging to this Afro-American heritage. He demonstrates how the 52s share aesthetic features with African-American musical and movement genres, including rap, jazz and breakdancing. Practitioners label the culturally appropriate application of individual 52s techniques as having 'flow', and evaluate movement and musical genres according to similar standards and using a common set of critical terms. In Chapter 10, Einat Bar-On Cohen examines the difficulties of transplanting religious ideas from 'foreign' cultural traditions, especially when translated into verbal and textual meanings. According to Bar-On Cohen, the embodied experience of martial arts render the spiritual aspect of such training graspable with no exegesis, in a way that is unrelated to verbal explanations. In Chapter 11, Raúl Sánchez García discusses the habitus in Eliasian terms, seeing the gym and the dojo as types of 'civilizing workshops'. He argues that specific habitus are dynamically produced in the gym and the dojo through a kind of habituation towards receiving and inflicting pain, to manage fear and to gain a sense of pride. In the cases of recreational boxing and in aikido, participants learn to deal with violence in a more detached and controlled way: that is, they gain a 'more civilized habitus'. In Chapter 12, Dale Spencer addresses the topic of cultural transmission of martial arts from East to West. Focusing on muay thai, he challenges the general assumption regarding the moral and philosophical Westernization of Eastern martial arts. In the process of acquisition of a muay thai fighter habitus, many Westerners feel the urge to travel to rural and urban areas of northern Thailand seeking 'authentic' Thai boxing. As part of this process, 'traditional', Eastern philosophical and religious aspects of the martial discipline are not only kept alive, but form the basis of an 'Easternization' of Western Thai boxers. This in turn creates complex hybrids that do not easily fit into the usual Westernization model of cultural appropriation. In the last chapter, the Conclusion to the volume, Raúl Sánchez García and Dale Spencer offer suggestions for future lines of ethnographic research. The epilogue 'Homines in Extremis' written by Loïc Wacquant offers an overall view of the volume as well as a critical review and rejoinder of some of the topics presented by different contributors.

Notes

1 Draeger's doctoral dissertation was entitled 'Kendo in Japanese Martial Culture: Swordsmanship as Self-Cultivation'.
2 Jack London also produced excellent ethnographic descriptions of big fights, transmitting the verve of the ring and the crowd surrounding the action. An outstanding example of this was his chronicle for the *New York Herald* of the Jeffries–Johnson fight (famous for its controversy on the 'race issue') that took place during 1910 in Reno, Nevada. Wacquant 2010 discusses the significance of London's involvement in and writings on the ring for the anthropology of boxing.
3 With this concept, Bourdieu was trying to explain social action avoiding the extremes of structuralism on the one side and subjectivist theories (of the symbolic interactionalist or rational-actor varieties) on the other. Wacquant also builds on Bourdieu's own ethnographic practice, especially his youthful field studies of honour, kinship and power in Kabylia and Béarn, and on the ethnographic tradition Bourdieu's research center has spawned in France (see Wacquant 2004c). Wacquant mentions specifically the works of Abdelmalek Sayad, Stéphane Beaud and Michel Pialoux, Yvette Delsaut and Monique and Michel Pinçon (Wacquant 2009b, 115). For a comprehensive review of the concept see Bourdieu 1977; Bourdieu and Wacquant 1992; Wacquant 2004d, 2009b and the Epilogue to this volume.
4 De Garis 1999 proposes a research programme in ethnography that resembles many of the tenets of a carnal sociology. The researcher *uses* her own embodied experience as a means of understanding an embodied, incarnate activity, avoiding the illusion of the figure of ethnographer as a so-called *transcendental subject*: distant from the activity, watching and taking notes, trying to convey with minimum distortion by avoiding any kind of direct participation (71). On the contrary, the ethnographer is an active agent who could gain a lot of insights by applying a sensuous, kinetic ethnography to the activity under study. In de Garis's own words: 'sensuous ethnography is also a performative ethnography; it is a lived experience performed by a lived body' (73).
5 The impact of the book has been felt well beyond academe: the book was enthusiastically reviewed in boxing magazines (*The Ring: The Bible of Boxing* called it 'a fresh and authoritative treatment') and it is a best-seller in several countries (it is taught in high schools in France). Wacquant reported to us that he has received countless missives from amateur and professional boxers (and from the girlfriends or wives of boxers) from around the world thanking him for having conveyed their world to outsiders. The work of the award-winning photographer Nicolas Wong was directly inspired by *Body and Soul*.
6 See *Qualitative Sociology* 28 (4) (2005) for Wacquant's rejoinder.
7 In *Theory & Psychology* (2009), see 'Special Section on Habitus in the Work of Loïc Wacquant', online at http://loicwacquant.net/debates/habitus/ (accessed 15 December 2012), with four more papers to come by John Martin, Gabriel Ignatow, Stephen Vaisey and Margaret Frye.

8 For a critical assessment of the potentialities and limitations of autoethnography (a research technique linked to the issue of apprenticeship) on the collaborative and contrastive engagement of two embodied experiences (one participating, the other just as an external observer) belonging to two different researches analysing the same activity (capoeira), see Sara Delamont and Neil Stephens (2006). Note that Wacquant is very critical of autoethnography on epistemological and methodological grounds. In his response to the special issue of *Qualitative Sociology* on *Body and Soul*, he firmly rejects Gary Fine's (2004, 505) proclamation of that book as the 'first sociological classic of reflexive autoethnography' in his review of the book in the *American Journal of Sociology*. Wacquant (2009b) makes his position clear: *Body and Soul* 'is absolutely not a fall into the bottomless well of subjectivism into which "auto-ethnography" joyfully throws itself, quite the opposite: it relies on the most intimate experience, that of the desiring and suffering body, to grasp *in vivo* the collective manufacturing of the schemata of pugilistic perception, appreciation, and action that are shared, to varying degrees, by all boxers, whatever their origins, their trajectory, and their standing in the sporting hierarchy. The central character of the story is neither "Busy" Louie, nor this or that boxer, and not even Dee Dee the old coach, in spite of his position as conductor: it is the gym as a social and moral forge. The intellectual model here is not Carlos Castañeda and his Yaquí sorcerers but the Gaston Bachelard of *Applied Rationalism* and of the materialist poetics of space, time, and fire' (Wacquant 2009b, 120).

9 Facing the difficult task of translating movement into language, Samudra opted for a kind of bodily communication between anthropologist and participants within a kinesthetic system. She encourages a type of 'somatic interview' to complement verbal interviews and field notes about the activity. In addition, kinesthetic translation of an activity may include a record of sensory impressions and the use of somatic narratives.

10 Sudgen's (1996) research is worth mention here, even though he did not rely on direct participation as a boxer but as a participant observer. He conducted an ethnographic comparative study of boxing cultures: Hartford (USA) Belfast (Northern Ireland) and La Habana (Cuba). His reports offer insightful information upon the relationship of the pugilist craft with the different social/ethnical stratification dynamics existing within these settings.

11 For example, at the beginning or end of the lesson, everyone stops to perform a short ceremony in front of the 'Wall of Honour'. Everyone bows in silence while the instructor talks about stories of injustice and disgrace, often referring to the Holocaust or terrorist threats, aiming at honouring those who gave their lives for the whole country.

12 For an arm's-length comparison of aikido across Japan and the US, see Jeffrey C. Dykhuizen (2000).

13 Wacquant (1996b) reports that the investigation of boxing 'has taken me from almost one extreme, the sociology of structural constraint and material inequality, to another, a phenomenological sociology of desire and carnal self-making. Much to my own surprise, the book that has helped me the most in effecting that passage and puzzle out that relation is Émile Durkheim's *Elementary Forms of Religious Life*. Certainly, when I signed up at the Stoneland Boys' Club and paid my twelve dollars to get my license and my ten-dollar annual gym dues and "gloved up" for the first time (really thinking that I was daydreaming and that it wouldn't go anywhere since I had never so much as seen a live fight in my life), I would have never thought I'd be talking about this – and certainly not in those terms, a few years later before an audience such as this one! If you had told me then that one day I would maintain that Durkheim has a close connection to boxing, I would have thought that to say this is proof that I'm punch-drunk before I've even gotten into the ring!' (22–3).

14 Another remarkable study on the role of oriental martial arts upon body/self transformation is Brown and Leledaki (2010). Qualitative in its methodological approach, it is based upon interviewing and documentary evidence but not on ethnographic research, so we do not treat it here in detail.

15 For an Eliasian sociohistorical analysis of the development of boxing and its relation to changes in habitus related to the Western civilizing process, see Ken Sheard (1997) and Sheard and Murphy (2006).
16 The meeting point between Bourdieu and Elias on the question of embodiment and social structure has been proposed by Wacquant (2004b, 2007b) in his analysis of the guetto using Elias's work; and Sánchez García (2006) in his analysis of the complex – and very problematic in the case of boxing – articulation of boxing and aikido practitioners' experience of their own activity with the general public images of those activities within Spanish society.

Chapter 2

HABITUS AS TOPIC AND TOOL: REFLECTIONS ON BECOMING A PRIZEFIGHTER

Loïc Wacquant

In this chapter, I recount how I took up the ethnographic craft; stumbled upon the Chicago boxing gym that is the main scene and character of my ethnography of prizefighting in the black American ghetto; and designed the book *Body and Soul* that reports on its findings so as to both deploy methodologically and elaborate empirically Pierre Bourdieu's signal concept of habitus (Wacquant 2004a). I draw out some of the biographical, intellectual and analytic connections between this research project on a plebeian bodily craft, the theoretical framework that informs it, and the macro-comparative inquiry into urban marginality of which it is an unplanned offshoot. I sketch how the practicalities of fieldwork led me from the ghetto as implement of ethnoracial domination to embodiment as a problem and resource for social inquiry. Through this reflection on becoming a prizefighter, I argue for the use of fieldwork as an instrument of theoretical construction, the potency of carnal knowledge, and the imperative of epistemic reflexivity. I also stress the need to expand the textual genres and styles of ethnography so as to better capture the *Sturm und Drang* of social action as it is manufactured and lived.

The concept of habitus supplied at once the anchor, the compass and the course of the ethnographic journey recapped in *Body and Soul*. It is the *topic* of investigation: the book dissects the forging of the corporeal and mental dispositions that make up the competent boxer in the crucible of the gym. But it is also the *tool* of investigation: the practical acquisition of those dispositions by the analyst serves as technical vehicle for better penetrating their social production and assembly. In other words, the apprenticeship of the sociologist is a methodological mirror of the apprenticeship undergone by the empirical subjects of the study; the former is mined to dig deeper into the latter and unearth its inner logic and subterranean properties; and both in turn test the robustness and fruitfulness of habitus as guide for probing the springs of social conduct. Contrary to a commonly held view that habitus is a vague notion that mechanically replicates social structures, effaces history and operates as a 'black box' that obviates observation and confounds explanation (see Jenkins (1991) for a standard regurgitation of these nostrums), it emerges that Bourdieu's sociological reworking of this classic philosophical concept is a powerful tool to steer social inquiry and trace out operant social mechanisms. Properly used, habitus not only illuminates the variegated logics of social action; it also grounds the distinctive virtues of deep immersion in and carnal entanglement with the object of ethnographic inquiry.

A Pathway to the Ethnographic Craft

Since the notion of habitus proposes that human agents are historical animals who carry within their bodies acquired sensibilities and categories that are the sedimented products of their past social experiences, it is useful to begin with how I came to ethnographic research and what intellectual interests and expectations I brought with me to the South Side of Chicago. My initiation to fieldwork predates my entry in graduate school at the University of Chicago in 1985. To fulfil my military duties (as every French male had to do back then), by a stroke of luck, I was assigned to do a stint of civilian service in the South Pacific as a sociologist in a research centre of the Office de la Recherche Scientifique et Technique d'Outre-Mer (Orstom), France's former 'office of colonial research'. So I spent two years in New Caledonia, a French island north-east of New Zealand, in a small research team – there were only three of us – at the time of the Kanak uprising of November 1984. This means that I lived and worked in a very brutal and archaic colonial society, because New Caledonia in the 1980s was a colony of the nineteenth-century type that had survived virtually intact to the end of the twentieth century (see Bensa 1995 for an account). It was an extraordinary social experience for an apprentice sociologist to carry out research on the school system, urbanization, and social change in the context of an insurrection, under a state of emergency, and to observe in real time the struggles between the colonials and the independence forces, and to have to reflect in a concrete way about the civic role of social science. For instance, I was privileged to participate in a closed congress of the Kanak Socialist National Liberation Front in Canala at the height of the clash, and I also travelled all the way around the 'Grande Terre' (the main island) and made several sojourns on Lifou island at the home of friends who were long-time Kanak militants at a time when practically no one was moving about in the territory.

The New Caledonian crucible sensitized me to ethnoracial inequality and to spatial consignment as a vector of social control – the Kanaks were largely relegated to isolated rural reservations and hypersegregated neighbourhoods in the capital city of Nouméa. It also alerted me to the variegated workings of rigid hierarchies of colour and honour in everyday life and to the crucial place of the body as a target, receptacle and fount of asymmetric power relations. And it exposed me to extreme forms of deprecative racial imagery: the native Melanesians were typically pictured as 'super-primitives' devoid of culture and history, even as they were rising to seize their historical fate (Bourdieu and Bensa 1985). All of this would prove immensely useful later, on the South Side of Chicago, where germane treatments of African Americans were current. It is in New Caledonia that I read the classics of ethnology – Mauss, Mead, Malinowski, Radcliffe-Brown, Bateson, etc. (especially works on the South Pacific: the Trobriand Islands were just nearby) – and that I kept my first field notebooks. The very first was scribbled among the tribe of Luecilla, in the Bay of Wé, at Christmas of 1983, about a year before the independentist uprising (the notebook's highlight was a section on going bat hunting and having to eat the roasted proceeds of our expedition at dinner that evening). Field notations found their way into my first publications on educational inequality, colonial conflict and the transformation of Melanesian communities under the press of capitalist expansion and French rule.

At the close of my Caledonian sojourn, I got a four-year fellowship to do my doctorate at the University of Chicago, the cradle of US sociology and home of the main tradition of urban ethnography. When I arrived in Upton Sinclair's town, my intention was to work on a historical anthropology of colonial domination in New Caledonia, but I got unexpectedly derailed and detoured into America's dark ghetto. On the one side, the New Caledonian gates were abruptly shut after I filed a complaint against the mediocre bureaucrat who was my supervisor in Nouméa and had forced his name as co-author of a monograph on the school system that I had carried out by myself (Wacquant 1985). The directors of the Institute in Paris hastened to cover up for the cheater and effectively banned me from the island. On the other side, I found myself confronted day-to-day with the gruesome reality of Chicago's ghetto, or what was left of it. I was assigned the last student-housing unit available on campus, the one nobody had wanted, and so I lived on 61st Street, at the edge of the poor black district of Woodlawn. It was a constant tremor and puzzlement to have right under my window this quasi-lunar urban landscape, with its unbelievable decay, misery and violence, backed by a totally hermetic separation between the white, prosperous and privileged world of the university and the abandoned African American neighbourhoods all around it. Coming from Western Europe, where such levels of urban blight, material destitution and ethnic segregation are unknown, this questioned me profoundly on a quotidian level, intellectually and politically. It is at this point that the second decisive encounter of my intellectual life took place, the one with William Julius Wilson (the first was with Pierre Bourdieu, five years earlier, when I decided to convert from economics to sociology after hearing a public lecture by him, see Wacquant 2002a).

Wilson is the most eminent African American sociologist of the second half of the twentieth century and the foremost expert on the nexus of race and class in the United States – his analysis of 'Blacks and Changing American Institutions' in *The Declining Significance of Race* (Wilson 1978) set the parameters for that subfield of social research in 1978. He was one of the faculty who had initially attracted me to Chicago, and so when he offered me to work with him on the big research project on urban poverty he had just started (roughly, the agenda marked out by his book *The Truly Disadvantaged*, Wilson 1987), I jumped at the chance, and I quickly became his close collaborator and co-author. This afforded me the opportunity to get straight to the core of the subject and also to get a close-up look at how this scientific and policy debate operated at the highest level, especially in the philanthropic foundations and 'think tanks' that shaped the resurgence of the problematic of race, class and poverty in the inner city. That is how I started my investigations, first as an acolyte of Wilson and then by myself, on the transformation of the dark ghetto after the riots of the 1960s, by striving to break with the pathologizing vision that pervaded and distorted research on the question.

I owe a huge personal and intellectual debt to Bill Wilson, who was a mentor at once demanding and generous. He stimulated and supported me, and he also gave me the freedom to diverge from his analyses, and at times to go in a direction diametrically opposed to his. By example, he taught me intellectual courage: to pursue the big picture, to dig deep into the details, to ask the hard questions, even when this entails ruffling a few social and academic feathers along the way. He also invited Pierre Bourdieu to speak to his research team on his Algerian research on urbanization and proletarianization from the early 1960s (Bourdieu et al. 1963). As it turns out, Bourdieu had tried to get *The Declining Significance of Race* translated into French a few years earlier. This meeting and the ensuing discussion solidified my sense that I could make a link between Bourdieu's early anthropological inquiries into the lifepaths of Algerian subproletarians and the contemporary predicament of the residents of Chicago's black ghetto that preoccupied Wilson. But I did not know just how yet.

Ethnography played a pivotal role at that juncture, on two counts. On the one hand, I took more anthropology than sociology courses, because the sociology department at the University of Chicago was very dull intellectually and because I was viscerally committed to a unitary conception of social science inherited from my French training. The courses, works and encouragements of John and Jean Comaroff, Marshall Sahlins, Bernard Cohn and Raymond Smith pushed me towards fieldwork. On the other hand, I wanted to quickly find a direct observation post inside the ghetto because the existing literature on the topic was the product of a 'gaze from afar' that seemed to me fundamentally biased if not blind (Wacquant 1997). That literature was dominated by the statistical approach, deployed from on high, by researchers who most often had no first-hand or even second-hand knowledge of what makes the ordinary reality of the dispossessed neighbourhoods of the Black Belt, and who fill this gap with stereotypes drawn from common sense, journalistic or academic. I wanted to reconstruct the question of the ghetto from the ground up, based on a precise observation of the everyday activities and relations of the residents of that *terra non grata* and for this very reason *incognita* (see Wacquant [1992] 1998a for an early effort).

I deemed it epistemologically and morally impossible to do research on the ghetto without gaining serious first-hand knowledge of it, because it was right there, literally at my doorstep (in the summertime, you could hear gunfire going off at night on the other side of the street), and because the established works seemed to me to be full of implausible or pernicious academic notions, starting with the scholarly myth of the 'underclass', which was a veritable intellectual cottage industry in those years (see Katz 1993 and Gans 1995 for critical accounts; Wacquant 1996a for a conceptual dissection). As a white Frenchman, my formative social and intellectual experiences made me a complete foreigner to this milieu and intensified the need I felt to acquire some practical familiarity with it. After a few aborted attempts, I found by accident a boxing gym in Woodlawn, some three blocks from my apartment, and I signed up, saying that I wanted to learn how to box, quite simply because there was nothing else to do in this setting. In reality, I had absolutely no curiosity about or interest in the pugilistic world in itself (but I did want to get good exercise). The gym was to be just a platform for observation inside the ghetto, a place to meet potential informants.

Figure 2.1. Urban desolution on 61st Street, near the Woodlawn boxing gym.

Photo by the author.

Habitus Comes to the Gym

But, very quickly, that gym turned out to be not only a wonderful window into the daily life of young men in the neighbourhood, but also a complex microcosm with a history, a culture, and a very intense and rich social, aesthetic, emotional and moral life of its own. In a matter of months, I formed a very strong, carnal, bond with the regulars of the club and with the old coach, DeeDee Armour, who became a sort of adoptive father to me. Gradually I found myself attracted by the magnetism of the 'Sweet Science' to the point where I spent most of my time in and around the gym. After about a year, the idea grew on me to dig into a second research subject, namely, the social logic of a bodily craft. What is it that thrills boxers? Why do they commit themselves to this harshest and most destructive of all trades? How do they acquire the desire and the skills necessary to endure in it? What is the role in all this of the gym, the street, the surrounding violence and racial contempt, of self-interest and pleasure, and of the collective belief in personal transcendence? How does one create a social competency that is an embodied competency, transmitted through a silent pedagogy of organisms in action? In short, how is the *pugilistic habitus* fabricated and deployed? That is how I found myself working on two connected projects simultaneously – two projects ostensibly very different from each other but in fact tightly linked: a carnal microsociology of the apprenticeship of boxing as subproletarian bodily craft *in the ghetto*, which offers a particular 'slice' of this universe from below and from inside (Wacquant 2004a); and a historical and theoretical macrosociology *of the ghetto* as instrument of racial closure and social domination, providing a generalizing perspective from above and from the outside (Wacquant 2008).

I had started writing a field diary after every training session from my first afternoon at the gym, initially to overcome the overpowering sense of being out of place on the pugilistic scene on so many levels and not knowing really what I would do with these notes. Now I shifted to taking systematic notes and to exploring the various facets of the 'Sweet Science'. The notion of habitus immediately came to me as a conceptual device to make sense of my personal experiences as a boxing apprentice and as a scaffold to organize my ongoing observation of pugilistic pedagogy. I had read Bourdieu's anthropological works front and back during my Caledonia years. So I was fully familiar with his elaboration of the notion, intended to overcome the antinomy between an objectivism that reduces practice to the mechanical precipitate of structural necessities and a subjectivism that confuses the personal will and intentions of the agent with the spring of her action (Bourdieu 1990b; see Wacquant 2004d for a genealogy and exegesis of the notion). The author of *Outline of a Theory of Practice* had retrieved habitus from a long line of philosophers, stretching from Aristotle to Aquinas to Husserl, to develop a dispositional theory of action recognizing that social agents are not passive beings pulled and pushed about by external forces, but skilful creatures who actively construct social reality through 'categories of perception, appreciation and action'. But, unlike phenomenology, Bourdieu insists that these categories, while being resilient and shared, are not universal (or transcendental, in the language of Kantian philosophy), and that the generative matrix they compose is not unchanging. Rather, as the embodied sediments of individual and collective history, they are themselves socially constructed.

> As the product of history, habitus produces individual and collective practices, and thus history, in accordance with the schemata engendered by history. It ensures the active presence of past experiences which, deposited in each organism in the form of schemata of thought and action, tend, more surely than all formal rules and all explicit norms, to guarantee the conformity of practices and their constancy across time. (Bourdieu 1990b, 91; my translation)

Four properties of the concept of habitus suggested its direct relevancy for disclosing the social making of prizefighters. First, habitus is a set of *acquired* dispositions, and no one is born a boxer (least of all, me!): the training of fighters consists precisely in physical drills, ascetic rules of life (concerning the management of food, time, emotions and sexual desire), and social games geared towards instilling in them new abilities, categories and desires, those specific to the pugilistic cosmos (Wacquant 1998b). Second, habitus holds that practical mastery operates *beneath the level of consciousness and discourse*, and this matches perfectly with a commanding feature of the experience of pugilistic learning, in which mental understanding is of little help (and can even be a serious hindrance in the ring) so long as one has not grasped boxing technique with one's body (Wacquant 1995a). Third, habitus indicates that sets of dispositions *vary by social location and trajectory*: individuals with different life experiences will have gained varied ways of thinking, feeling and acting; their primary dispositions will be more or less distant from those required by the Sweet Science; and thus they will be more or less invested in and adept at picking up the craft. This certainly accorded with my personal experience and notations on the disparate

Figure 2.2. DeeDee at work, keeping time from the back room of the gym.

Photo by the author.

behaviours of my gym mates over time, as they tangled with the competing lure of the street and the gym, adapted to the authority of our coach, and sought to remake their self in accordance to the exacting demands of the trade. Fourth, the socially constituted conative and cognitive structures that make up habitus are malleable and transmissible because they result from *pedagogical work*. If you want to pry into habitus, then study the organized practices of inculcation through which it is layered (Wacquant 1995b).

The 'magical moment' of fieldwork that crystallized this theoretical hunch and turned what was initially a side-activity into a full-blown inquiry into the social logics of incarnation was a rather inglorious one: it was getting my nose broken while sparring in May 1989, about nine months into my novitiate. This injury forced me to take a long 'time out' away from the ring, during which Bourdieu urged me to write a field report on my initiation for a thematic issue of *Actes de la recherche en sciences sociales* in preparation on 'The Space of Sports'. The result was a long article that showed me that it was both feasible and fruitful to convert the theory of action encapsulated by the notion of habitus into an empirical experiment on the practical production of prizefighters at the Woodlawn gym (Wacquant 1989, 2002a). This article was soon augmented by more direct engagement with habitus on the theoretical front.

While I was carrying out my investigations on boxing and on the ghetto, I was in constant contact with Pierre Bourdieu who encouraged and guided me. Upon learning that I had signed up to learn how to box at the Woodlawn Boys Club, he had written me a note that said essentially, 'Stick it out, you will learn more about the ghetto in this gym than you can from all the surveys in the world.' (Later on, as I got deeper into my immersion, he got a bit scared and tried to get me to pull back. When I signed up to fight in the Chicago Golden Gloves, he first threatened to disown me as he feared that I would get hurt, before realizing that there was no need to panic: I was well prepared for this trial by fire.) Bourdieu came to Chicago several times, visited the gym, and met DeeDee and my boxer friends (I introduced him to them as 'the Mike Tyson of sociology'). During one of these visits, we hatched the project of a book that would explicate the theoretical core of his work, aimed at the Anglo-American readership, since it was on this front that there were the strongest distortions and obstacles to a fertile grasp of his models. We devoted three years to writing this book across the Atlantic (by fax, phone, letters and meetings every few months), entitled *An Invitation to Reflexive Sociology* (Bourdieu and Wacquant 1992), in which we disentangle the nexus of habitus, capital and field. During those years I led a sort of Dr Jekyll and Mr Hyde existence, boxing by day and writing social theory by night. In the afternoon I would go to the gym, train, hang out with my buddies, and 'conversate' on end with our coach DeeDee before driving him home at closing time. And, later in the evening, after having typed my field notes, I would switch to the book manuscript with Bourdieu. It was in turns intoxicating, invigorating and exhausting. But the daytime sessions as a student of pugilism offered both a respite from theoretical cogitation and powerful stimuli for thinking through the abstract issues tackled in the book in very mundane empirical terms. The sociology of the ghetto (which I had extended to encompass a comparison with the postindustiral transformation of the French urban periphery), the carnal ethnography of the skilled body, and theoretical work with Bourdieu: all these strands were elaborated together and at the same time, and they are all woven together.

The boxing project is an ethnography in a very classic mould in terms of its parameters, a sort of village study like the ones British anthropologists conducted in the 1940s, except that my village is the boxing gym and its extensions, and my tribe the fighters and their entourage. I retained this structural and functional unity because it encloses the boxers and carves out a specific temporal, relational, mental, emotional and aesthetic horizon, which sets the pugilist apart, pushes him to 'heroize' his lifeworld, and thereby raises him above his ordinary environs (Wacquant 1995c). I wanted, first of all, to dissect the cloven relation of 'symbiotic opposition' between the ghetto and the gym, the street and the ring. Next, I sought to show how the social and symbolic structure of the gym governs the transmission of the techniques of the Manly art and the production of collective belief in the pugilistic *illusio*. And, finally, I wished to penetrate the practical logic of a corporeal practice that operates at the very limits of practice by means of a long-term apprenticeship in 'the first person'. For three years, I melted into the local landscape and got caught up in the game. I learned how to box and participated in all phases of the preparation of the pugilist, all the way to fighting in the big amateur tournament of the Golden Gloves. I followed my gym buddies in their personal and professional peregrinations. And I dealt on a routine basis with trainers, managers, promoters, etc., who make the planet of boxing turn and share in the spoils of this 'show-business with blood' (Wacquant 1998c). In so doing, I was sucked into the sensuous and moral coils of pugilism, to the point where I seriously envisaged interrupting my academic trajectory to turn professional.

But, as the foregoing should have made clear, the object and method of this inquiry were not of the classic mould. *Body and Soul* offers an empirical *and* methodological

Figure 2.3. 'Busy' Louie caught sparring with Ashante.

Photo © Jimmy Kitchen.

radicalization of Bourdieu's theory of habitus. On the one hand, I open the 'black box' of the pugilistic habitus by disclosing the production and assembly of the cognitive categories, bodily skills and desires that together define the competence and appetence specific to the boxer. On the other hand, I deploy habitus as a methodological device, that is, I place myself in the local vortex of action in order to acquire through practice, in real time, the dispositions of the boxer with the aim of elucidating the magnetism proper to the pugilistic cosmos. This allows me to disclose the powerful allure of the combination of craft, sensuality and morality that binds the pugilist to his trade as well as impresses the embodied notions of risk and redemption that enable him to overcome the turbid sense of being superexploited (Wacquant 2001). The method thus tests the theory of action that informs the analysis according to a recursive and reflexive research design.

The idea that guided me here was to push the logic of participant observation to the point where it becomes inverted and turns into *observant participation*. In the Anglo-American tradition, when anthropology students first go into the field, they are cautioned, 'Don't go native'. In the French tradition, radical immersion is admissible – think of Jeanne Favret-Saada's ([1978] 1980) *Deadly Words* – but only on condition that it is coupled with a subjectivist epistemology that gets us lost in the inner depths of the anthropologist-subject. My position, on the contrary, is to say, 'go native' but *go native armed*, that is, equipped with your theoretical and methodological tools, with the full store of problematics inherited from your discipline, with your capacity for reflexivity and analysis, and guided by a constant effort, once you have passed the ordeal of initiation, *to objectivize this experience and construct the object*, instead of allowing yourself to be naively embraced and constructed by it. Go ahead, go native, but come back a sociologist! In my case, the concept of habitus served both as a bridge to enter into the factory of pugilistic know-how and to methodically parse the texture of the work(ing) world of the pugilist, and as a shield against the lure of the subjectivist rollover of social analysis into narcissistic storytelling.

From Guts to Paper

Some of my critics, conflating the narrative form of the book with its analytic contents and mistaking my work for an extension of the 'study of occupations' in the style of the second Chicago School (Hughes 1994), did not even notice the double role that the concept of habitus played in the inquiry and even complained about the absence of theory in the book (Wacquant 2005c). In fact, theory and method are joined to the point of fusion in the very empirical object whose elaboration they make possible.

Body and Soul is an experimental ethnography in the originary meaning of the term, in that the researcher is one of the socialized bodies thrown into the sociomoral and sensuous alembic of the boxing gym, one of bodies-in-action whose transmutation will be traced to penetrate the alchemy by which boxers are fabricated. Apprenticeship is here the means of acquiring a practical mastery, a visceral knowledge of the universe under scrutiny, a way of elucidating the praxeology of the agents under examination, as recommended by Erving Goffman (1989) in a famous talk on fieldwork – and not the means of entering into the subjectivity of the researcher. It is absolutely not a fall into the bottomless well of subjectivism into which 'auto-ethnography' joyfully throws itself (Reed-Danahay 1997), quite the opposite: it relies on the most intimate experience, that of the desiring and suffering body, to grasp *in vivo* the collective manufacturing of the schemata of pugilistic perception, appreciation and action that are shared to varying degrees by all boxers, whatever their origins, their trajectory and their standing in the sporting hierarchy (Wacquant 2005a). The central character of the story is neither 'Busy' Louie, nor this or that boxer, and not even DeeDee the old coach, in spite of his central position as conductor: it is the gym as a social and moral forge.

Indeed, I hold that, with this project I did in an explicit, methodical and above all *extreme* manner that which every good ethnographer does, namely to give herself a practical, tactile, sensorial grasp of the prosaic reality she studies in order to shed light on the categories and relations that organize the ordinary conduct and sentiments of her subjects. Except that, usually, this is done without talking about it or without thematizing the role of 'co-presence' with the phenomenon being studied, or by making (herself and others) believe that this is a mental process, and not a bodily and sensual apprenticeship that proceeds beneath the level of consciousness before it becomes mediated by language. *Body and Soul* offers a demonstration in action of the distinctive possibilities and virtues of a *carnal sociology* that fully recounts the fact that the social agent is a suffering animal, a being of flesh and blood, nerves and viscera, inhabited by passions and endowed with embodied knowledges and skills – by opposition to the *animal symbolicum* of the neo-Kantian tradition, refurbished by Clifford Geertz (1973) and the followers of interpretive anthropology, on the one hand, and by Herbert Blumer (1966) and the symbolic interactionists on the other – and that *this is just as true of the sociologist*. This implies that we must bring the body of the sociologist back into play and treat her intelligent organism not as an obstacle to understanding, as the intellectualism drilled into our folk conception of intellectual practice would have it, but as a vector of knowledge of the social world.

Body and Soul is not an exercise in reflexive anthropology in the sense intended by what is called 'poststructuralist' or 'postmodern' anthropology, for which the return of the analytic gaze is directed either onto the knowing subject in her personal intimacy or onto the text that she delivers to her peers and the circuits of power-knowledge in which it travels, in a contradictory and self-destructive embrace of relativism (Hastrup 1995; Marcus 1998). Those forms of reflexivity, narcissistic and discursive, are rather superficial; they certainly constitute a useful moment in a research undertaking by helping to curb the play of the crudest biases (rooted in one's identity and trajectory, affects, rhetorical effects, etc.). But they stop the movement of critique at the very point where it should start, through the constant questioning of the categories and techniques of sociological analysis and of the relationship to the world these presuppose. It is this return onto the *instruments of construction of the object*, as opposed to the subject of objectivation, which is the hallmark of what one may call *epistemic reflexivity* (Bourdieu and Wacquant 1992, 36–46; Bourdieu 2002a). And here is another difference with the 'egological' or textual reflexivity of the subjectivist anthropologists: epistemic reflexivity is deployed not at the end of the project, *ex post*, when it comes to drafting the final research report, but *durante*, at every stage in the investigation. It targets the totality of the most routine research operations, from the selection of the site and the recruitment of informants to the choice of questions to pose or to avoid, as well as the engagement of theoretic schema, methodological tools and display techniques, at the moment when they are implemented.

So *Body and Soul* is a reflexive book in the sense that the very design of the inquiry forced me to constantly reflect on the suitability of the means of investigation to its ends, on the difference between the practical mastery and the theoretical mastery of a practice, on the gap between sensorial infatuation and analytic comprehension, on the hiatus between the visceral and the mental, the *ethos* and the *logos* of pugilism as well as of sociology. Likewise, *Urban Outcasts* (Wacquant 2008), the companion book of macrosociology which draws up a comparison of the structure and experience of urban relegation in the black American ghetto and the French urban periphery, is a work of reflexive urban sociology because it ceaselessly interrogates the very categories it puts into question and into play – underclass, inner city, *banlieues*, hyperghetto, anti-ghetto, precariat – in order to think through the novel configurations of marginality in the city. And because it rests on a clear-cut demarcation between folk categories and analytic categories, which is for me the plinth of reflexivity.

Epistemic reflexivity is all the more urgently needed by ethnographers as everything conspires to invite them to submit to the preconstructions of common sense, lay or scholarly. By methodological duty, they must be attentive to the agents they study and take seriously their 'point of view'. If they do their job well, they also find themselves bound to these agents by affective ties that encourage identification and transference (for an astute analysis of the methodological use of transference in *Body and Soul*, see

Manning 2005). Finally, the public image of ethnography (including, regrettably, in the eyes of other social scientists) likens it to storytelling and diary writing, if not to epic. So much to say that the anthropologist or sociologist who relies on fieldwork must *double the dose of reflexivity*. This is what I tried to demonstrate in 'Scrutinizing the Street' about recent trends and foibles in US urban ethnography (Wacquant 2002b). The considered target of my critique is not the three books on race and urban poverty that I subject to a meticulous analytic dissection (and still less their authors, who are here simply points in academic space, or their political positions, to which I am completely indifferent), but a certain epistemological posture of unreflective surrender to folk apperceptions, to ordinary moralism, to the seductions of official thought and to the rules of academic decorum. This posture is the fount of serious scientific errors, as these errors are systematic and have both ordinary and scholarly common sense on their side.

To enable the reader to experience the thrills of the apprentice boxer and to make palpable both the logic of the fieldwork and its end product required adopting a quasi-theatrical mode of writing. How to go from the guts to the intellect, from the comprehension of the flesh to the knowledge of the text? Here is a real problem of concrete epistemology about which we have not sufficiently reflected, and which for a long time seemed to me nearly irresolvable (notwithstanding the varied attempts at and discussions of formal innovation and poetic construction among anthropologists). To restitute the carnal dimension of ordinary existence and the bodily anchoring of the practical knowledge constitutive of pugilism – but also of every practice, even the least 'bodily' in appearance, including sociological analysis – requires indeed a complete overhaul of our way of writing social science. In the case at hand, I had to find a style breaking with the monological, monochromatic, linear writing of the classic research account from which the ethnographer has withdrawn and instead elaborate a multifaceted writing mixing styles and genres, so as to capture and convey 'the taste and ache of action' to the reader (Wacquant 2004a, vii–xii).

Body and Soul is written against subjectivism, against the narcissism and irrationalism that undergird so-called 'postmodern' literary theory, but that does not mean that we should for that deprive ourselves of the literary techniques and instruments of dramatic exposition that this tradition gives us. That is why the book mixes three types of writing, intertwined with each other, but each given priority in one of the three parts, so that the reader slides smoothly from concept to percept, from analysis to experience. The first part anchors a classic sociological style in an analytic mould that identifies at the outset structures and mechanisms so as to give the reader the tools necessary for explaining and understanding of what is going on. The tone of the second part is set by ethnographic writing in the strict sense, that is, a dense depiction of the ways of being, thinking, feeling and acting proper to the milieu under consideration, where one encounters again these mechanisms but in action, through the effects they produce. The experiential moment comes in the third part, in the form of 'sociological novella' that delivers felt action, the lived experience of a subject who also happens to be the analyst.

The weighed combination of these three modalities of writing – the sociological, the ethnographic and the literary – according to proportions that become gradually inverted as the book progresses, aims to enable the reader to feel emotionally and understand rationally the springs and turns of pugilistic action. For this, the text weaves together an analytic lattice, stretches of closely edited field notes, counterpoints composed by portraits of key protagonists and excerpts from interviews, as well as photographs whose role is to foster a synthetic grasp of the dynamic interplay of the factors and forms inventoried in the analysis, to give the reader a chance to 'touch with her own eyes' the beating pulse of pugilism. Here again, everything hangs together: the theory of habitus, the use of apprenticeship as technique of investigation, the place accorded to the sentient body as vector of knowledge, and formal innovation in writing. Indeed, there is no point in carrying out a carnal sociology backed by practical initiation if what it reveals about the sensorimotor magnetism of the universe in question ends up disappearing later in the writing, on the pretext that one must abide by the textual canons dictated by Humean positivism or neo-Kantian cognitivism.

Many social researchers view theory as a set of abstract notions that either float high up in the pure sky of ideas, disconnected from the nitty-gritty of the conduct of inquiry, or constitute responses to the empirical questions that the latter raises, to be discovered in the real world, as in the approach labelled 'grounded theory'. This is a misconstrual of the relationship of theory and research, and ethnography in particular. Whether the investigator is aware of it or not, theory is always driving field inquiry because, as Gaston Bachelard (1971) taught us, 'the vector of knowledge goes from the rational to the real', and not the other way around. And it must of necessity engage observation in order to convert itself into propositions about an empirically existing entity. This applies to habitus, which, like every concept, is not an answer to a research question but an organized manner of asking questions about the social world − in the case recounted here, a methodical plan to vivisect the social fabrication of pugilists in their workaday environment.

Chapter 3

IN SEARCH OF A MARTIAL HABITUS: IDENTIFYING CORE DISPOSITIONS IN WING CHUN AND TAIJIQUAN

David Brown and George Jennings

Introduction: The Problem of the Martial Habitus

In the last 10 years, the field of scholarly study of martial arts and combat sports has been expanding steadily. For example, a range of empirical qualitative (particularly ethnographic) research has been produced within capoeira (Delamont and Stephens 2008; Joseph 2008a), Venezuelan stick and machete fighting (Ryan 2011), military and 'reality' schools of fighting (Bar-On Cohen 2011), mixed martial arts (MMA) (Downey 2007a; Spencer 2009; Abramson and Modzelewski 2011) and Chinese martial arts (Jennings, Brown and Sparkes 2010). A number of these make quite extensive use of the concept of habitus as developed by Bourdieu (1977) and Bourdieu and Wacquant (1992). This concept has provided a powerful analytical tool for making sense of the reflexive cultural dynamics taking place between these arts as transcultural practices, their specific sociocultural contexts of adoption and adaption, and the pedagogical and transformative nature of these practices for their practitioners.

The notion of a martial habitus has apparent interpretive connections with Wacquant's (1992, 2004a) work on the 'pugilistic habitus' (for example, certain key dispositions are seemingly shared such as Wacquant illustrated, the near monastic devotion to routinized training practices). However, unlike the field of boxing, which is the product of a long and increasingly globalized process of standardization of pugilistic logics of practice (i.e. winning, losing, professional, amateur, legitimate, illegitimate, types of body (weight, condition, age, gender) and uses of the body techniques, etc.), at this point in time there are difficulties with accounting for the commonalities and differences of dispositional schemata that might be constitutive of a martial habitus covering the range of martial arts and combat sports that currently exist (Sánchez and Malcolm 2010). This is due to their immense variety, cultural location and associations, lack of standardization, various intended outcomes of practice and, crucially, body pedagogies. Contrastingly, attempts to isolate a habitus to a particular martial/combat art (e.g. a capoeira or wing chun kung fu habitus) are also fraught with the opposite problems tending towards the magnification of differences between arts in general, whilst at the same time assuming a dispositional sameness within a given art (there are also many practical and contextual variations of an individual martial art form to account for). These problems of theoretical universalism and particularism become especially apparent in non-reductionist empirical research, however aesthetically appealing either of these interpretations may be conceptually.

In response, this chapter critically reflects upon conceptions of a universal 'martial habitus', and also any particularist 'genus' of martial habitus, and presents an emergent examination of this concept that has developed from analysis of data gathered in an ongoing study of the Chinese martial arts of wing chun and taijiquan conducted by authors in the UK context. In what follows, we explore the idea emerging from our data that there may be multiple core dispositions observable within the habitus of any single martial art, but that these dispositional schemata also tend to have some significant congruence across martial arts as well. With this seemingly paradoxical backdrop in mind, we propose that it is nevertheless possible and desirable to identify three co-present, yet differentially valued and positioned, practically oriented dispositions in relation to the arts and practitioners we studied. We refer to these as the combat efficacy–efficiency disposition, the practice–perfection–mastery disposition and the body–self–environment awareness disposition respectively. Through focusing on dispositions in this way, we also show how these dispositions act as three interlaced continua comprising a schema or martial habitus, each disposition ranging from focal to peripheral orientations for practical action for a given martial practice. In addition, the subjective element of our data informs us that a distinction between the 'in situ' dispositions forged from practice in a 'delimited field' such as a specific martial arts club, and general dispositions (those that pertain to the net effect of engagement with a range of fields in toto) is both empirically evident and theoretically useful.

We conclude by considering how such a variegated, dynamic and reflexive view of the 'martial habitus' formed through practice also acts as a 'generative grammar' for future action, change and continuity within a specific delimited martial field of practice. These dispositions, we argue, might be taken to constitute a 'core martial schema of dispositions' or 'martial habitus' for the arts we have studied. While we are not in a position to extrapolate these dispositions to other martial practices at this time, we nevertheless sense from our own experiences that these dispositions may also be constitutive in other martial practices as well. In this sense, the analysis presented in this chapter is intended as a cautious beginning at exploring ways of understanding how martial practice gives rise to similar dispositions that might form a martial habitus within and across arts and, crucially, become further variegated by individual martial artists' own practice and interpretation. Finally, in presenting this analysis we are also conscious that further developing the idea of a core schema of dispositions of the martial habitus is likely to need the addition of further dispositions. We return to these points in our conclusions.

The Martial Habitus as a Continuum of Interlaced Dispositions

Bourdieu (1990b, 53) has defined habitus in the following terms:

> The conditionings associated with a particular class of conditions of existence produce habitus, systems of durable, transposable dispositions, structured structures predisposed to function as structuring structures […] objectively 'regulated' and 'regular' without

being in any way the product of obedience to rules, they can be collectively orchestrated without being the product of the organizing action of a conductor.

Furthermore, according to Bourdieu (1990b, 55–6) a degree of alignment between the internalized dispositions forming the habitus and those that form the practical orthodoxies (doxa) of any given field is to be expected:

> Being the product of a particular class of objective regularities, the habitus tends to generate all the 'reasonable', 'common sense' behaviours (and only these) which are possible within the limits of these regularities, and which are likely to be positively sanctioned because they are objectively adjusted to the logic characteristics of a particular field, whose objective future they anticipate.

Therefore, in relation to any given field of activity, the concept of habitus describes not a fixed set of dispositions but rather an emergent set of dispositions formed in relation to the conditions of existence in particular historically and culturally located fields of activity. Habitus, therefore, is likely to vary in its specific forms, at the same time as being recognizable in terms of its emergence as a response to a practical need or function. In this sense, as Kasper (2009, 320) contends, the habitus always describes a continuum of dispositions forged through practice within an identified field of activity. She continues, 'the question is not whether a person or group is this or that but where they fall on the continuum that can provide a sense of the direction they tend toward presently and how their position relates to others in that space'.

Following Kasper, the very notion of a martial habitus is best seen as an heuristic that can sensitize us to the range of dispositions that may emerge from engagement in the field of martial practices and will likely be differentiated by the continuum of possible positions that agents may adopt (or be assigned) within a field. Nevertheless, we believe there is at least one identifiable, consistent practical logic underpinning all martial practices (if they are to be considered martial practices at all): this is to provide a structured and coherent response to the material, practical and symbolic phenomenon of interpersonal human conflict. Furthermore, because interpersonal human conflict can and does take place in a wide variety of physical and cultural settings, a wide range of embodied practical permutations are observable (e.g. open scenarios such as one versus one/many, larger versus smaller, strong versus weak, armed versus unarmed etc., and also closed situations such as the strongly codified conditions of engagement existing within martial/combat sports), importantly also are a range of scenarios in which physical conflict may only be a threatening possibility or even 'merely' a symbolic conflict and combat (Read 2010). In short, while a core schema of dispositions may be recognizable, considerable variation should be expected. How such variation might be interpreted conceptually occupies our attention next.

Dispositions as Delimited Field Specific and General Continua

Given the above, the field of martial practices form a wide-ranging and dynamic continuum of delimited fields of practice. However, we further suggest that it is not only the schemata of dispositions that might be seen as a continuum, but also the more discrete dispositions themselves. In order to explore this it is necessary first to consider what is meant in a sociological sense by the term disposition. Bourdieu (1977, 214) provides the following elucidation:

> The word disposition seems particularly suited to express what is covered by the concept of habitus (defined as a schema of dispositions). It expresses first the result of an organising action, with a meaning close to that of words such as structure; it also designates a way of being, a habitual state (especially of the body) and, in particular, a predisposition, tendency, propensity, or inclination. [The semantic cluster of 'disposition' is rather wider in French than in English, but as this note – translated literally – shows, the equivalence is adequate. Translator.][1]

Figure 3.1. Dispositions as a continuum from focal to peripheral.

Figure 3.2. General and de-limited field dispositions.

A disposition that forms through sustained practice in a martial field is one that guides and informs (rather than determines) an individual's way of being or orientation towards a specific practical exigency, and by dint of this, their propensity for future action. Applied discussions of habitus quite rarely get past the focus on schemata of dispositions and devote attention to highlighting and articulating singular dispositions. However, the idea of disposition as a continuum, ranging from the focal to the peripheral (see Figure 3.1), attempts to capture a way of being that is differentiated for practices and individuals. Therefore, the notion of a continuum of a disposition provides opportunities for a far more specific contextual analysis of habitus through the myriad ways in which a single disposition can be interlaced into the body and mind of a given individual, group culture, or even society. When entire schemata of dispositions are seen interlaced in this manner it is not difficult to see how a wide array of dispositional profiles might emerge from the same schema of dispositions.

There is one further conceptual distinction that needs to be made at this point. Stones (2005) argues that it is possible and desirable to distinguish between the habitus and other internal structures. Stones (2005, 85) defines these as: 'Internal structures within the agent, which can themselves be divided analytically into two components, namely conjuncturally specific internal structures and general dispositional structures, or, following Bourdieu, habitus'. The point we wish to extract here is that Stones's distinction between the general and the specific is of central importance. Specific internal structures can be understood as delimited field dispositions (those evolving from a very specific field of martial practice and conjunctural because they take place in a specific time and place). While these may be analytically separated from general dispositions (those which pertain to the net effect of engagement with a range of fields in toto, see Figure 3.2), this is not meant to intimate that they are experienced separately. Rather, dispositions constituting the martial habitus may potentially evolve over time from being delimited dispositions to general dispositions and in our view this necessarily occurs through the constant interlacing of these at the individual practical/experiential level. Such a view helps to redress the problem of agency, subjectivity and change that a singular notion of habitus has been criticized for not embracing (Shilling 2004). We return to these relationships in our conclusions.

Methodological Strategy

The methodological strategy for this chapter is informed by Wacquant (2011) who argues that the habitus can serve as a topic and a tool for social scientific investigation. In pursuing this reasoning he argues for a methodology that encompasses 'the use of fieldwork as an instrument of theoretical construction, the potency of carnal knowledge, and the imperative of epistemic reflexivity' (2011, 81). The first element of this view, that fieldwork and the data generated can be used to develop pre-existing theory, is also supported by Plummer (2001, 159) who argues that 'theoretically we can use life stories in at least three ways'; he proposes that we can 'take a story to challenge some overly general theory […] to illustrate or illuminate some wider theory […] as a way of building up some wider sense of theory'. The use of the life-history extracts in this chapter pertains most obviously to senses two and three of Plummer's uses. The specific data used to illustrate the ideas in this chapter are life-history extracts taken from a three-year (2006–2009) ethnographic and life-history study that focused upon practitioners of wing chun kung fu and taijiquan. These data were collected by the co-author (George Jennings). The individual voices presented here comprise of Terry (wing chun), Chris (chen-style taijiquan practitioner), Ted (wing chun), Zack (wing chun), Kelly (various including wing chun and lau gar) and Will (mixed traditional Chinese arts practitioner including taijiquan and praying mantis). Further biographical details are woven into the analysis below, and all names and places mentioned are pseudonyms.

These life-history data were derived from specific researched contexts and emerged from ethnographic fieldwork. Drawing on Hammersley and Atkinson (2003), George became an overt participant observer and immersed himself in a number of martial arts settings and, informed by Emerson and colleagues (1995), gathered detailed field notes. Additionally, this approach shared similarities with Samudra's (2008) notion of thick participation, in that it attempted to capture something of the multisensorial nature of these martial art practices in the settings studied. Illustrations of this can be found elsewhere (see for example, Jennings, Brown and Sparkes 2010). This approach, as Sparkes (2009, 30) confirms, displaces the privilege normally accorded the occularcentric in ethnographic research, commenting that all the senses 'have their part to play, in different degrees at different times, in how sport and physical activity are experienced and understood'. As George's insider knowledge evolved, he began interviewing key individuals and drawing on fieldwork data to enrich the lines of questioning in the interview process.

Following the second and third elements of Wacquant's (2011) methodological view there is a need to connect with an additional flow of influence from the fieldwork and, beyond this, also from the longer-term life experiences of both authors. This comes in the form of strands of dispositions formed through years of martial arts practices engaged in by us. Therefore, although the circumstances for us as martial artists researching martial arts are very different from Wacquant's own pugilistic experiences, the way in which we 'tap into' our relative carnal knowledges has some similarities. In short, we are not only investigating habitus as a topic but also as a 'tool of investigation' (Wacquant 2011, 82), as Wacquant comments: 'The practical acquisition of those dispositions by the analyst serves as technical vehicle for better penetrating their social production and assembly. In other words, the apprenticeship of the sociologist is a methodological mirror of the apprenticeship undergone by the empirical subjects of the study' (2011, 82).

Prior to beginning this study, George, (a white, able-bodied male in his mid-20s, at that time studying for a doctorate) was already an established and regular member of Bridge's Wing Chun Association and had studied with various instructors in this academy since 2002. George's habitus had evolved from that of an outsider with previous wing chun experience into one of the trusted core members who holds a prized black sash and is a qualified instructor in this system. George also has experience of other schools of martial arts including tae kwon do, kendo, judo, taijiquan and, more recently, xilam. George's martial habitus, developing both before, during and after the study period in question, served as a powerful dispositional resource to draw on in terms of focusing on elements to observe, participate in and discuss with participants.

This chapter's other co-author David (also a white, able-bodied male, in his early 40s, a university lecturer and former doctoral supervisor of George) has also experienced a variety of martial arts including Shotokan, Wado ryu and kempo karate, aikido, a little taijiquan and was a practitioner of wing chun for around five years. In this context, the idea of using habitus as a tool has been fruitful for the way in which it guides an examination of our own orientations as well as the embodied schemata of perception to key martial orientations in others. This approach contrasts with a traditional ethnographic perspective of the sort outlined by Hammersley and Atkinson (2003) in which the potential for George and David to 'go native' and affect our ability to analytically engage with the field of martial practices generally, and those delimited fields in which we are invested specifically, would be seen as a limiting factor. Using the concept of habitus as a tool opens up a different view of its value for the invested researcher and the research process, because to various degrees we cannot 'go native' because we are native! However, our collective collaboration and considerable dialogue helped to bring to conscious attention our interest, investment and, specifically, as Bourdieu (1998, 77) terms it, our illusio or 'feel for the game' and how through 'being caught up in that game' we possess the 'dispositions to recognize the stakes at play'.

Lastly, as indicated earlier we have identified a few core dispositions and the nature of the representation of these is significant. Deliberately each of the dispositions is not presented as a keyword. There are two reasons for this. First, because habitus, and thereby dispositions, relate to states of being that have been formed by practice, rather than practices per se, any articulation of a disposition needs to be reflective of a state and for this reason clusters of nouns are used. Second, these noun clusters connect with Frank's notion of narrative habitus, which in an interview with Eldershaw, Mayan and Winkler (2007) he defines (in part) as, 'a certain repertoire of stories we know […] and these stories direct us to have a certain sense of the world and our possibilities and constraints of action in the world' (128). With these elements in mind, we now turn to our data to illustrate the three incorporated dispositions as interlaced continua.

The Combat Efficacy–Efficiency Disposition

The problem of interpersonal human conflict leading to actual physical combat is fundamental to human existence and has to be addressed by everybody in some way or another. Notwithstanding the huge cultural and historical range of contexts in which this physical combat might take place (and how martial practices are generally evolved for specific types of conditions of combat), the combat efficacy–efficiency disposition emerges strongly from this practical logic.

Terry typifies an advanced martial artist with a focal combat efficacy–efficiency disposition. Indeed, Terry is in many ways an archetypical 'street fighter' and as such he expresses the combat efficacy–efficiency disposition in its purest form, when he comments:

> GJ: So what do you understand martial arts to be now?
> TM: An efficient way of fighting… That's what my training's for, that's why I do it. The same as when I first started. I knew how to fight anyway. That's not why I started wing chun anyway. It was to tidy up what I already had. To get better. (Terry, interview 1, 12 February 2008)

At the time of the study Terry was 39, the top student and assistant instructor through 20 hard years of training in a wing chun academy. Originating from a tough working-class background in Grimethorpe, a town in north-west England, Terry has had countless street fights throughout his youth and adulthood. Terry's general disposition has drawn him towards a particular type of martial art renowned for its direct, effective street-fighting style. This interlacing of the general disposition and the delimited field-specific disposition is emphatically illustrated in the following statement by Terry:

> It's from what my dad taught me: you're either fighting, or you're not fighting. If you are fighting, you're fighting. You're not talking about it. You're not shouting your mouth off. You're dropping the fucker as quick as you can. Cos he'll generally have mates with him, and they can get you to the floor, then they'll kick you to death. So, that's what put me off other martial arts, because there was too much standing up, backing away, and giving each other too much room. Being short of stature, I'm not massively small, I'm 5 ft 10. I have to get inside people quickly, because they're always bigger than me for some reason. So I can't stand up and give other

people the reach, I can't stand up. My arms aren't long enough. So I learnt through my teenage years to get in sharpish and get in there and finish it. And when I saw this Gary [a friend and doorman who introduced him to the art] fella, I thought, 'Fuck it. I like that. He's fighting like me. He's doing what I do.' (Terry, interview 1, 12 February 2008)

Terry's comment here has echoes of Wacquant's (1992) 'self-selecting' street-fighting boxers and is also illustrative of Bourdieu's (2003, 241) approximation of the Weberian notion of 'elective affinity' to 'taste', when he comments, 'taste is what brings together things and people that go together'. Terry's general disposition towards street combat, already established through street-fighting practice, gives rise to a 'taste' for a particular style of martial art that was stimulated when he first witnessed a friend performing wing chun. Exposure to this martial practice (and it must be said the local interpretation of it in the academy where Terry practises) helped Terry to develop his focal combat efficacy–efficiency disposition, which is interlaced in a complementary fashion with his general disposition for efficacy formed from street fighting. Indeed, while Terry is now an accomplished martial artist who has competed in full-contact British competitions, he still dislikes these kinds of competitions for their lack of reality as compared with street fighting.

If Terry represents a martial artist with a focal combat efficacy–efficiency disposition, then Ted illustrates a more moderate position on this dispositional continuum. Like Terry, Ted claims that for him martial arts are still centrally focused around combat efficacy–efficiency; however, for Ted the practical logic of combat is orientated towards self-defence rather than fighting:

I would say for me, the purpose of a martial art is to be able to look after yourself in a fight situation. You talk about discipline of the mind and body and all that kind of stuff. Getting the benefit, blah, blah, blah, but to me, at the end of the day it should be that in a fighting situation, you should be able to avoid that situation. And if you can't, you have to stand and fight, not run, then it stands you with a far better chance. (Ted, interview 2, 4 June 2008)

Like Terry, Ted drew on his general dispositions (as a former Royal Marine) initially to orientate him towards an 'effective' martial art first and foremost, his efficacy–efficiency disposition in the service of fighting is not as strong as Terry's and is more orientated to self-defence as last resort. Therefore, while combat efficacy is clearly central, an individual's orientation towards 'fighting' can be varied from focal to peripheral indicating a continuum of orientations driven by this disposition. An overly narrow interpretation of the term fighting can be misleading as it actually often implies a level of actual physical cooperation in human conflict (in the sense that both parties capitulate in the 'game' of physical combat that is street fighting). Many self-defence arts tend to see a combat situation as less of a 'fight' in which there are willing participants, winners and losers, and more of a critical incident in which the protagonist 'forces' someone to defend themselves from the threat of actual bodily (or psychological) harm. Approaching human combat with this interpretation is likely to shape considerably the nature of the response and the practical mode of engagement. For example, these self-defence arts typically contain within their skill sets relatively fewer techniques and emphasis on pre-emptive striking, and so tend to generate less of this protagonist approach in their disposition-forming practices.

Chris provides a strong illustration of the 'peripheral' end of the combat efficacy–efficiency dispositional continuum. It is instructive for the way in which it indicates that even in many 'softer' arts such as taijiquan, the combat efficacy–efficiency disposition remains apparent:

> I think it's really important to have a good balance in your life of all of the emotions and all of your experiences. All humans are a mixture of the quieter aspects of human nature, the passive, and the outgoing active aspects. This is the yin-yang balance. If you allow yourself to go too far down the yin way, too passive, too receptive, then you're not experiencing life to the full, to the maximum. It's not that I want to go out fighting people. I never would do. I've never been an aggressive person. I'm not aggressive. But I think I need to develop the controlled potential for aggression. That's an aspect of myself that I want to explore more. It's not pure aggression, but I think I need to be more yang in my life. Just that aspect of who I am. So fighting, developing fighting skills in Chinese martial arts helps you to fulfil that condition, or create that condition. (Chris, interview 1, 20 September 2008)

Chris's background is not one in which there is an identifiable general disposition oriented towards fighting, or even the need for self-defence combat, and so the efficacy–efficiency disposition is more exclusively emergent from the delimited field of taijiquan and more peripherally influential in his martial habitus. Therefore, if there is a single core disposition that is constitutive of the martial arts, then the combat efficacy–efficiency disposition is probably it. However, on its own the combat efficiency–efficacy disposition is insufficient to be constitutive of a martial habitus. A partial reasoning for this is that the learning of efficacious and efficient combat techniques is almost universally agreed (except for certain short-term commercial self-defence programmes) as requiring considerable amounts of practical investment and real-world experience over extended periods of time (years) if appropriate responses are to be naturalized. Through this time investment, two other core dispositions (in these data) also emerge strongly as a practical logical consequence. It is to these that we now turn.

The Practice–Perfection–Mastery Disposition

The second core disposition in the martial habitus emerging from the practical pedagogic logic observed by generations of different master martial practitioners is simply that in order for a skill to become a 'naturalized' response, it has to be practised thousands of times. This realization has recently been further confirmed by social psychologists studying the qualities of experts. For example, Ericsson, Prietula and Cokely (2007) comment that 'the would-be expert needs to demythologize the achievement of top-level performance, because the notion that genius is born, not made, is deeply ingrained'. Indeed, this issue is pertinent for Wacquant, (1992, 249) who contends that:

> What fighters take for natural ability ('You gotta have it in you' […] 'you're born a boxer') is in effect this peculiar nature that results from the long process of the inculcation of the pugilistic habitus […] The native concept of 'natural' […] denotes this cultivated nature whose social genesis has become literally invisible to those who perceive it through the mental categories that is its product.

In many traditional martial cultures this idea of cultivated nature is widespread and accompanied with a consistent call for a submission to the doxa of practice and that practice reigns supreme over natural 'ability'. This is simply because of the practical logic that even the most able can be improved with practice, and that with human conflict and fighting one can never be over-prepared. Moreover, as practitioners configure these skills sets into pedagogic units for daily practice they also give a 'form', in an aesthetic sense, to these cultivated natures and represent movement expressions of ideas and principles that underpin a given approach to combat (wing chun is often described as a 'concept'), thereby creating a style in which form rises to a competing and sometimes more significant prominence than function: 'Thus within the class of worked-upon objects, themselves defined in opposition to natural objects, the class of art objects, would be defined by the fact that it demands to be perceived aesthetically, i.e., in terms of form rather than function' (Bourdieu 2003, 29). This gives these martial forms a living, moving 'artistic' dimension and through practical mimesis an aesthetic disposition emerges that is captured in the idea of practice–perfection–mastery. As a dispositional continuum this resonates with Bourdieu's (1977) own reasoning of the dynamic embodied relations embedded in the practice and interpretation of art, in which he argues:

> To treat a work [read performance] of plastic [read martial] art as a discourse intended to be interpreted, decided, by reference to a transcendent code analogous to the Saussurian 'langue' is to forget that artistic production is always also – to different degrees depending on the art and on the historically variable styles of practising it – the product of an 'art', 'pure practice without theory', as Durkheim says, or to put it another way, a mimesis, a sort of symbolic gymnastics, like the rite of a dance; and it is also to forget that the work of art always contains something ineffable, not by excess, as hagiography would have it, but by default, something which communicates, so to speak, from body to body, i.e. On the higher side of words or concepts, and which pleases (or displeases) without concepts. (Bourdieu 1977, 2–3)

In application, the practice–perfection–mastery disposition emerges as artistic in orientation because of the way in which martial practice can be seen as 'pure' practice passed on through body to body by mimesis, and which manifests itself in a styled performance of techniques that is not (in most of these practical cases) a real fighting performance (although it can be), but rather a physical performance of technical execution (akin to a symbolic gymnastics) in which perfection-in-movement is sought as a central valued form of incorporated capital.

As a dispositional continuum this is distinctive from and often paradoxically disruptive of the combat efficacy–efficiency disposition, as its core logic of movement perfection is ultimately different from combat efficacy. This disposition as a focal orientation is well illustrated by 27-year-old Will, a keen advocate of taijiquan and several other traditional Chinese martial arts:

> I will always be restricted by my body and myself. But within that, I can just be the best that I can and follow my teaching the best that I can. For me, it's just doing that. Perfection for me, it's listening to what I'm being told, absorbing it, and trying to let it radiate from within me. If perfection, in inverted commas, is the beautiful taiji form, 20 minutes long, fully relaxed, but if I don't know the form or if I can't relax properly, I can still be as perfect as I can be. I may never be as perfect as top masters, but it's an individual thing. Everyone, if you're putting the effort in, then you're getting as far as you can get. That is your own personal perfection. And that's all you can hope for. (Will, interview 2, 13 September 2008)

As illustrated here, Will's interpretation of perfection is self-referenced, which is distinctive from the combat efficacy–efficiency disposition because the latter presupposes that the barometer for one's skill needs to be tested against others in order to find out if it works, whereas the practice–perfection–mastery emerges as primarily self-referential and therefore self-legitimizing. The practice–perfection–mastery disposition was also strongly illustrated by Zack, a wing chun practitioner:

> Nobody can be perfect, but trying to be the best that you can. In yourself. In all areas of your life. Using wing chun as the first step to achieve that. Because you're trying to achieve perfection in your technique. So hopefully that quest for perfection, that will go into other areas of your life. Whether it be your relationship. With family, or work relationships. Or just in dealing with people, I think. (Zack, interview 1, 15 March 2008)

Zack's comment is also instructive because it suggests a deliberative interlacing of the practice–perfection–mastery disposition learned through the delimited field of this martial art with more general dispositions in other contexts of his life. Significantly, even those with the focal combat efficacy–efficiency disposition still tend to display the practice–perfection–mastery disposition prominently, although it remains subordinate to efficacy–efficacy, as evidenced by Terry:

> In the safety of the gym, you get the practice without the danger. You get to act without a reaction. You get to practice without getting a busted lip. Obviously, we get some accidents, but it's a safe environment. Whereas in the fighting environment, you haven't got time to think about what you're doing. You haven't got time to feel anything. So, the different between the two is… I have a phrase I use: 'In the gym, you want to give 100 per cent.' Because it's the only place you'll get perfection. When you actually go, the adrenaline's up, the fear, the circumstances, the fact that

the guy's actually going your way, will all, all bubble together, and will all cut down how efficient you are, how correct you are with your technique. You'll never be 100 per cent in a fight. That's why you've gotta try to achieve it in the gym. If you lose it when the real fight happens, then you're left with 50 per cent. Whereas when you only train at 50 per cent, well, half of 50 per cent is 25 per cent. So I'll be fighting as good as a quarter of what I could be. So the better I try in the gym, the more I practise, the harder I get, the better people I have fighting in the gym, the more I have to fight people outside the cash point. (Terry, interview 1, 12 February 2008)

There is an additional dimension with the artistic practice–perfection–mastery disposition, which is that while the goal of martial arts practice may be 'perfection' in self-defence terms, the aesthetic, the self-referential nature of this disposition means that there is a realization that this is ongoing and, in practical terms, a never-ending and unachievable pursuit, which perhaps explains why so many martial practices are pursued as a lifelong activity. This is seemingly embraced by many practitioners who have a focal leaning towards this disposition, as illustrated by Kelly:

Self-defence is just being able to react to a situation once it occurs. Martial arts is a whole different state of mind. It's a whole change in lifestyle. It's dedication, it's commitment to what you're doing… that commitment towards constantly achieving. Whereas in self-defence, you learn: 'Oh, if someone grabs you from behind, this is what you do.' And that's that. That's the whole story. Whereas martial arts, there's just a whole different aspect that you're just constantly learning. You think you get to the end of one style, and you can go onto another one, or learn another aspect of that style. It's just never ending. It's brilliant. (Kelly, interview 1, 20 February 2008)

The time that Kelly has spent training in a variety of martial arts has led to the practice–perfection–mastery disposition becoming focal, to an extent that it challenges the combat efficacy–efficiency disposition for primacy, although both are clearly present. In short, this focal disposition becomes an end in itself and begins to illustrate how it is that the idea of disposition continuum generates spaces for reinterpretation, variation and change in practice. These variations contain considerable scope for subjectivization: like Will, Kelly has studied numerous martial arts and while her core dispositions are recognizable in relation to individual arts they also begin to break free from any one art as these dispositions interlace with her general habitus, a point we shall return to later. Both of these dispositions – efficacy–efficiency and practice–perfection–mastery – are strongly expressed in the presence of another, what we refer to as the body–self–environment awareness disposition.

The Body–Self–Environment Awareness Disposition

The prolonged practical study of these martial arts appears to instil a third disposition that is constitutive of the martial habitus, which we refer to as the body–self–environment awareness disposition. Body–self–environment awareness is taken to mean a progressive 'tuning in' or sensitivity to one's embodied self and the external environment, including other people, objects, social and natural contexts (in short, one's place in the world, in relation) as training progresses.

However, in addition, the body–self–environment awareness disposition also has a constitutive function of its own, which is that such awareness comes to be viewed as a 'valuable end in itself'. In the following statement Will illustrates this disposition as focal in his martial habitus:

> I want the martial arts to be used in the West to their full potential. And I want people to benefit from them in the way that I have. And that's not in a violent capacity, that's not in a particularly self-defence capacity either. I think you should learn martial arts, particularly internal arts, as a child, to develop the skills of being at one with yourself, being rooted, being relaxed and just being more secure in yourself and to have that more positive outlook on life that it gives you. It's not about having power and exerting power over others; it's just about empowering yourself and being strong within yourself and therefore not needing to try to beat other people. So you understand the power, you have control over the power. And you use it applicably. It comes into more of the hippy ideals that I have, like one love, and that sort of perspective of a world where we all relate with each other rather than fighting against each other. Martial arts for me isn't about fighting. That's just the medium through which you train. But it's so much more than that, and hopefully I can pass that on a little bit to the people that I train with. (Will, interview 1, 20 August 2008)

In addition, it is the body–self–environment awareness disposition (coupled with an emphasis on practice) that opens many martial arts styles to spiritualized and/or sacralized self-developmental interpretations (Brown, Jennings and Molle 2009). Chris Armstrong, age 44, a chen-style taijiquan instructor based in south-west England, with over 12 years' experience in the art, commented:

> I've had moments where I've had outer-body experiences where I've had a standing posture. Where all of a sudden, I could see my whole body, but without flesh and skin and stuff like that. I could see bones and vessels and stuff like that. Not many [times]. Sometimes, quite often if I go outdoors and practise Taiji… when you fully relax into the postures and you go into the flow with the movement of the body, then you perceive the world, all the colours seem sharper and seem brighter. Your hearing seems to be more acute. Everything seems much more… the world seems to flow through you, a much more powerful connection to it. So you get those situations… And also, on occasions, I kind of wish it would happen more often, but sometimes when I've been practising taiji, I feel like my whole body is breathing. It's not that my body is breathing, but it's that the universe is breathing my body. (Chris, interview 1, 20 September 2008)

Chris's body–self–environment awareness disposition is clearly a focal element of his taijiquan practice and one that he then begins to interpret according to the specific Taoist metaphors that are abundantly utilized in his own taijiquan style. In a similar vein, Zack reflects on how martial arts practice has instilled in him a 'way of being' that is more body–self and environmentally aware:

> Well, it's just changed everything really. It's given me a lot more focus in my day-to-day life. It's given me a lot of positive spin offs in other areas of my life. Such as motivation. Awareness. I've become very aware of what I want to achieve. What I'm capable of. It cancelled a lot of negativity out of my life. It's given me a good focus. Plus it's the physical attributes, extra coordination, energy levels, fitness... just clarity of mind in a lot of things, has really helped. (Zack, interview 1, 15 March 2008)

Again, Zack illustrates the interlacing of the disposition of body–self–environment awareness coming from practice in this delimited martial arts field and his general dispositions. A similar story albeit with differing qualities is told by Terry, who began wing chun to improve his fighting capabilities, but gradually discovered that the discipline instilled through wing chun practice assisted him in becoming a little more self- and socially aware. Specifically, he found that training helps 'to stop the head mist' that he experienced in tense situations on the street, which usually led to his beginning fights quickly and also to him overacting in these situations:

> I always dissociated myself from the act [of fighting and violence]. It was never me doing it. That's why I think I blacked out. Because I couldn't accept that I had my thumb that far into someone's eye (laughs). It's not a pleasant thing to look at. Whereas, now, over the years, it's took years for me to rationalize it, but I accept now that there's a little Grimthorpe animal out there, and he's a nasty bastard. So I can't let him be out in the general world, because the civilization we live in has rules, and I'll go to jail if I do that in the general world. So what I do now is I lock him up in his box in my head. He's quite happy in his box. But I let him out sometimes. And because he knows he can come out sometimes, I can put him away. (Terry, interview 1, 12 February 2008)

It is clear that, for fighters such as Terry, the body–self–environment disposition is peripheral and subordinate to the combat efficacy–efficiency disposition (in the sense that greater awareness is developed in the service of combat efficacy–efficiency) in Terry's martial habitus. Nevertheless, body–self–environment awareness had a demonstrable impact on his general dispositions over time and, accordingly, a positive impact on his general health (through training he also gave up a 'punishing' involvement in the 'rave' scene) and social behaviour through the reduction in the amount of street fighting he now gets involved in, and also the extent of his actions if he does get involved.

Concluding Comments

The view of the martial habitus suggested here is not one of stasis (hexis) but rather one of constant revision and adaption, permanent mutation (Hilgers 2009), invention and emergence (Spencer 2009) or, as Bourdieu and Wacquant (1992, 133) put it, as a generative grammar for practical action in which habitus can be seen as an 'open system of dispositions that is constantly subjected to experiences, and therefore constantly affected by them in a way that either reinforces or modifies its structures'. We have attempted to illustrate that the range and dynamic nature of dispositions themselves are strongly implicated in this generative practical process, invoked by engagement in the specific delimited fields of wing chun and taijiquan that we have studied.

Figure 3.3. General and de-limited field dispositions interlaced and aligned.

When martial practices are focused on instilling gradual change through pedagogies that extend the capacities of individuals in incremental ways, dispositional change at the individual, subjective level, can take place slowly and almost imperceptibly. In some of Bourdieu's later writing (2005, 45) he intimated that habitus can be subjected to purposive and conscious attempts to change: 'habitus is not something natural, inborn: being a product of history, that is of social experience and education, it may be changed by history, that is by new experiences, education or training'. Therefore, as martial practice is generative of martial habitus and vice versa, there are always possibilities for mutation or regeneration, but equally we must account for the development of particular tastes that are often already strongly informed by life experiences prior to beginning or even knowing about a martial practice. That general dispositional resource is taken into the martial practice in question and may also inform the actual choice of the practice itself, as we saw with Terry. However, once one submits to (develops illusio for) a given practice and its doxa, changes to body and mind can be observed as interlacing with the general dispositions comprising the habitus of an individual (see Figure 3.3).

Following Wacquant's (2011, 81) consideration of the 'imperative of epistemic reflexivity', in this chapter we have drawn on our habitus to inform our observations of others and to develop understandings of the martial habitus for the Chinese arts of wing chun and taijiquan. In this sense, we have come to agree with Wacquant (2011, 82), who says that, 'habitus not only illuminates the variegated logics of social action; it also grounds the distinctive virtues of deep immersion in and carnal entanglement with the object of ethnographic inquiry'.

In so doing, we have extended the idea that the martial habitus is not merely a schema of dispositions which may be considered as a continuum of orientations towards a particular field of practice (in this case the martial arts of wing chun and taijiquan). Our principle interest has been to forward the relatively underexplored idea that the martial habitus is a continuum of dispositions that are themselves (the dispositions) configured in terms of an interlaced series of more discrete continua of 'ways of being'. In doing this, we identified three dispositions (combat efficacy–efficiency, practice–perfection–mastery and body–self–environment awareness dispositions), each of which are configured through practice in relation to the specific dynamics of the delimited fields of the specific martial arts of wing chun and taijiquan that we studied both as researchers and participants. Crucially, we have also shown these to be configured by the specific subjective orientations (informed by the general dispositions of individual practitioners). Put simply, while these dispositions are widely present, their significance, intensity (focal or peripheral) and practical impact seem clearly variable across individuals, arts and associations in a way that suggests a dispositional continuum. Such a view provides some possibility of addressing simultaneously the universalizing and particularizing tendencies of theorizing using the habitus/disposition concepts in relation to martial practices. The multiple dynamics illustrated by dispositional continua on the one hand, and delimited field specific/general dispositions on the other, suggests that there is a spectrum of positions possible, and that the martial habitus, while being universally recognizable in relation to a core schema of dispositions, might also be radically differentiated in their actualization across particular practical cultural contexts and individuals.

Clearly, in spite of the congruence of these dispositions across the arts we have studied, a considerable degree of caution is required in extrapolating these ideas to other martial practices at this point in time. This caution is reflected in three caveats that we would wish to make by way of conclusion. First, while we remain committed to the idea that identifying something that might be termed the martial habitus is valuable for better understanding the phenomenon of martial practices in our societies, we in no way suggest that the dispositions we identify here will be focally present in all arts across this diverse field of human activity. This will require further research and also significantly (given Wacquant's habitus as tool method) dialogue between researcher-practitioners of different martial practices within the field. Second, this 'search' for the martial habitus is not a search for essences or ideal types, but rather for ongoing constructions emerging from lived 'carnal' dispositions that are simultaneously shifting in convergent and divergent directions. Following this, the third caveat is that we would logically expect that further key dispositions might be added to the three we have identified here. We are conscious that in many martial arts the orientation towards competition is focal. This might be expressed through the dispositional state suggested by the verb cluster of compete–test–progress. We therefore hope that this analysis will serve to stimulate further dialogue into the dynamic nature of the dispositions comprising the martial habitus.

Note

1 Translator's note in the original, by Richard Nice.

Chapter 4

EACH MORE AGILE THAN THE OTHER: MENTAL AND PHYSICAL ENCULTURATION IN *CAPOEIRA REGIONAL*

Sara Delamont and Neil Stephens

Introduction

Our title is from Jorge Amado's (1993) novel *The War of the Saints* set in Salvador, Brazil. The romantic hero is an African-Brazilian taxi driver, and a student (*discipulo*) of respected capoeira teacher Master (*Mestre*) Pastinha. Capoeira is an African-Brazilian dance-fight game, which has become globalized in the last 30 years.[1] In the title scene two advanced students, Traira and 'Good Hair',[2] are playing a capoeira game:

> In the centre of the room *Traira* and Good Hair performed, each more agile than the other, more in control of himself, more tricky and unexpected, more dazzling. No one who saw them leap their leaps will ever forget the roguishness of their wily thrusts, the blows that were the most difficult of ballet steps: capoeira kills! (Amado 1993, 232; emphasis in original)

The goal of serious capoeira learners is to be more agile physically and mentally than the other player he or she meets in the *roda*, the circle in which games are played.

We have structured this chapter to introduce capoeira, explain and illustrate our fieldwork and then to explore our own embodiment as fieldworkers (Herzfeld 2009). The project is an example of the carnal sociology called for by Crossley (1995) in that it focuses not only on the bodies of others but on our own embodied selves. The core point of the chapter is encapsulated in the quote from Amado, because the embodied habitus of capoeira is both physical and mental. Acquiring the physical skills does not make a good capoeirista. The mental agility is fundamental. We reflect on our two-handed ethnography drawing on Bourdieu in the main part of the chapter.

Capoeira Explained

Capoeira consists of attacks (mostly kicks) and escapes, plus acrobatic flourishes, and many moves take place with the participants upside down: 'standing' on their hands or their heads (Lewis 1992; Downey 2005a, 2010; Willson 2010). Games also involve trying to deceive your opponent with false movements so that they defeat themselves, and this deceit (*malicia*) is what Amado means by Traira and Good Hair being 'tricky' and 'unexpected'.

Originally capoeira was a male activity learnt by playing in the streets of Brazilian cities (Assunção 2005, 2007; Holloway 1989). Today, all over the world, men and women are taught the moves and practice them in formal classes (Almeida 1986; Butler 1998; Capoeira 1995, 2002, 2006; Joseph 2008a, 2008b; Reis 2005; Travassos 1999; Vieira 2004). These involve warm-up and stretching, the practice of moves and short sequences of moves in lines and then in pairs for about 90 minutes, before a *roda* takes place: games in a circle. Capoeira is an unusual martial art because music is essential. The *roda* includes people playing instruments and a lead singer who 'calls' verses. Everyone is required to respond to the singer by chorusing simple lines in Brazilian Portuguese and clapping the rhythm. A typical chorus is:

Oi, Sim, sim, sim, sim
Oi, Nao, nao, nao, nao
(Which means 'oh, yes, yes, yes, yes; oh, no, no, no, no'.)

In capoeira the agility desired is both mental and physical – and both agilities are centred either metaphorically or actually on the waist (*cintura*). Learners work to achieve an actual bodily change: the development of a flexible waist, or at least the loss of the hard waist (*cintura dura*) that northern Europeans, especially men, have developed by adolescence. Downey (2005a, 129) explores the strong conviction among Brazilian capoeiristas that men in northern Europe and North America are enculturated into a bodily style, or habitus, that trains them to hold their torso inflexibly rigid, not to dance but to resist sensuous, sinuous movement of either the upper or lower body: 'European soccer players, like novice *capoeiristas*, are said to suffer from a *cintura dura*, a hard waist, and thus are likely to be "unnerved" by the Brazalain "*jogo de cintura*" (literally the game of the waist).' In this stereotype is an assumption that: 'Adaptability and responsiveness appear to be located in the torso' (Downey 2005a, 129). Good capoeira students have to loosen their waists physically, and adopt the game of the waist symbolically: i.e. become devious when they play opponents in games. The skill and flair of Brazilian soccer players is widely recognized in Europe. Brazilians attribute this success to a mixture of physical skill due to flexible waists, and mental agility and cunning: that is, playing the game of the waist. Downey (2005a, 128) says that Brazilian soccer players 'like *malandros* and *capoeiristas*, have "good *jogo de cintura*".' A *malandro* is a man who dresses well, dances beautifully, is irresistible to women, yet has no job. It is the characteristics of the *malandro* that Amado is invoking when he describes Traira and Good Hair as 'roguish' and 'wily' (da Matta 1991; Lewis 1992). We have explained elsewhere (Stephens and Delamont 2009) how Brazilians expect capoeiristas to use deceit (*malicia*) for survival in everyday life as well as in the gym.

Our fieldwork is on capoeira classes in the UK. Classes are to be found throughout the UK, especially in university towns and cities. Assunção (2005) has researched the history of disaporic capoeira with particular emphasis on the UK and the representation

Figure 4.1. Capoeira *roda*: Students perform attack and evasion movements in front of the *bateria* of musical instruments.

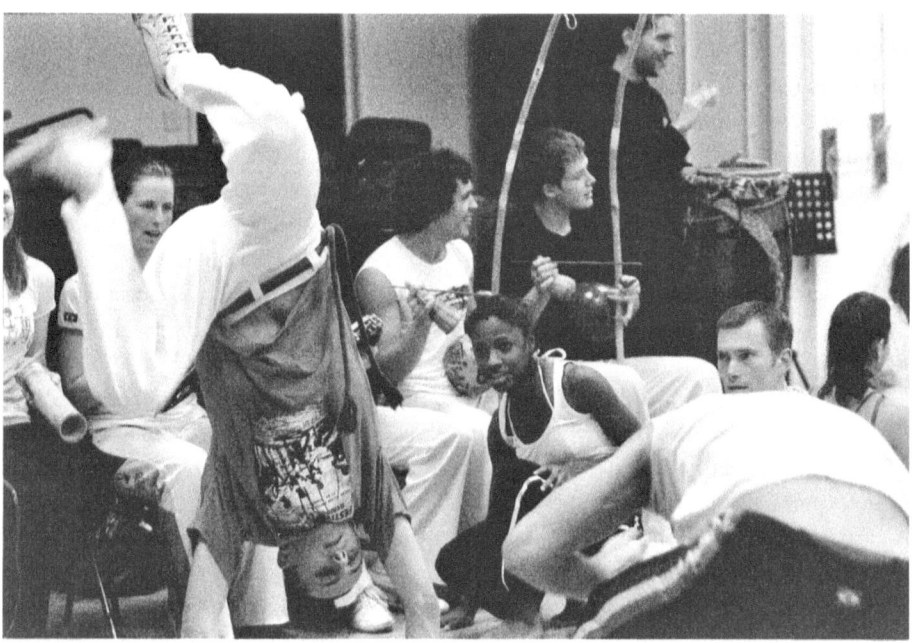

Photo © Paul Atkinson.

of the major Brazilian groups there. Each Brazilian group has a different account of UK capoeira and no consensual story exists. There are some *mestres* who have been teaching, and overseeing teaching, in the UK for more than 30 years, and some groups have provided classes throughout that time. Other groups have existed and vanished, because many capoeira teachers live and work in the UK for a few years and then move to other countries, including a return to Brazil. Those *mestres* who have settled in the UK are producing a few British capoeiristas advanced enough to be teachers themselves. Allegiances to specific teachers and to groups are often deeply felt by serious students. The Brazilian nature, or Afro-Brazilian nature of capoeira is fiercely guarded, so that Portuguese singing is required, and serious students are expected to learn the language and to visit Brazil.

Classes attract students of many nationalities. There are few data on the typical student experience, but many students 'do' capoeira enthusiastically for two to four years before moving on to other leisure activities. Some capoeira teachers have developed outreach and social change agendas, working in prisons or community development projects, and with African-Caribbean schoolchildren. Capoeira teachers are also under-researched, but Rosario, Stephens and Delamont (2010) present the perspective of a young man who is, in our experience, fairly 'typical' of UK capoeira teachers. The biggest difficulty that capoeira teachers face is economic: it requires a great deal of effort to recruit and retain enough paying students to cover room hire and to provide a living.

We now take the reader straight into 'normal' or 'routine' classes led by Achilles,[3] a Brazilian who teaches in two British cities: Cloisterham and Tolnbridge.[4] The following field notes from Tolnbridge in 2006 show a typical UK lesson in which the instructor is not only explicitly teaching physical movements (kicks and escapes) but also implicitly teaching the use of *malicia* in capoeira:

> Achilles teaches a trick: stop the *ginga* (swing) in first position, do a *laterale* (a sideways escape), come up right, feint an *armada* (a spinning kick), as if you are going to kick from left to right, but in fact, do the real kick from right to left, so the opponent has leant into your kick to escape it but because of your trickery she is making herself vulnerable to it. They train this in lines, 10 to each side: that is they do a *laterale* to their right side, stand up, feint an *armada* from right to left, but actually deliver one from left to right, then *ginga* again until Achilles yells 'now' and indicates (with an arm signal) to the left when they do a *laterale* to their left and so on. (Lesson 148)

This chapter's co-author Neil Stephens is present in those lines, while the other co-author, Sara Delamont, sat in a corner watching the class. These were our usual fieldwork roles.

In this short extract the two types of agility are being taught at once. The physical agility comes from practising the kicks and escapes, done repeatedly in sequences. A particular aspect of the training is doing all the moves with both legs, with both arms, to both sides (see Stephens and Delamont 2010b). The mental agility comes from learning how to escape, prepare for being tricked (so that the escapes have to be done very fast in unexpected directions) and how to deceive the opponent by feinting to one side and then attacking from another.

Given that these two aspects of agility are equally important, the methods we chose to study capoeira needed to ensure that both were explored (Stephens and Delamont 2006b, 2013). Capoeira classes, from the initial warm-up and stretching through the capoeira instruction and practice to the warm-down at the end, focus explicitly on re-enculturation of the body, especially the male body. The tacit, 'not-taught' change, acquired by listening to stories, watching games in the *roda*, peer interaction and conversations with teachers, is also about the waist, but metaphorically. The 'game of the waist' (*jogo de cintura*) is the capoeira equivalent of 'ducking and diving', i.e. surviving in tricky situations, or being 'streetwise'. When Jorge Amado wrote of two players 'each more agile than the other', he meant both varieties of agility. Achilles explains *jogo de cintura* as follows:

> Game of the waist? *Jogo de cintura* means when someone knows how to get out of any difficult situation. You know, for example, I am in the game of capoeira, I have planned to take up one position but it is quite impossible because the guy who kicked at me is so low in his kick and I don't know how to escape it, how to get out of the way. So I change my idea. I'm not going for a dodge, I'm going to jump up him, spring up close to his body so I leap over his kick – and that's a kind of *jogo de cintura*. To have a solution for difficult questions in the game, you know. So that's a *jogo de cintura*.
>
> In life – we have this expression in Brazil – when you have *jogo de cintura* that means you know how to get out of difficult situations.
>
> Bruxa: So it's used in capoeira and in life?
> Achilles: Exactly. In capoeira and in life.

Malicia and *jogo de cintura* are not explicitly taught in routine UK classes but are demonstrated in the *roda* by teachers and some advanced students. By watching games, novices learn about the trickery, what Lave and Wenger (1991) call legitimate peripheral participation (see Stephens and Delamont 2009, 2010a).

Agile Methods for an Agile Topic?

We reflect on how two sociologists learnt about both types of agility while doing a two-handed ethnographic project on how capoeira is taught and learnt in the UK.[5] Initially Stephens learnt capoeira from Achilles as a hobby, having done karate to black-belt level as a boy and a young man. He brought embodied knowledge of one martial art to his apprenticeship in capoeira as a man in his twenties when a postgraduate student in the sociology of science and technology (Stephens 2007). Delamont came to capoeira as an ethnographer seeking an interesting fieldsite, and found Stephens, whom she knew as a graduate student, already a *discipulo* in Achilles's classes. We began to discuss what was happening, initially with Stephens as a key informant, but quickly moved on to develop joint insights and publications (Stephens and Delamont 2006b, 2009, 2010a).

Over eight years we have developed a shared sociological understanding of the habitus of capoeira in the UK, paralleled by Jennings, Brown and Sparkes's (2010) study of wing chun kung fu. Delamont is still doing fieldwork on capoeira, augmented by some observation of savate (French method of kickboxing), while Stephens has ceased to do capoeira due to recurrent knee injuries, and spent a year training in Shaolin nam pai chuan kung fu, but is still involved with his capoeira friends and organizing Brazilian music events (McGowan and Pessanha 1998; Murphy 2006; Vianna 1999).[6]

The research on capoeira has been a traditional, or people-centred ethnography (Hammersley and Atkinson 2007; Fine 2003; Brown-Saracino, Thurk and Fine 2008) that can be used to produce a 'thick' (Geertz 1973) or 'luminous' (Katz 2001, 2002) description. Bruxa writes field notes in classes and produces narrative accounts of them (Walford 2009). When we plan to write about capoeira, and when Bruxa is puzzled about the embodied enculturation that is being produced, we sit and discuss what Bruxa has observed. The advantages of a two-handed approach to an embodied activity, where one person's body changes and another watches those changes, are explored in Stephens and Delamont (2006a). Students of capoeira are engaged in what Crossley (2006a, 2006b) called a body project, and for any 'body project' the dynamic relationship between one social scientist who is actively changing his embodiment and another who concentrates on watching the embodiment changing is sociologically productive. When Stephens was still training in capoeira he was actively moving his body, and acquiring both types of agility, for 4 to 12 hours per week. Capoeira play is foundationally dialogic: teachers stress that games consist of questions and answers (attacks and escapes and counterattacks). We have sought, by our two-handed data collection and dialogic analytic and writing strategies, to reproduce the style of capoeira itself (Stephens and Delamont 2006a). The theoretical ideas of Bourdieu are another way in which we conceptualize the methods we use and we return to Bourdieu after some further data are presented on the inculcation of both agilities.

Figure 4.2. Capoeira lesson in the UK: Students practicing movements in pairs.

Photo © Paul Atkinson.

Back to the Class: Work on the Waist

Capoeira teachers begin the task of altering the waists of their students very early in lessons, with the warm-up exercises. Any student (*discípulo*) in the UK would recognize the warm-up routine described below, which Bruxa observed in a routine class taught by a Brazilian, Scinnius, in a London gym in 2006. It included, as well as running around the room, circling the arms vigorously and rotating the upper body from the waist. Scinnius led the students through a set of stretching exercises as follows:

> bending to touch the floor with the hands, legs kept together; spreading the legs as far apart as possible and bending forward to get the forearms (bent at the elbow) and the head onto the floor; then with the legs still spread turning the torso first left, then right to hold each ankle in both hands with the body bent down the leg. This is followed by bending sideways down each leg to pull up the toes of each foot in turn, and then by swivelling the torso from left to right. Next the students sit and put their legs as wide apart as they can. Once again, the body is bent forward from the waist to get the head onto the floor, with the teacher walking round pushing people down further. Again the *discípulos* are ordered to lean along each leg to touch their feet, pulling their body down along the leg. Suddenly the instructor orders them to do a bridge, then relax, then a second bridge, then relax, then a third. Then they sit up, with one leg straight in front, the other bent at the knee across it, hugged close to the body, with the torso turned to look backwards. This is done six times, three to each side. (Lesson 197)

The precise sequence was observed by Bruxa on one specific day, but it was entirely familiar and Trovao would have found the exercises 'normal'. These warm-up exercises involve increasing the flexibility of the waist: students may be urged to repeat them at home twice a day. Then the capoeira class itself begins, and nearly every move taught increases the flexibility of the waist, and every sequence of moves – every question posed to an opponent – also builds the metaphorical game of the waist. Classes involve practice of the basic step, the *ginga*, a triangular step sequence done with one arm raised to protect the face, which should be done with a flexible waist. The *rabo de arraia* kick is practised, delivered with the body bent double and both hands on the floor. The *queixada* and *armada* kicks involve spinning, and the torso must move fluidly with the attacking leg. A typical sequence drilled in a class might involve a *ginga*, with a *rabo de arraia*, followed by an escape that involves bending the torso forward low over the front leg, and then a *rolé* (a turn, through 180 degrees, bent at the waist), followed by the *ginga* again. Students repeat this 20 times, first to the left and then to the right, and then, in pairs, repeat the sequence a further 20 times. Every repetition both increases the students' flexibility and relies upon it.

Such a warm-up and sequence of moves are a central part of every European capoeira class and form a core part of teaching students how to move like Brazilians. Beginners report that they were racked with pain the day after their first class because the moves are so unfamiliar to them; even if novices are fit, capoeira uses different muscles from their normal exercise – in strange ways. Regulars, especially those who have been in training for several years, recognize that they have developed a new relationship with their body: a relaxed comfort and pride. This is captured by Barbara Browning (1995, 87–8) who recalled learning capoeira when it first reached New York, and the pleasure she and her friends took in walking through Central Park: 'Capoeiristas in New York... my friends and I used to stride through the park, leonine and muscular, feeling the mechanism of our bodies walking.' Recalling one of the first capoeira teachers in New York, Loremil Machado, she writes: 'all his friends and students... say he taught them this: how to throw themselves headlong into the pleasure of having a body'.

Browning is a scholar of dance, and draws explicit comparisons between samba and capoeira. Comparisons to dance are useful and simultaneously misleading. The body movements required to play capoeira properly do require rhythmic, sinuous, sensuous actions, like dance. Seeing a rhythmic action done in time to music and the general gaiety, a superficial exposure to capoeira can be misleading, it can look spontaneous and even undisciplined. A casual observer could be misled into thinking that capoeira bodies are not disciplined as compared to those of exponents of karate (Ashkenazi 2002) or other eastern martial arts (Holcombe 2002; Twigger 1999; Donohue 2002). In fact, capoeira bodies are disciplined by hours of drill and practice to appear to be fluid and acting spontaneously and exercising their abilities to play with *malicia*. As the *discipulos* have been acquiring bodily skill, they have also been acquiring the mental agility.

So far the field notes quoted have been from 2006 when Trovao was in full training. While he is now doing kung fu, we can both 'see' what was happening when we discuss together field notes from 30 September 2011 taken during Mestre Hermes's London class:

> At 6:35 the class is about to start. Lines form facing the mirror, but Mestre Hermes signals that they should turn 90 degrees so they are facing the *bateria* (the seats where the musicians sit) and asks for volunteers to play the instruments set out there. Nine advanced students come out of the lines and pick up the instruments. One starts to sing, they all play, and Mestre Hermes sets off with his back to the lines in a fast, light-footed, 'dancey', fluid, 'mazey' *ginga*. Once they have got a rhythm going, Hermes adds a hop and a 360-degree spin to the left and then to the right side. When they have done 10 of those to each side, Hermes goes back to the basic *ginga*, but with 'freezes': i.e. he signals to the musicians, the music stops, the class have to stand stock still in the position they are in, until he signals for the musicians to play again.
>
> 6:55 Hermes leads the class in the *frevo* – a side step with the legs crossed – followed by a false *rabo de arraia* and a real *queida de rins*. They drill 10 of that to each side. (Lesson 653)

The class continue to train a mix of dancey moves, explosive moves and holding still ('statues') until 7:04 when Hermes divides the class into two halves. One half stand along the wall and clap and sing, while the other half practise a short sequence with more space, the halves are rotated every three minutes. For the next 40 minutes, the class practised short sequences of increasing difficulty: the moves became progressively harder for the students. At 7:35 Hermes called them to a *roda*, swapping the musicians out of the *bateria* and calling those who had by then been playing instruments for an hour to come and play him at capoeira. Hermes does not often play students in the *roda* at the end of a routine class, usually preferring to lead the music. To play the teacher, and be first into the *roda* is a great treat. Delamont wrote:

> Hermes plays Mowgli and three other advanced men – very fast, very serious, very tricky, very acrobatic, lots of *malicia*. E.g. Hermes steals the hat off a man's head, puts it on his and avoids it being snatched back.

This was an advanced class and Hermes spoke only Portuguese to the students. It was very hot, and the exercises were taxing for the students, although they worked extremely hard at trying to do them. The nine musicians, who had played and sung for an hour, were rewarded by being exposed to the *malicia* of the teacher. Playing the teacher tests the physical and mental agility of the students, and that test is itself a reward for their commitment. *Malicia* is not used on beginners, who are focused on the physical skills, but is routinely deployed among advanced capoeiristas because it is part of their acquired habitus.

We have presented field notes from a regular class of Achilles's, in which Trovao trained his own body, and two regular classes of London groups, taken between 2006 and 2011, in which Trovao could have participated, and which he can understand when he sees the narrative account that Bruxa has produced for discussion. We now reflect in a more theorized way on that fieldwork.

Bourdieu, Wacquant and Our Fieldwork

Wacquant (2011, 1) argues for 'the use of fieldwork as an instrument of theoretical construction' and in his study of a boxing gym in Chicago the theory constructed was drawn from Bourdieu. As Wacquant puts it, 'The concept of habitus supplied at once the anchor, the compass and the course of the ethnographic journey' (2011, 1) because the research 'dissects the forging of the corporeal and mental dispositions' (2011, 2) of the boxer.

The sociological and anthropological concept of habitus originates with Mauss ([1950] 1979), whose work on techniques of the body focused on the socially constructed customary habits of moving bodies, which vary across societies, social classes and systems of training and education. For Mauss, the bodily techniques were interconnected with modes of life and systems of manners. Bourdieu (1962, 1977) elaborated sociological and anthropological thinking about the concept and enthroned it at the centre of cultural sociology, from his early writing on bachelors in the Béarn, his study of photography (Bourdieu et al. 1965) through *Outline of a Theory of Practice* (1977). Bourdieu argued that any habitus is socially produced (Reed-Danahay 2005). Dispositions are a core part of habitus: socially produced bodily postures, tastes, thoughts and feelings. They are closely linked to stratification and social class, and that link is central to grasping what Bourdieu meant in his 'classic' definition of habitus:

> Systems of durable, transposable dispositions, structured structures predisposed to function as structuring structures, that is, principles of the generation and structuring of practices and representations which can be objectively 'regulated' and 'regular' without in any way being the product of obedience to rules […] Collectively orchestrated without being the product of the orchestrating action of a conductor. (1977, 72)

Subsequently Bourdieu (1990b, 166) argued that 'the teaching of a bodily practice' such as a sport or dance form was an excellent location in which the researcher could gather data on 'a set of theoretical questions of the greatest importance'. His work on habitus has been used by many scholars focusing on changes in embodiment and performativity in dance or sport, anthropologists such as Downey (2010) and Herzfeld (2009), and sociologists such as Crossley (2004c, 2006a, 2006b) and Wainwright, Williams and Turner (2006). Habitus is both a state of mind and a bodily state of being. At the individual level, a person's biology, and their biography, gives him or her a unique habitus. Simultaneously, however, that person is also shaped by the collective history of any group(s) to which he or she belongs. Thus the enculturation and socialization that an individual receives in any educational setting, formal or informal, in any occupational context they enter and in any leisure activities they practise contribute to the individual habitus.

Many Anglophone scholars have offered interpretations of Bourdieu and casuistic disputes abound. Jenkins (2002), for example, claims that personal factors of habitus are lost due to the overdetermination of historical and cultural structures. Such a position reduces Bourdieu's sociological imagination to the flat sterility of Talcott Parsons, and is an approach we reject. A capoeira student who works to acquire and deploy the two types of agility in the *roda*, and then beyond it as Browning (1995) did, like the student of wing chun kung fu (Jennings, Brown and Sparkes 2010), is actively changing her or his individual habitus.

Wacquant's (2004a, 98–9) elaboration of these ideas is central to his ethnography of boxing in Chicago: a study of what he called the 'pugilistic habitus'. Denial of individual agency in developing new individual habituses reduces Wacquant's work to meaninglessness. Capoeira shares some features of the pugilistic habitus but it is also a variety of dance habitus. Like boxing, capoeira is an embodied activity, with a strong performative element. Elsewhere (Stephens and Delamont 2006b) we have contrasted the expert body of the capoeira *mestre* with the novice bodies of the *discipulos*. Here we deploy the theoretical idea of habitus to compare the acquisition of the mental agility and the physical agility. Wainwright, Williams and Turner (2006) draw on the same set of ideas when they explore three varieties of habitus in the field of ballet. Capoeira, being both dance and martial art, sits comfortably between the pugilistic habitus of Wacquant and the balletic habitus of Wainwright and his colleagues. Wainwright, Williams and Turner argue that sociological work on the body has been overly theoretical, a critique they extend more generally to cultural studies. Building on Atkinson's (2006) ethnography of an opera company, they focus on the 'balletic body as a series of cultural practices' (2006, 392). They separate an individual's habitus (e.g. the ballet dancer Carlos Acosta), the institutional habitus (e.g. the Royal Ballet) and the choreographic habitus (e.g. a particular role choreographed for Acosta). Wainwright, Williams and Turner use the life histories of two dancers who left the New York City Ballet for the American Ballet Theatre, with consequent changes to their individual bodily habituses to illustrate their argument. As we have studied capoeira we have been increasingly acquainted with its pugilistic and its dance habituses (Stephens and Delamont 2012).

The idea of the institutional habitus is central to capoeira, and we briefly discuss it, before moving on to the individual habituses of ourselves as ethnographers and of capoeiristas. Wainwright, Williams and Turner (2006) use the term 'institutional habitus' to encapsulate the style and culture of the Royal Danish Ballet as compared to the Kirov or London's Royal Ballet. The capoeira equivalent is the group 'founded' by a famous historical *mestre*; a lineage with Brazilian origins such as Senzala, Cordão d'Ouro, Abolição, União and Beribazu. These have pedigrees of varying depths and complexity, and serious students will argue about their merits or the authenticity of their specific style and conventions. Senzala, for example, traces its origins to a specific period in the history of capoeira. After the liberation of the slaves in Brazil (in 1888) capoeira appeared dangerous to the white ruling class, and was made illegal (Holloway 1989; Assunção 2005). In the 1930s, when the next generation of the elite were actively sculpting a multi-racial Brazilian national identity and culture (Burke and Pallares-Burke 2008, 90), an African Brazilian man nicknamed Bimba started teaching white men capoeira in private gyms in Rio. His work led to *Capoeira Regionale*, to the legalization of capoeira and to its incorporation into a multi-racial Brazilian set of cultural forms. Two of his students,

Paulo and Rafael Flores, are today honoured as the founders of Senzala: an origin story that gives that group a powerful authenticity claim in a contested field. Senzala groups now exist all over the world, and their institutional habitus is characterized by Assunção (2005, 173–6) as involving high kicks, some particular throws and 'unbalancing techniques' (*rasteiras*) not emphasized in other lineages.

A core value of capoeira is loyalty and fidelity to one's *mestre* or teacher (Lewis 1992) and his group. The first public expression of that loyalty is joining their teacher's group. Downey (2005a), for example, joined the Group de Capoeira Angola Pelourinho (GCAP) in Salvador, and later took GCAP classes in New York. Downey describes his immersion in GCAP as an apprenticeship, and likens his time in Salvador to Wacquant's (2004a) period in the Chicago gym. He acquired an individual capoeira habitus and the GCAP's institutional habitus. Students in Tolnbridge, including Trovao, acquire the institutional habitus of their teacher, Achilles.

The ballet 'insiders' interviewed by Wainwright and his colleagues (2006) by watching the performers dance could tell where they had trained and been socialized (a Russian, French or Cuban dance apprenticeship); capoeira experts can tell which diasporic lineage experienced players belong to by the style of their game. In December 2006, Perseus's festival included a public display by the best students and their teachers. Visiting the event, Bruxa heard an advanced student comment to her friends that: 'You can really see who is Cordão d'Ouro and who is Abolição can't you?' Aiming to understand the institutional habituses of different capoeira lineages is an active ingredient in the ongoing fieldwork. When Bruxa is asked by *mestres* how much longer she plans to study capoeira, the answer 'until I can tell an Abolição capoeirista from a União or Nago player by their style in the *roda*' is treated as a sensible goal. Mestre Hermes, for example, said warmly in 2010, 'That is a *good* ambition, Bruxa.' Here we are concerned with the individual habitus, focused on ourselves as researchers and the *discípulos*, but these are contextually grounded in wider capoeira institutions.

Individual Habitus: Researchers and Capoeiristas

Herzfeld (2009, 139) claims that 'it is often anthropologists who are less aware of their embodied self-expression than are their informants'. He commends those who use the comments of their informants to reflect on their own bodily style, doing carnal sociology as Crossley (1995) advocated, and did when learning muay thai himself (2007). When Herzfeld began fieldwork in Bangkok, ordinary Thais would not speak to him in Thai. He got annoyed, and said 'But I'm speaking to you in Thai', which did not produce any greater cooperation because, as he realized later, he was using gestures from his previous fieldwork in Rome. The embodied style he was using signalled 'foreign', 'not-Thai' far more strongly than his Thai speech signalled 'reply to this man in Thai'. When he next worked in Bangkok, with the 'correct' posture and gestures – that is Thai postures and gestures – people spoke Thai with him. In that insightful and amusing reflexive paper, Herzfeld uses his successful and unsuccessful mastery of, and performances as, an embodied Cretan, Italian and Thai, contrasted with his routine everyday life as an academic at Harvard. In the funniest anecdote in the paper, Herzfeld describes how he found himself behaving like a Thai at an international academic meeting in Paris, and unintentionally offended friends by, for example, flinching when one came to embrace him, something that male Thais do not do. Wacquant's (2004a, 2011) reflections on life in Dee Dee's gym are a parallel case, especially when he focuses on how he got his nose broken.

We address our embodied self-expression and that of the advanced students in Achilles's Tolnbridge class, the people who had started learning when Trovao did, starting from a fieldwork extract:

> 7:54 Achilles calls them back to lines. He demonstrates a sequence of moves: *ginga*, first position, a false move, swiftly followed by a 'flying' *martelo rodado* (a kick launched in mid-air with both feet off the ground). Achilles does this, and he can deliver the kick, without apparent effort. Achilles demonstrates this leading (that is kicking) with his left leg, then with his right, four times each. Then he says 'Can you see? It's easy.' The experienced class members including Trovao laugh, as whenever Achilles says 'It's easy' and demonstrates something that appears effortless for him, the move is at the limits of what they can do. Achilles never says 'It's easy' when demonstrating anything the advanced students can do easily. I smile, as I know that only two or three of the students will be able to do that move. (Lesson 168)

There were 23 students present, of whom 8 were relatively experienced: that is they had the second, third or fourth belt.[7] These *discipulos* could either perform this move and practice it or, like Trovao, could try to do it and realistically be expected to master it and add it to their repertoire with further practice:

> When they have drilled this short sequence five times to the left and five times to the right, Achilles calls them to form a circle round him and signals for Jagai to be his demonstration partner. Achilles tells Jagai what he wants to demonstrate. Jagai does a *rabo de arraia*, Achilles dodges that kick, and comes up right to do the *martelo rodada*. This is a 'flying' kick, delivered in mid-air with both feet off the ground, which Jagai escapes. They demonstrate the sequence four times with Jagai attacking Achilles's *martelo rodado* counterattack, then once with Achilles doing the *rabo de arraia*, and Jagai counterattacking with the *martelo*. Typically, Achilles does not content himself with a simple escape from the 'flying' *martelo*. Instead Achilles shows his superiority by doing a counterattack on Jagai who falls to the ground. Everyone laughs, including Jagai. They go into pairs to practice that routine.

The capoeira teacher wants to show how much better he is than any student, *and* to teach the class never to relax or think the game is over, but always to be mentally agile. Achilles adding to the rehearsed routine to do that counterattack is typical. In that ordinary class, Achilles is teaching both types of agility. The physical changes needed in the embodied performance are explicitly taught and practised. The mental agility needed to escape *malicia* was being demonstrated by its absence: Jagai was not mentally agile enough to have thought of any escape or counterattack to use on Achilles. It is the job of the capoeira teacher to expose students to *malicia* (Stephens and Delamont 2009). The eight men and women, including Trovao, were developing physical agility and being exposed to *malicia*, acquiring more of the habitus of capoeira. None was yet 'dazzling' like Traira and Good Hair in Amado's novel, but they were working to be so.

Not all the students present in that advanced class are still in capoeira: Vainateya is a teacher earning his living giving capoeira classes; Jagai is a regular student, still a favourite demonstration partner of Achilles, being tricked and falling to enculturate new students; but others have left Tolnbridge or capoeira or both. However, all those eight people had the bodily and mental agility with which they entered capoeira changed by capoeira. Achilles judges Trovao to have a flexible waist and much greater self-confidence in life because of capoeira, and Trovao concurs. Like for Wacquant, there has been a synergy between a changed bodily habitus and a research project.

For Bruxa, there is no obvious relationship between her embodied habitus and the capoeira fieldwork. She is over 65, fat, unfit, not at all physically agile and entirely lacks musical and rhythmic skill, as a series of autobiographical papers (Delamont 2005a, 2005b, 2005c, 2006, 2009) explore. The main change for Bruxa has been in her research habitus: publications and conferences with different discourse communities such as those who contribute to this volume. It can be argued that Bruxa has 'moved' intellectually as much as Trovao has changed his waist. Following Herzfeld (2009) she has learnt to present herself in a more 'Brazilian' way in the capoeira fieldwork, and occasionally found herself embracing non-capoeira people, 'forgetting' that they are not inhabitants of such a tactile culture; but these are minor issues compared to the intellectual journey.

Conclusions

In this chapter we reflected on the use of Bourdieu's concept of habitus in capoeira scholarship, our own embodiment as researchers (Herzfeld 2009) and issues of embodiment in dance and martial arts (Bar-On Cohen 2009c; Wulff 2008; Woodward 2008). We retain a Bourdieu-based theoretical stance although we recognize that previous use of Bourdieu as a theoretical frame (e.g. Delamont and Stephens 2008; Rosario, Stephens and Delamont 2010) has been challenged explicitly by the work of Downey (2010). While we have deployed Bourdieu's concept in several papers we have also interpreted our data using Jamous and Peloille's (1970) dimensions of indeterminate and technical knowledge (Stephens and Delamont 2009), suggested that students learn by what Lave and Wenger (1991) call 'legitimate peripheral participation' (Stephens and Delamont 2010a) and drawn upon Herzfeld's (1985) theories about the poetics of manhood. Because the research has involved both our movement and the movements of others we have also explored how the capoeira ethnography is an example of what Urry (2007) calls the mobilities paradigm, because the nine types of mobility that he argues require social science attention are all present in globalized capoeira. The teachers, the *discipulos*, and us as researchers are, as we demonstrate in Stephens and Delamont (2010b), all moving in real space and in cyber space, in order to make capoeira movements or to observe them being made.

Wacquant (2011) shows how it is possible to use Bourdieu's concept of habitus in a reflexive way to explore the scholar's ethnographic processes. In this chapter we have used the concept to reflect on a two-handed ethnographic project, in which two very different scholars have each changed their habitus. The next 'journey' for Trovao and Bruxa into their bodies, minds and publications is for Trovao his new enculturation into kung fu and for Bruxa more fieldwork on savate.

Notes

1 There are two main styles of capoeira today, *angola* which is held by its adherents to be more African and is played slowly and close to the ground, and *regional* which is played faster, upright and includes kicks that are similar to those used in karate. Pastinha is credited in the histories with ensuring that *angola* survived and was not superseded by Mestre Bimba's *regional* (Assunção 2005).
2 In capoeira, the players are often given a nickname by their master: 'Good Hair' is such a nickname. In capoeira regional groups, after a student has studied for a few months they attend a *batizado* (baptism) when they get their nickname and their first belt. Neil Stephens was given a nickname by Achilles in 2003, with his initial blue belt. Sara Delamont was honoured with a nickname in 2004. To protect our friends in Achilles's classes, while we both have a real capoeira nickname bestowed by Achilles we appear in our capoeira writings with pseudonymous nicknames Trovao (Thunder) and Bruxa (Witch) for Stephens and Delamont respectively.
3 All the teachers and students mentioned have pseudonyms. The teachers are protected by names from Greek mythology (Achilles, Scinnius), the male students by names from Kipling's *The Jungle Book* e.g. Bagheera; the females have the names of flowers e.g. Hibiscus. These pseudonyms reflect the ways in which capoeira operates: teachers are usually known by one name (e.g. Mestre Zulu, the founder of Beribazu), male students are given nicknames which are either martial (Hammer or Bad Guy) or funny (Big Nose or Idiot), with females usually having pretty or 'girly' nicknames. In UK capoeira the authors are better known by our real nicknames than as Neil Stephens and Sara Delamont. Hence our use of pseudonymous capoeira nicknames in publications.
4 All the places mentioned in the chapter except London are protected by pseudonyms.
5 Delamont has also observed capoeira classes in New Zealand and Holland. British capoeira classes are similar to those in other diasporic locations outside Brazil. Trovao's main teacher was Achilles, although he started with Cadmus, had a variety of other guest instructors and has trained briefly in Canada. Bruxa has watched Achilles teach over 400 times and has watched a further 300 classes led by other teachers. We have only experienced two women instructors, and for this chapter refer to all the teachers as 'he'.
6 Trovao developed an interest in African-Brazilian music and organizes Brazilian-themed club nights. Capoeira festivals usually include at least one dance-focused event in a night club, and capoeira clubs perform at these events in order to raise funds and publicize themselves.
7 Regional capoeira groups usually have a system of coloured belts (*cordas*) like karate. Each group has its own hierarchy, so a blue belt is the first level in Beribazu but a fifth level (indicating eight or nine years of hard training) in cordão d'ouro. In 2006 no one in Tolnbridge had a fourth or higher belt, but two of Achilles's Cloisterham students, Mysa and Vainateya, who had the brown and green (fourth) belt had come with Achilles that night.

Chapter 5

'THERE IS NO TRY IN TAE KWON DO': REFLEXIVE BODY TECHNIQUES IN ACTION

Elizabeth Graham

Introduction

Tae kwon do (TKD), 'a version of unarmed combat designed for the purpose of self-defence' (Choi 2008, I: 23), is a young martial art emerging in the mid-twentieth century in Korea. Despite an emphasis on Korea in discussions of TKD's history, it shares with many martial arts a history that can be traced to the Chinese martial art of tang soo do, which dates back more than 2,000 years to warriors in the T'ang Dynasty (Lake Norman Tang Soo Do Academy 2001).[1] The minimal recognition of non-Korean influence in the development of TKD has been discussed in relation to national identity. Presented as a Korean martial art, TKD encouraged a sense of nationalism that Koreans needed following the end of Japan's occupation in 1945 (Gillis 2008). However, the political and ideological split between North and South Korea filtered into historical accounts of TKD's beginnings and development with each laying claim to the art. Additionally, significant variations of TKD have developed; practitioners have divided into multiple groups all claiming greater authenticity than the others. The most well-known variants of TKD are the World TKD Federation (WTF) and the International TKD Federation (ITF). Although WTF is more popular (Gillis 2008), in this research I focus on ITF.[2]

General Choi identified nine training secrets that every TKD practitioner must memorize. They illustrate Choi's awareness of the necessity to see oneself through the statement 'I am a body' rather than 'I have a body' (Turner 1992). Each secret requires that the practitioner not simply act following thought but act in a thoughtful, purposive way. Together they constitute the foundation upon which all TKD learning must stand.

During my years of training in TKD there are two ideas I have heard repeatedly from my instructor that are the focus of this chapter. The first is 'There is no *try* in tae kwon do' [emphasis in original], a phrase that I understand as highlighting the interdependence of thinking and doing in TKD training. The second is being a *technician*, a term used to refer to practitioners who have achieved a level of skill and precision that alters how they see themselves as well as how others see them. The purpose of this chapter is to explore these ideas through the application of two concepts: habitus and reflexive body techniques (RBTs). Through this exploration, 'There is no *try* in tae kwon do' encourages the adoption of RBTs and highlights the interdependence of thinking and doing. In addition, the TKD technician habitus is shown to be an embodied understanding of 'There is no *try* in tae kwon do'. The discussion of these concepts offers insights into TKD and contributes to and highlights the necessity for a carnal sociology.

While there has been research focusing on martial arts, much of it either takes martial arts as a collection, not distinguishing among the different forms, or it focuses on more popular forms such as karate. However, in the limited research that focuses on TKD or includes it as one of many forms, the primary concern is the possible benefits of martial arts for children and adolescents. For example, some researchers have concluded that among these age groups martial artists score higher than non-martial artists on self-concept and personality trait indexes and scales. The more advanced their training, the greater their difference in relation to the non-martial artist. Additionally, much of this research focuses on self-correction through martial arts training. Researchers conclude that martial arts training effectively reduces aggressive behaviour or improves the self-esteem of adolescent boys (see: Chami-Sather 2004; Endresen and Olweus 2005; Lakes and Hoyt 2004; Zivin et al. 2001). Much of the remaining literature concentrates on high-level professional or Olympic competitors (Parmigiani et al. 2006), and physiological research focusing on the body and bodily injury among high-level athletes (Zetaruk et al. 2005; Burke et al. 2007). The remaining smattering of investigations explore women's interest in fighting arts with some identifying self-defence as an explanation for their interest (Angleman et al. 2009; Burrow 2007; Himmelsbach 2007; Lawler 2002).

Habitus and Reflexive Body Techniques

Most notably associated with Bourdieu, habitus is typically defined as 'a lived-through structure-in-process' (Spencer 2009, 120). It is the socially structured practice that moulds our behaviour, invites the belief that the behaviour is somehow natural (Alexias and Dimitropoulou 2011) and influences 'our bodies, tastes, knowledges, competencies, and ways of thinking' (Wade 2011, 225). However, it is also subject to change through body techniques or corporeal schemata that are learned through imitation and repetition (Spencer 2009). As such, habitus 'is not an independent thing but rather a flexible dispositional structure formed within and by the body, *qua* inter/action system, in the context of its ongoing interactions with the world' (Crossley 2004c, 40).

According to Crossley (2004c), the general concept of body techniques emphasizes 'that structured forms of bodily activity […] embody a practical understanding and meaning' and 'social facility'. They are both biological and psychological facts that vary across societies and groups within a society (2004c, 37–8). He further explains in relation to his work on circuit training that 'mastery of body techniques […] must entail the capacity to tackle the "double contingency" (Luchmann, 1995) incurred by having to perform them in environments which are simultaneously physically and socially structured' (2004c, 40).

The more specific concept of reflexive body techniques, which is of particular importance in my research on TKD, refers to 'body techniques which act back upon the agent, modifying him or her, and which are employed specifically for this purpose' (Crossley 2004c, 38). They 'are integral to the production of a reflexive sense of self' (Spencer 2009, 133; Crossley 2004c). The process by which they work indicates that mind and body are not separate as Descartes would have us believe. Rather, the RBTs generate the split of Mead's (1934) 'I' and 'Me' components of the self. It is from this split that we are rendered capable of objectifying our embodied experiences and fashioning the 'Me' (Spencer 2009; Crossley 2004c).

The discussion in this chapter is broken down into four sections beginning with a brief contextual and methodological discussion. In the three remaining sections, I provide a context in which to understand the experience of TKD. Then I explore the understanding and experience of 'There is no *try* in TKD' as a mantra meant to encourage the development of reflexive body techniques (Crossley 2004c). I conclude the chapter by discussing the TKD technician habitus as an embodied understanding of that mantra and illustrative of the need for a carnal sociology.

The Study: Context and Methodology

I was first introduced to TKD by a former sociology student. She had a second-degree black belt and was interested in teaching a TKD class at the university where I am on faculty. When she approached me to enroll in the class I was reluctant, given that I was 40 years old and in terrible physical shape. I did not think I would last, but more than six years later TKD has become an integral part of my life and the focus of a multiyear research project (Graham 2010, 2009).[3]

When I began the multiyear project in 2007 my objectives were to identify whether specific types of individuals choose to train in the martial arts, the reasons people begin to train as adults, their reasons for continuing, and finally to determine whether those reasons vary according to gender and over time. The project has three phases. Phase One is the source of information for this chapter.[4] It employed the ethnographic methods of participant observation and qualitative interviews. Participant observation occurred from 2007 to 2010 at five clubs in Ontario, Manitoba and British Columbia. The field notes I discuss in the following pages are limited to notes from the club in which I am a member and one club in British Columbia. The club where I train has approximately 75 members of which roughly 25 per cent are adults who train year-round. The British Columbia club has approximately 140 members. I observed that the percentage of adults was similar to that in my club. Supplementing this data is information collected during the qualitative interviews. I conducted 32 interviews, face-to-face or by telephone, with adult TKD practitioners from Ontario, Manitoba, Saskatchewan and British Columbia between the spring of 2008 and fall of 2010.[5]

This methodological approach allowed me not only to watch and listen but also to *feel* with my body what it is to do TKD as an adult in various *do jangs* under different instructors with different styles and expectations.[6] While adopting a classical participant observation approach, focusing considerable attention on the social context and the manner in which individuals construct and maintain the space and experience of a *do jang*, I also used my 'body as a tool of inquiry', thereby adopting a more nuanced form of this method which Wacquant refers to as 'observant participant' (2004a, viii). Similar to Spencer (2009, 124), I believe the use of this method 'has allowed me to observe and participate in the ways in which fighters learn body techniques and transform' their bodies.

I also had the advantage of being an insider for this research. At the beginning of this project I had achieved the rank of blue belt and participated in two tournaments. By the end of Phase One, I had advanced to the rank of black stripe, and participated in two additional tournaments. My insider status translated into a certain degree of cultural capital with research participants. Many felt confident in my familiarity with TKD and bypassed explanations that an outsider would be required to give. Similar to claims made by Abramson and Modzelewski (2011), this insider status afforded me 'near total access' to my research sites, an ability to understand 'behavioural and speech cues' and gave me 'enough status in the subculture [...] to make successful authenticity claims' (2011, 149). These advantages were particularly important in the quasi-militaristic environment of TKD. While my rank indicated experience, I held no position of authority in relation to my research participants.

Figure 5.1. TKD class reciting oath.

Photo courtesy of the author.

There is no doubt that the observant participant method enabled me to collect information that otherwise would have never emerged. However, the qualitative interviews were also essential because the nature of TKD classes allows for few opportunities to talk unless you are instructing the class. The majority of the interviewees were members of the two clubs I described above. They ranged in age from 18 years to over 70 years. The gender distribution was approximately two-thirds male and one-third female with a range of ranks from white belt (beginner) to advanced black belts. Through the interviews I explored the personalities and character traits of participants, their vision of TKD and their attraction to it. The interview guide was designed to be flexible in order to ensure that issues of importance to the participants were included in the information collected. It was because of this flexibility that the primary ideas discussed in this chapter revealed themselves as worthy of focused attention.

'There Is No *Try* in Tae Kwon Do'

The mantra of my head instructor, 'There is no *try* in tae kwon do' is meant to encourage 'doing' over 'thinking'. However, it is not meant to imply a lack of thought. Rather it simultaneously recognizes the physical and mental demands of the art and the requirement that the TKD practitioner cease to understand the mind and body as separate. As phenomenologists explain, there is 'an organic synthesis of mind and body' that produces a TKD practitioner and 'his/her social behavior' (Alexias and Dimitropoulou 2011, 88). Understanding the mind/body relationship as a synthesis is necessary in order to avoid the otherwise inevitable problem of the mind causing delayed action of the body. To *try* denotes conscious thought preceding bodily movement. Bodily speed is essential in TKD; however, there cannot be speed or movement without purpose. As such, the mantra should be understood to mean *there is only doing with understanding*. As in the case of Crossley's (2004c) circuit trainers and Spencer's (2009) mixed martial arts (MMA) fighters, successful enactment of this mantra in TKD is achieved through the acquisition of RBTs.

The transition from thinking to doing

As in any other context, gaining body techniques in TKD can then be used to modify oneself through repetition of structured bodily activity (Crossley 2004c). In TKD, to instil the importance not just of repetition but precise repetition, training involves strenuous regimented physical components, including a warm-up routine, TKD exercises and patterns (*tuls*), kicking techniques (*bal gisool*), prearranged sparring (*yaksok matsogi*), free-sparring (*jayu matsogi*) and self-defence (*hosin sul*), paired with an understanding of how these are done and to what purpose.

TKD instructors recognize that for the beginner to move towards the body/mind synthesis (Alexias and Dimitropoulou 2011) initially requires an unbalanced relationship in which the mind dominates. Therefore, they require beginners to focus their attention on patterns, kicks and prearranged sparring while reserving free-sparring and self-defence for students who are familiar with basic techniques. Such techniques are broken down into step-by-step movements that students repeat innumerable times. As the training regimen is repeated, the body begins doing without the deliberate conscious thought of *how*. In the process of achieving a TKD technician habitus, such repetition gradually transitions to RBTs. The individual reaches a point at which feet, hands, breath and eyes come together at the moment of contact to form a single fluid movement. With the aid of my field notes and interviews concentrating on patterns and free-sparring, the following section provides a glimpse of this transition.

Learning and practising: Thinking before doing

The beginner's preoccupation with thinking inevitably means that movements, whether actions or reactions, will be deliberate and ensue more slowly and awkwardly than is the case of the seasoned TKD practitioner. This is apparent as one observes a beginner learning the motions of their first exercise, a precursor to patterns.

Like patterns, exercises teach 'flexibility, grace, balance and coordination' (Choi 2008, I: 75). They 'are various fundamental movements, most of which represent either attack or defence techniques, set to a fixed and logical sequence'. Consistent practising of exercises and patterns enables the student 'to develop sparring techniques, improve flexibility of movements, master body shifting, build muscle and breath control, develop fluid and smooth motions, and gain rhythmical movements' (Choi 2008, I: 144). Optimally, each motion should be done with maximum power, appropriate speed and total coordination of the body. Because each exercise or pattern builds on the previous one, a student is required to become proficient in one before learning the next (Choi 2008, I: 144–5). Acquiring and maintaining such proficiency requires 'practice, practice, practice' (Mr Andrews, head instructor).[7]

As an example, *sagigurugi*, or four directional block, is the first exercise learned in TKD. While learning this exercise I quickly realized the difficulty of full body coordination when enacting each of the 14 motions. The detail necessary to perform only the first motion illustrates the complexity of such learning and the necessary preoccupation with thinking that every beginner experiences. To perform a walking stance with a low block a student must learn:

> The length between the feet must be one shoulder width from the big toe of the left (front) foot to big toe of the right (back) foot and the width between the feet must be one shoulder width. The left foot must be turned out 15 degrees and the right foot turned out 25 degrees. The left knee should be bent to the middle of the foot and the right leg must be straight. The hips and shoulders need to be straight so that the individual is full-facing. The left forearm should be down with the hand in a fist, thumb across the first two fingers, forming a low block at a 25 degree angle, which is meant to protect the lower abdominals. The right arm should be pulled back with the fist resting at the belt. Eyes must be forward, looking into the eyes of the opponent. As the motion reaches the target it should be accompanied by a sharp exhalation. Successfully performing this motion requires that each of these movements begin and end at exactly the same time. (Field notes, 15 June 2008)

TKD terms such as walking stance and low block are 'meaningless to a beginner, but they become gradually loaded with significance, and their meaning shifts as the students' understanding of them is modified through somatic experience' (Bar-On Cohen 2006, 75). Additionally, initially enacting the required physical coordination seems impossible. Students attempt to minimize their incompetence by mentally working through what they are supposed to do and how to do it, before they engage in the movement. The mental process is practically visible to an observer. The beginner looks around to observe what others are doing, what direction they are facing, where their feet and hands are positioned. The movement of feet, hands, eyes and breath never seem to happen together. Feet get tangled. People face the wrong direction, use the wrong arm for the block or move the wrong foot back for the stance. Similar to the newcomers in Crossley's circuit training classes, the habitus of these TKD beginners is unstructured and as such 'demonstrates that the habitus of the circuit trainer [or TKD technician] is both structured and structuring' (Crossley 2004c, 47).

The beginner quickly realizes that knowing a walking stance with a low block 'is a matter of practical bodily know-how rather than conceptual knowledge-that'. To know this technique is 'to be able to do it [...] at the right moment, without first having to think about it' (Crossley 2004c, 45). However, it is still necessary that 'conceptual knowledge-that' precede 'practical bodily know-how'. As Choi explains, 'It is this mental conditioning that separates the true practitioner' from others (2008, I: 23).

While visiting a TKD club in British Columbia, Canada I participated in a class in which the head instructor encouraged students to strive for bodily know-how but simultaneously reinforced the need for conceptual knowledge:

> Following a warm-up, we began to practice patterns, starting with the lowest (first learned) and working our way up. Mr Barry, the head instructor, had us do each pattern one motion at a time as he walked around the *do jang* correcting everyone's body positioning. However, he added a mental component to the situation. As he examined each student's body positioning he shouted out questions about the angle of the arms, the position of the feet, and the purpose of the technique. At one point I heard 'Ms Graham what is the target for your reverse knife hand?' He noted my surprise at having a question directed to me, a guest, and said 'Aaah, you didn't expect that. You're part of the class.' I offered an answer. In a jesting manner, he replied, 'That is incorrect. But thank you for playing', and then repeated the question directing it to another student. (Field notes, 13 April 2010)

So, while each motion was expected to be done on command without hesitation, without thought, Mr Barry was instilling in his students the need to always know the what and why of each movement. He encouraged the adoption of somatic codes which 'have the capacity of succinctly focusing the participants' awareness onto a certain aspect of training' (Bar-On Cohen 2006, 75). However, the student must eventually come to know that 'conceptual knowledge-that' is 'an impediment to learning body technique' (Spencer 2009, 128). This realization is reinforced each time a student moves up in rank as they revisit the experience of transitioning from thinking to doing. They must learn new patterns, new kicks, new prearranged sparring. However, the transition progresses more quickly each time, as their prior embodied knowledge is more structured than at less advanced ranks. Despite this difference between the beginner and more advanced TKD student, the purpose of the exercises and patterns remains the same, to learn methods of attack and defence that can be used in free-sparring and self-defence.

Learning and practising: Intertwining doing and thinking

Free-sparring, in particular, reveals the transition to 'practical bodily know-how'. Free-sparring 'is essentially an open combat with controlled attacking and prohibition of attacking to certain vital spots' (Choi 2008, V: 234). It is the unchoreographed application of acquired techniques that highlight the necessity of precision, 'speed, balance, flexibility, adroitness, coordination, and so on' (Choi 2008, IV: 10). 'In the case of the students of Taekwon-Do who have been in constant practice or the experts themselves, they spend no time thinking, as such an action comes automatically to them. Their actions, in short, have become conditioned reflexes' (Choi 2008, I: 25).

Figure 5.2. Western Regional Tournament: Sparring match between Graham and anonymous woman.

Photo courtesy of the author.

In a typical class, an individual will spar with four to six people of varying rank, age and sex. The variety encourages students to become flexible and fluid in relation to their opponents. Sparring with more experienced individuals is the best way to practise and experiment with new techniques. However, sparring with less advanced individuals is also advantageous because they provide the more advanced opponent the opportunity to perfect techniques. My field notes on the sparring in one class illustrate these benefits and reinforce the importance of the mind/body balance:

> My first sparring match is with Ms Jones, a second *Dan*. We stand at attention facing each other in the centre of the ring. Hearing the command, 'Stepping back guard. And, begin', we begin [...] As the more senior ranking person, Ms Jones bounces around waiting for me to attack. I move in with a front leg turning kick to her abdomen followed

by a punch to the head. She blocks the kick and instantly retaliates with a reverse back kick, which pushes me back so that my punch does not make contact. We both bounce back briefly. Ms Jones moves in with a double turning kick. I block the first and simultaneously retaliate with a reverse back kick, which moves my body so that her second kick misses […] Ms Jones does a downward kick catching my collar bone. She has devised a way of doing the kick faster than the traditional method of execution. She pauses and motions for me to try the technique on her. I surprise myself by successfully making contact but my targeting is off – I only grazed the edge of her shoulder. We continue. She easily blocks my turning kick and reminds me to avoid overuse of a single technique, 'I knew that was what you were going to do. You've done it so many times that I expected it.' We hear 'TIME' and everyone stops. (*Reflective note: I intentionally seek out another black belt, Mr Peterson who is a large man. Because of the size difference, sparring with Mr Peterson gives me the opportunity to push myself harder and use as much power as I can, within reason, without being concerned that I may injure him. It is an opportunity for me to let go and not get caught up in thinking too much. It is purely act and react. He never goes easy on me because I am small and female.*) At the command we begin the match. Like Ms Jones, he waits for me to attack. He uses his entire body, including his face, to let me know that I am not pushing myself hard enough. He does a side kick that pushes me completely out of the ring. I move back into the ring. He lunges at me with multiple punches to the head and ribs. My blocks are nearly completely ineffective but then, as his momentum is pushing me backward, I land a punch to his face. He pauses and nods in approval while motioning for me to follow-up the blow with others. We continue in this way until we hear 'TIME'. I pair up with Mary who is a lower rank. I am exhausted so I am happy to pair up with her. However, because of this difference in rank it is now my responsibility to help her in the same way that the black belts helped me, while still getting something out of it for myself. At the command, we begin the match. Mary is reluctant to attack and somewhat fearful of my attacks. I motion for her to attack. She tentatively approaches me and attempts a front snap kick with minimal power and apologizes even though I successfully blocked the kick. I shake my head indicating that she should not apologize and encourage her to attack again. She does a turning kick, which I easily block and follow-up with a back kick and punch to the head. She almost blocks the kick but is unprepared for the punch. The pace is also much slower and Mary's movements are visibly more awkward compared to my partners in the first two matches. (Field notes, 21 February 2009)

As my notes reveal, more experience means that the habitus of the practitioner is more structured. Sparring is a concrete reminder that while the mind always needs to know what the body is doing and why, the body should never need the conscious mind to move. There is no time to consciously consider what vital spot on the opponent should be attacked. Such conscious thinking makes you an open target for your opponent, as I was for the black belts and Mary was for me. In addition, the less experienced practitioner tends to repeatedly enact only those few techniques that have become part of their evolving habitus. Their actions are therefore predictable and easily thwarted by the more advanced practitioner. Concurrently, such an opponent, with a more structured habitus, can easily identify an open vital spot on your body and attack as automatically as breathing. These abilities of the advanced practitioner only develop through repetition. As Mr Andrews says, practise that kick or that combination 'thousands, millions of times'.

The TKD Technician Habitus

While free-sparring encourages the student to pit their newly acquired skills against a living opponent, it is not the ultimate objective. TKD is an art of self-defence 'which aims at a noble moral rearmament, high degree of intellectual achievement, graceful techniques, formidable power and beauty of physical form, it can be considered as a part of one's daily life, just as are breathing and thinking' (Choi 2008, I: 14). Some who persevere ultimately modify their sense of self by acquiring a TKD technician habitus.

A TKD technician habitus is essentially the embodied understanding and consequence of 'There is no *try* in tae kwon do'. It is the successful manoeuvring through the interactive process of thinking and doing with the body to a state of bodily knowing. Specifically, a technician is a practitioner who has reached an 'embodied form of "knowing without knowing" […] a form of unformulated and perhaps unformulable knowledge which consists only in the capacity to do' (Crossley 2001, 122). The technician is someone who has acquired near perfect precision and accuracy in every movement, as well as the ability to effectively evaluate each movement; they have adopted the identity of a martial artist and the ability to effectively teach TKD to others. However, underlying all of these is one characteristic. The technician understands that this habitus emerges through an 'organic synthesis' of body and mind (Alexias and Dimitropoulou 2011, 88), which evolves through acceptance of the mantra 'There is no *try* in tae kwon do'.

There is a level of precision among technicians that suggests an embodied intentionality, as described by Crossley (2004c). They have the ability to tune-in to the class and tune-out of their everyday attitude more adeptly than the beginner. They are able to 'obey automatically […] without question' (2004c, 53) and without hesitation. Their focus is undeniable.

Mr Barry and Mr Andrews are two of many technicians I now know who have repeatedly demonstrated an ability to consistently hit or kick a target as if they were targeting the centre of a dart board. Adept at 'tuning in', neither of them any longer requires time to mentally shift in and out of a TKD mindset; the target is the only thing in their centre of vision. Kathy, one of the people I interviewed from Mr Barry's club, told a story illustrating this ability:

> There is a story about him doing that kick (she points to a picture of Mr Barry doing a jumping front-snap kick). He was at a tournament, not competing. He was a judge for the speciality kicks so he didn't have his *do bok* on. He was wearing a suit. All the young black belts were complaining, 'the board is too high', 'we can't reach that', that sort of thing. Rather than criticizing them for allowing themselves to adopt a defeatist attitude, he simply walked over, took off his jacket, shoes and socks, jumped up and with one attempt split the board in half. It was 9 feet high. He turned to them and said, 'It's not too high', and walked off the floor. (Interview, 13 April 2010)

Nearly everyone I talked with from Mr Barry's club told some version of this story. They were exceedingly pleased to have an instructor capable of 'tuning in' so effectively. Many of them hoped to acquire RBTs that would allow them to accomplish similar feats. Mr Barry's habitus inspired his students to strive for a TKD technician habitus.

Similarly, in another class, Mr Andrews illustrated to his students the ability that comes with precision when he demonstrated the 'one inch board break' (a punch that breaks through a board held only one inch away from the fist). His fist moved through the board as if it was a potato chip, one easy snap and the board was in pieces. During this class, he explained to students that 'anyone, no matter their size, can break a board, can break many boards, if their technique is correct'. 'You can practise over and over but if your technique is wrong, if you're off target, it won't matter.' 'It only hurts when you don't break the board', he says (field notes, 28 January 2008). Precise repetition is required. Practising the same kick over and over, and ensuring proper targeting, are essential, so that all parts of the body (mind, eyes, hands, feet and breath) are acting in sync. This cannot be achieved when conscious thought interferes. It must become an RBT.

Mr Andrews further encouraged his students to strive for a TKD technician habitus with his slogan for the club: 'Be a Black Belt'. He teaches his students that anyone can be a black belt even if they do not yet *have* a black belt. It is a TKD state of being. To be a black belt is to engage in RBTs with the intention of achieving and maintaining a TKD technician habitus. The student who is willing to invest the time and effort required to remould his or her body and mind is a black belt.

As Mr Andrews' slogan illustrates, identifying oneself as a TKD martial artist means more than being able to physically defend yourself. While the TKD technician aims for 'intellectual achievement, graceful techniques, formidable power and beauty of physical form' (Choi 2008, I: 14), the aims and philosophy of the art become part of the technician's sense of self. Mr Andrews, for example, described himself in the following way:

> I'm a martial artist. I'm a leader. Uh, I'm a teacher. I'm a student… I'm, I don't know, expert is too grand a word… I am a philosopher, an athlete, I'm an organizer… I am someone that will spend a great deal of time doing the same thing over and over. I am traditional. I am someone that thinks outside the box. I uh, I am someone that can generate a lot of ideas. (Interview, 15 February 2008)

During an interview, Mr Peterson described himself in the following way:

> I'm all over the place. Depends on what the situation needs. Do you need me to be caring and listen to you and say 'yes dear, yes dear', well I can do that. Do you need me to say 'no, cut it off', absolutely I'll do that too. Fluid, how 'bout that? It's like water flowing over the rocks. I'm not saying it takes the easiest way but it does what it needs to do to get where it's going. (Interview, 8 June 2008)

For Mr Stevens, another interviewee, the impact of TKD training on his everyday life has been very subtle. His TKD technician habitus emanated from him as a quiet confidence that both he and those he interacted with were cognisant of, whether or not they knew he was a black belt in TKD. Knowing that he is able to physically defend himself if necessary has been coupled with a sense of social responsibility and social justice consistent with the teachings of Choi. He told me of an experience involving a confrontation with a number of young men on his street that illustrates his TKD-influenced self. The men had been harassing older residents in the neighbourhood. He 'simply approached them and explained that their behaviour was unacceptable'. He was aware that a physical confrontation could have easily resulted but was pleased it did not. He was also keenly aware that it was his TKD training that counteracted any fear that might have prevented him from confronting the men (interview, 29 August 2009).

It is no coincidence that all three of these individuals are TKD instructors. Officially, anyone who has achieved a black belt is qualified to teach TKD. However, effective teaching requires a *technician* self – someone able to encourage habits that 'materialize into techniques that are the work of "collective and individual practical reason rather than, in the ordinary way, merely the soul of its repetitive faculties" (Mauss, 1973:73)' (Spencer 2009, 125). Repetition in its simplest form implies mind over body. A technician is able to instil in students the necessity of rejecting such an imbalanced, dualistic view of mind and body in favour of a view acknowledging the intertwining of the two. She or he assists the student in recognizing that the body is more than an object upon which the mind imposes its will; it is an essential component in the formation of social action (Turner 1995).

Technicians recognize that 'There is no *try* in tae kwon do' and that 'bodily memories change over time and in and through social working and re-working of bodies' (Spencer 2009, 132). They are able to instil these things in their students through their own being. In addition, they bring together all they have learned: the importance of precision and the use of RBTs in achieving it, the relationship between body and mind in the construction of a TKD martial artist identity, and how to maximize the transmission of this knowledge in a sufficiently fluid manner to ensure students' potential to become technicians. The technician has achieved a state of being in which she or he is not only aware of the necessary synthesis between body and mind but also embodies it.

Conclusion

This work adds to the growing body of research focusing on bodies in settings devoted to bodily moulding and modification, and fighting (e.g. Abramson and Modzelewki 2011; Spencer 2009; Bar-On Cohen 2006; Crossley 2006b, 2005, 2004c; Wacquant 1995b, 2004a). Following the work of Spencer (2009), it is intended to assist in filling the gap in the literatures devoted to the sociology of sport and the sociology of the body 'regarding the processes related to the actual acquisition of embodied knowledge and concrete practices of accomplishing sporting activity' (120). Bodies engaged in such activities are fluid in the sense that they are influenced by multiple factors in multiple ways, they constantly adapt, and consequently influence the impact of the factors that influence them.

As illustrated throughout this chapter, to achieve a TKD habitus necessarily means that one has reached an embodied understanding of 'There is no *try* in tae kwon do'.

There is doing without thinking, a 'practical bodily know-how' (Crossley 2004c, 45). Such a state emerges through repetition and RBTs, which act back upon the agent and transform him or her. As a technician, the TKD practitioner comes to know as well as to illustrate the necessity of rejecting the Cartesian mind/body dualism so common in the literature that relegates the body to the position of object. This ethnographic project, therefore, adds to the literature intent on a rethinking of the role of the body in social life. It contributes to the burgeoning area of carnal sociology that is 'concerned with *what the body does* and examines the necessarily embodied bases of the praxical-symbolic constituents of the social formation' (Crossley 1995, 43).

Consistent with other martial artists (Bar-On Cohen 2006) and fighters (Wacquant 2004a), TKD practitioners learn the importance of embodied knowledge. Such shared experiences leave little doubt that the adept and committed can achieve a habitus comparable to the TKD technician habitus I have discussed. Yet, it takes someone who achieves precision and accuracy but has also self-identified as a martial artist, recognizing and embracing the resulting change in their sense of self. To illustrate this commonality, Wacquant's description of habitus in relation to boxers applies equally to that of a TKD technician:

(1) 'a set [of] *acquired* dispositions', (2) 'holds that practical mastery operates *beneath the level of consciousness and discourse*', (3) indicates that sets of dispositions *vary by social location and trajectory*' and (4) its structures 'are malleable and transmissible because they result from *pedagogical work*'. (2011, 85–6)

Clearly the path to a technician habitus is through the acquisition of RBTs. However, an individual will not succeed in acquiring RBTs without accepting the mantra 'There is no *try*'. Essentially, as Crossley (1995) explains, 'habitus [...] is the basis of choice. It is a structure of preferences and a means by which situations are made meaningful' (56). To achieve a TKD technician habitus requires 'distanc(ing) oneself from one's ways of being' (56), specifically distancing oneself from there *is try*. The student must understand that to *try* is to put thinking before doing, and that prioritizing thought in this way denies the possibility of becoming a technician.

While Merleau-Ponty does not use the term habitus, he essentially offers us a 'carnal version' of the concept. For him, our bodies are our way of being-in-the-world. The body knows itself and its world 'by way of its active relation to its world' (Crossley 1995, 54). However, this understanding is not primarily achieved through cogitation but rather through repetition. Carnal sociology 'addresses the active role of the body in social life. It is concerned with *what the body does*' (Crossley 1995, 43). The body, rather than being the object upon which the mind exercises control, is understood as intelligent in itself. Body and mind are not distinguishable attributes but rather intertwined necessities of being.

As my discussion throughout this chapter indicates, sociological inquiries that involve only information regarding intellect are insufficient. Who we are is a product of what we know, but to know is more than thought. To know is to do. Like Merleau-Ponty we must acknowledge 'the body as an effective agent' (Crossley 1995, 44–5).

The transition from 'conceptual knowledge-that' to 'practical bodily know-how' (Crossley 2004c, 45) is evident in the TKD beginner's experience with *sagigurugi*. It demonstrates that 'Our principle relation to our world is not a matter of "I think" [...] but rather "I can"' with 'can' illustrating 'that our primary relation to our environment consists in practical competence' (Crossley 1995, 53).

More generally, the acquisition of RBTs, which are purposively taken up in order to modify the self, offers us a viable process by which the mind/body synthesis plays out. While repetition appears to operate at the level of *action follows thought*, RBTs transition us to habitus and a carnal vision of the human subject as acting agent. It is through the acquisition of RBTs that we cease to 'reflect upon the "hows", "whats" and "wheres" of our body movements' (Crossley 1995, 53), and it is through examination of this acquisition that sociologists illustrate that 'we do not relate to our bodies as we do to an external object' (Crossley 1995, 53) when we go about doing and being in the world. It is only when the body technique is novel to us that there is any real comparison between how we relate to our bodies and how we relate to external objects. And, it is in these instances that we see the awkward, inept execution of body techniques.

In TKD, as in other martial arts and fighting traditions, the ceaseless repetition of body techniques invites individuals to enter into a process whereby doing is not hindered by thought. Practitioner's action and thought must be one. Acceptance of this invitation ultimately leads to a modification of the practitioner's sense of self – 'I am a martial artist.' Successfully manoeuvring through the process of acquiring RBTs, during which mind and body alternately dominate, ultimately results in a state of bodily knowing that is at the core of a TKD technician habitus. The meaningful behaviour indicative of this success illustrates that 'mindedness and embodiment are aspects of a single structure' (Crossley 1995, 48). Similar to Wacquant's apprenticeship, there is a:

> corporeal intelligence that tacitly guides social agents [...] It enables us to grasp human conduct [...] as a mutual moulding and immediate 'inhabiting' of being and world, carnal entanglement with a mesh of forces pregnant with silent summons and invisible interdictions that elude the scholastic distinction between subject and object. (Wacquant 2005a, 465–6)

The exploration of RBTs and habitus as they are discussed here should not be restricted, however, to social extremes such as fighting arts. As Wacquant comments in relation to his work on boxing, 'carnal sociology is [...] a general approach to social life because *all agents are embodied and all social life rests on a bedrock of visceral know-how*' (2005a, 467; emphasis in original). Since to be a social being by necessity means doing, being an active agent should mean that a carnal approach is necessary in any examination of social life. The attraction of carnal sociology is that by redesigning the mind/body relationship out of the Cartesian dualism we are able to explore the ways that the social world in which the body is located 'is made both functional and meaningful for it. Practical action [...] [comes to] be understood as a way of taking up a meaningful position in the world' (Crossley 1995, 56). In addition, it advocates that 'the world of shared meanings is effectively constituted not only by speech acts, but by other forms of bodily action and comportment' (Crossley 1995, 56). However, so long as many of us continue to '"forget" that the social is embodied and that the body is social' (Crossley 1995, 44) we will continue to fall victim of the Cartesian view of the body.

Notes

1 General Choi, the founder of TKD (Gillis 2008), attempted to amalgamate the various martial arts in Korea under the name TKD. Hwang Lee, the leader of tang soo do in Korea, rejected Choi's plan and remained independent (Lake Norman Tang Soo Do Academy 2001).
2 From this point forward, TKD will refer to ITF TKD unless otherwise stipulated.
3 While I began in September 2005 my participation has not been consistent due to injuries and health problems.
4 Phase Two involves an online survey and will be completed in the summer of 2012. Phase Three is planned for 2013 and will be an ethnography similar to Phase One.
5 Three of the individuals who were interviewed are not affiliated with ITF TKD. However, the style of TKD that they train in is more like ITF than different.
6 *Do jang* is the English spelling for the Korean word that refers to the physical space in which TKD training takes place.
7 In TKD individuals who have a white belt to red belt are often referred to by their first names, those who have a first- to sixth-degree black belt are referred to as Mr or Ms, those with a seventh- or eighth-degree are Master and those with a ninth-degree are Grand Master. For this chapter, participants have been given pseudonyms appropriate for their rank.

Chapter 6

'IT IS ABOUT YOUR BODY RECOGNIZING THE MOVE AND AUTOMATICALLY DOING IT': MERLEAU-PONTY, HABIT AND BRAZILIAN JIU-JITSU

Bryan Hogeveen

Introduction

> Where two flashing swords meet there
> is no place to escape;
> Move on coolly, like a lotus flower blooming
> in the midst of a roaring fire,
> And forcefully pierce the heavens.
> (Zen Koan, cited in Stevens 2001)

My entry into the world of Brazilian jiu-jitsu (BJJ) was circuitous. I have always been involved in combative sports. I have been pinned to the mat by wrestlers, been punched in the face during muay thai classes and slammed to the ground by judoka. For the last seven years I have been immersed in a different martial art that has put me on the receiving end of countless chokeholds and joint locks. In addition to practising and teaching BJJ five or six days a week, understanding perception and the grappler's body has captivated my intellectual work. Initially I had no intention of studying BJJ from a scholarly perspective. It merely represented a means through which to increase my physical fitness and a way to better understand myself. Today, BJJ is more than a martial art, more than a passion; it has become a central object of my intellectual energies.

BJJ has forced me to rethink much of what I held certain. Its practice has continuously enriched my being. Academic demands often contribute to a cloistered and sedentary lifestyle where the mind is the foundation of being. I barely decamped from my computer or library study carrel during my doctoral studies, which contributed momentously to not only my expanding knowledge, but also my waistline. I barely knew this body. This was not the body that so efficiently carved its way down the ice during hockey games or twisted (or was twisted by) wrestling opponents. During my doctoral studies and the early years of my academic career, this drive and enthusiasm for corporeal activity remained dormant. I was so fully immersed in intellectual pursuits that the way out was (almost) unrecognizable. Stepping on the mats for the first time with young men a decade my junior (or more) intent on demonstrating their dominance at my expense was a shock to my complacency. My ego took a terrible beating.

Becoming a part of the BJJ milieu meant not only learning the grammar, lexicon and norms that would help me to survive, but also questioning my being in the world. I increasingly found it disagreeable being an 'out of shape' and slovenly academic with a penchant for the delectable. Learning to fight forced me to call my corporeal schema fully into question. My entire being was out of tune and out of sync – I was overweight and physically unfit. I have made many discoveries while travelling along the BJJ fighter's path. While unearthing details of my carnal being, the physical demands of training have challenged my taken-for-granted (mis)assumptions about being-in-the-world. Immersion in the world of arm locks and chokes has put me more fully in touch with my carnal being. I have learned to feel the almost imperceptible shifts of my opponents' weight and am now acutely aware of the subtle changes in their breathing patterns. These skills and insights that were acquired through blood and sweat have not remained firmly ensconced in the academy: my (re)awakened sense of carnal being is fully on display throughout this chapter.

In this chapter we follow Maurice Merleau-Ponty's (2002) understanding of embodied perception and habit as a way into the complex and nuanced world of grappling. An exploration of BJJ provides an opportunity for critical reflection on habit and a launching site from which to explore and deepen Merleau-Ponty's reconception of human perception. His conception of carnal being invigorates debate about the body and habit in a social milieu. This is not to say that there are not others whose tenets could be expounded to this end. Pierre Bourdieu's (1990b) richly textured detailing of the habitus could usefully be employed in a fashion similar to that of his student Loïc Wacquant's (2011, 2004a) exceptional exploration of the corporeal world of boxers. Nevertheless, because there is much to be gained from an approach that returns to some of the phenomenological antecedents underpinning Bourdieu's work, this chapter highlights the contributions that Merleau-Ponty's conception of habit might furnish for carnal sociology (Crossley 2001a, 1995).

In an article that is neither a critique nor an addendum to Bourdieu's work, Nick Crossley (2001a) maintains that meditating on phenomenological contributions to this oeuvre encourages enrichment and elaboration. I agree with Crossley's (2001a, 99) argument that we need 'to bring the insights of phenomenology into the otherwise very powerful theory of practice' that Bourdieu developed. It is not my intention to delve more fully into the spaces of convergence and discord between Bourdieu and Merleau-Ponty.[1] My claim on the phenomenological habit is relegated to how it aids in sketching the contours of the grappler's body and contributes to carnal sociology. The latter attends to the 'active role of the body in social life' and highlights 'what the body does' (Crossley 1995, 43). Merleau-Ponty's work 'provides for the paradigm shift that a carnal sociology of the body entails' and 'the basic conceptual tools which we require to incorporate the body, more fully, into sociological theory and analysis' (Crossley 1995, 60).

Habit, for Merleau-Ponty, provides the corporeal schema necessary for smooth and effortless navigation and negotiation of the world. Habit is 'knowledge in the hands' that readies the understanding body for meaningful interface with the world. Grappler's corporeal schema consists of particularly nuanced and timed movements gradually forged through practice. Habit, then, allows us to think through how the grappler's body perceives its world and explore how beings assimilate BJJ strictures into a body that understands. Through a critical analysis of the temporality and spatiality of habit, as evidenced in the practice of BJJ, I highlight the structure of embodied perception as pre-reflective solutions to a given situation or stimuli of a general and recognizable form. My intention is to draw inspiration from Merleau-Ponty's understanding of habit in order to sketch an exposition of BJJ that shares his understanding that the 'body is our natural self and, as it were, the subject of perception' (Merleau-Ponty 2002, 239).

Training ligaments, muscle fibres and tendons to perform BJJ's many sweeps and submissions demands countless hours consigned to the mats. Objective and macro elements of these positions may be gleaned through mere observation, but the fine gradations of feel and leverage that render the techniques effective and efficient are largely invisible and thus must be discerned through a body that is acting and reacting to stimulus. In BJJ, study that is detached from immersion in the grappling milieu is a poor substitute for authentic bodily immersion in combative space. As I will demonstrate, the grappler's body is forged in the space between and among active bodies. Training partners are vital to the process of assimilating BJJ habits and developing a grappler's corporeal schema. As we will see, this 'other' becomes an extension of the self.

Linkages between intellectual pursuits and martial arts may seem a priori tangential. But there are fundamental epistemological principles held in common. For instance, BJJ and philosophy are both primarily problem-solving exercises. John Danaher (cited in Hanley 2011, 63), who holds a black belt in BJJ and pursued a PhD in philosophy from Columbia University, explains the study of philosophy:

> [...] gave me the greatest skill that any man can have [...] the skill of critical thinking that enables a man to gain knowledge through rational enquiry. To look upon the world through the eyes of a problem solver. Jiu-Jitsu is [...] a course in problem solving, namely, the problem of how to control and submit a resisting opponent who is attempting to do the same to you. As such, it shares with the study of philosophy the deal of rational solutions to difficult problems. They differ only in subject matter.

Martial arts and philosophy are also linked ontologically. Eastern philosophy has inspired and been inspired by martial arts (Stevens 2001). This chapter follows in this tradition. Both martial arts, in this case BJJ, and academia can be enriched through mutual study and exploration.

I am not the first to draw these connections. Recent years have witnessed scholars from a number of intellectual traditions more fully concentrate their capacities on fighting traditions. Loïc Wacquant's (2004a) exceptional ethnographic exploration of the boxer's habitus has paved the way for scholars to delve more deeply into the sociological and philosophical implications of fighting. Intellectual engagement with more established combative sports and martial arts have seen much ink spilled since Wacquant's seminal work (Downey 2005a; Spencer 2009). Despite BJJ's popularity and extremely rapid diffusion, it has received comparatively little scholarly attention (Green and Svinth 2003; Hogeveen 2011). Drawing on my ethnographic study of the art, my experience training in Brazil and interviews with 30 athletes,[2] this chapter examines how experienced BJJ players perceive the grappling milieu and acquire habits that organize the combative experience. Following a description and compressed history of BJJ, the chapter explores Merleau-Ponty's concept of habit. Next, I consider how the grappler's body schema is forged through concerted and dedicated training.

Brazilian Jiu-Jitsu: The Game of Human Chess

> You can bend a man's arm forward up to his shoulder, but if you bend it backward, first thing you know he has two elbows. That's jiu jitsu. (Anon. 1942)

Few people outside of the relatively small circle of adepts and mixed martial arts (MMA) aficionados are well acquainted with BJJ. According to an official history written several years ago by Kid Peligro (2003), the art emerged in the opening years of the twentieth century when Helio and Carlos Gracie refined traditional judo techniques for the rough-and-tumble streets of Rio de Janeiro, Brazil.[3] Countless North Americans were incited to learn the art in 1993 when the comparatively diminutive Royce Gracie (Helio's son) quickly dispatched three opponents in a single night on his way to winning the inaugural Ultimate Fighting Championship (UFC). The initial UFC events pitted martial artists from various fighting styles against each other in a no-holds-barred event that was broadcast to the world via pay-per-view television. Nourished on a steady diet of boxing and Bruce Lee films, North American fighting audiences were convinced that effective fighting technique involved flashy strikes delivered from a standing position. On 12 November 1993 the Gracie family effectively turned traditional self-defence and fighting wisdom on its head when Royce took his opponents, most much larger than himself, down to the mats and forced them to submit using a combination of choke holds and joint locks. Today, BJJ is taught in almost every major urban centre and is considered one of the world's fastest growing martial arts.

BJJ, often called the game of human chess,[4] is a martial art of leverage and feel. Practitioners struggle for control of opponents' bodies and create opportunities for locks and choke holds.[5] With leverage as its backbone rather than raw power, feel as its cornerstone rather than pure strength, BJJ has broad appeal. Those with physical and visual impairments all compete and practise the art. Subjects are drawn to this martial art for a variety of reasons: some consider it an efficient form of self-defence, others see it as an uncompromising discipline that is well suited to combat sport, and still others follow its strictures for fitness or spiritual inspiration. Whatever the case, BJJ cuts across socioeconomic, cultural and political lines. Although it may seem trite to say: once on the mats one's substance matters little. Rigan Machado (2002) writes that 'so many times I have seen millionaire white belts turn to poverty-stricken black belts for advice, support and technical assistance'. He concludes that 'wealth in jiu jitsu is determined by what is in your heart, not by what you have in your wallet'.

A typical class involves a short but vigorous warm-up, instruction in two or three techniques, drilling these movements and 30 to 45 minutes of sparring or 'rolling' as it is referred to in the vernacular. BJJ is practised in a gi or kimono – woven cotton pants and a jacket with a thick lapel and tapered sleeves. To withstand the rigorous grabbing, twisting and pulling that is characteristic of the training, BJJ gis are typically manufactured of thicker cotton material than traditional martial arts uniforms. Author and veteran fighter Sam Sheridan (2007, 116) maintains that BJJ 'is all about the gi, you grab it at every turn, pulling pant legs, twisting sleeves, gripping and pulling the belt, the lapels, untucking your opponent's gi and twisting the lose ends around his body to turn him, to choke him. The cloth controls the body underneath, and the body controls the cloth and breaks the grips'.

Two differences (there are certainly others) can be cited to help differentiate BJJ from many traditional martial arts. The first lies in how the art is practised. Instead of throwing punches at imaginary opponents or kicking heavy bags, BJJ players practise technique at close to 100 per cent of their strength, speed and effort. A great number of injuries could legitimately be expected from this manner of training. Allowing practitioners to 'tap out' or otherwise signal submission (i.e. verbally) whenever they feel uncomfortable from a choke or lock mitigates risk. 'Tapping out' signals surrender and indicates that the opponent should instantly release the hold. Training in this way allows students to practise and perfect their techniques against opponents of differing sizes and abilities who provide unfixed levels of resistance.

The development of the guard represents a second means through which to distinguish BJJ. While an argument can be made that early judo masters employed one form of guard or another, the Gracies in the mid-1900s and contemporary practitioners have refined and revolutionized it in ways that would seem almost unrecognizable to these early practitioners. A recent article in an issue of *Gracie Magazine* dedicated to the guard proclaimed that this position is the 'essence of Jiu-Jitsu' (Dunlop 2009, 34). Guard occurs when a player has his/her back to the mat with their legs wrapped around an opponent. Their feet may or may not be clasped behind their challenger. Among BJJ players, the guard is celebrated for its versatility. It can be an advantageous position from which to launch submissions and sweeps – techniques that invert position from the bottom to the top. Guard is also a site of respite from an overly aggressive attacker.

Traditional martial art and combat wisdom held that an opponent on their back was defeated. Because of the vast array of submissions and sweeps available to guard players, many BJJ players choose to start the fight from this position. In addition to the traditional or closed guard, innovations have produced an increasing number and array of guard positions, including the spider guard, de la riva guard, hook guard, butterfly guard, x-guard, quarter guard, 50/50 and, but not limited to, rubber guard.

Expertise in BJJ demands years of training and dedication. A decade or more of concentrated effort is often necessary to obtain a black belt – the most elevated belt colour utilized in many martial arts. Finite timing and fine tuning the body's muscles and ligaments is required to successfully execute the techniques and movements camped under the BJJ rubric. As such an intricate and complex art, it provides an excellent springboard from which to begin thinking about habit and the body and/ in martial arts.

Forging the Grappler's Body

How do experienced BJJ players understand how to efficiently and expertly apply their holds and techniques on resisting opponents? Towards coming to terms with this phenomenon I take Merleau-Ponty's (2002) manner of conceptualizing habit as my starting point. He was convinced that the 'phenomenon of habit is just what prompts us to revise our notion of "understand" and our notion of the body. To understand is to experience the harmony between what we aim at and what is given, between the intention and the performance—and the body is our anchorage in a world' (Merleau-Ponty 2002, 167) There is much at stake in Merleau-Ponty's conception of habit. In addition to forcing us to rethink contemporary knowledge about the body, habits enable our bodies to gear with the demands of our worlds and to seamlessly weave their way through space. Only bodies that are fully immersed in this space acquire the requisite corporeal schema to grasp its significance. Habit is not won solely through imagination or intellectual engagement. For example, I can read about how to perform a particular hold or dream about 100 chokes, but until my body experiences the feel of the kimono, the angle of my opponent's body, the comportment of my hands and the opponent's resistance, the movement will not be fully assimilated into my body and activated when appropriate. My body will not perceive its essence and will not have understood.

Habit permits smooth navigation and negotiation of subjects' worlds. It is what allows for pre-reflective negotiating and navigating the world. Habit is carried with the individual and employed in similar situations that need not share the same exact conditions and alignments. Thus, acquiring skill in one domain does not limit its expression to this singular locale, instance or expression. Habit permits bodies to adapt to unfamiliar situations and contexts evidencing recognized and accustomed demands. Through an examination of an organist who is asked to play an unfamiliar organ, Merleau-Ponty (2002, 168) clarifies the adaptability of habit. 'He sits on the seat, works the pedals, pulls out the stops, gets the measure of the instrument with his body, incorporates within himself the relevant directions and dimension, settles into the organ as one settles into a house.' This example highlights how habit provides bodies with the ability 'to respond with a certain type of solution to situations of a certain general form' (164).

The organist's body understands and comprehends its situation as being familiar – it catches on. Familiar demands placed on the body initiate or activate the embodied 'habits' that have been ingrained over years of practice. While the corporeal schema and bodily demands diverge, the organist and grappler hold much in common. Like the organist who spends incalculable hours before the organ, the expert BJJ athlete is forever on the mats sparring with partners and drilling technique. Training or experience in the grappler's and organist's particular milieu constitutes a body project that fashions a schema geared to that setting. Drilling and practice is more than the mere repetition of acts, however; it is what permits facile functioning in a world that presents us with differential situations. Familiar demands or stimulus encountered by a practised body initiate or activate the embodied 'habits' that have been ingrained over years of practice.

Training, practising and otherwise experiencing the movements intrinsic to BJJ carries my body forward in time. Habit certainly implies repeatable skilful activity that is woven within the corporeal schema. But, perhaps more important, because replication underpins habit it implies future significance. Heidegger (1962) was convinced that beings are always already living ahead of themselves and working towards some end that is not yet fully in view. As we move through our world and gather more experience we become something other. The body is being pulled ahead of itself in time as it struggles to greater efficiency and to becoming more functionally geared to its milieu. With each BJJ practice my body is being pulled ahead of itself to a future time to come – a time I cannot yet foresee.

Oriented to a Future to Come: Forging a Grappler's Corporeal Schema

My body's shape, comportment and grappling ability have been altered significantly through my grappling experience. I weighed 230 lbs when I entered a BJJ academy for the first time – a situation that felt severely awkward given my previous sports-centred life. But, this is what happens when under the stress and time crunch of a demanding PhD programme. During those four years I was, save for a few rounds of golf every year, basically sedentary. I now look back upon my first BJJ class with equal degrees of embarrassment and satisfaction. I felt not a little bit of shame over my body that refused to comport itself to the rigours of the class. I was 'winded' after only a few jumping jacks and push-ups – and the formal part of the class had yet to begin. I recall that a simple arm lock from inside the guard was the lesson of the day and that my body awkwardly fumbled along. My unfortunate training partner left with bruises on his legs and shoulders from my flailing feet. Nevertheless, this was where my current grappler's body was initiated – a future I could not yet know. Today, I am 65 lbs lighter and regularly teach that same arm lock from guard. How did this happen? Habit entails a body that grasps the significance of particular movements. Thus, only through repeating the arm-lock movement and drilling the position with training partners of different sizes and shapes did my body come to understand what was being demanded.

Efficient being in the world requires the meshing of the motor and the perceptual in a way that pulls the individual body into the future (Weiner 1990). Preparing for approaching competitions finds top BJJ players, such as multiple time world champion André Galvão, dedicating hours of practice to repeating movements that replicate positions they are likely to encounter. Galvao explains that:

> For me, drilling is very important because you teach your body to move naturally into these positions. You can't think too much when you're fighting. You just have to do. You get that from drilling [...] When you drill, your body gets conditioned to naturally get into the proper positions [...] If you drill positions you don't know or are weak in, you're going to make bigger gains. Drilling helps you learn. (Inside BJJ 2011)

Drill produces a body that is capable of efficient and pre-reflective action when in the heat of competition. Abiding in the minutiae of existence during a match would surely cost Galvão a victory and/or result in an injury. Practice and repetition is what fashions bodies proficient at pre-reflectively seizing hold of significances.

While sparring my body is in constant motion. I am grabbing, twisting, shifting my centre of gravity, defending, reaching and sweeping. Despite this motility, which to the outside observer might appear frenetic, I have intimate knowledge of where my hands are located without calling them to mind. Such pre-reflective familiarity with my body as it moves through space and bumps up against another has been acquisitioned through hours and hours on the mat. I do not have to consciously think about moving my hand to grab my partner's collar to pull and squeeze in the appropriate fashion. It is already done. Transferring my hand to my opponent's collar is not a movement that is or needs to be chronicled by my conscious mind. It is, rather, a certain 'adjustment of motility, physiognomically distinguishable from any other' (Merleau-Ponty 2002, 166). Grabbing the collar is a pre-reflective movement of my body through space intended to accomplish a very specific and dedicated end – choking my opponent. Merleau-Ponty (2002, 166) describes the typist's movement over the space of the keyboard in a very similar manner:

> It is possible to know how to type without being able to say where the letters, which make the words, are to be found on the banks of keys. To know how to type is not, then, to know the place of each letter among the keys, nor even to have acquired a conditioned reflex for each one, which is set in motion by the letter as it comes before our eye.

Many world-class athletes are at a loss when requisitioned to describe how they accomplish unprecedented levels of efficiencies, or they describe movements that are at odds with their performance. Vic Braden has interviewed numerous world-class tennis stars and is amazed by how they are routinely unable to effectively describe their bodily formula for smashing tennis balls. Braden explains that: 'Out of all the research that we've done with top players, we haven't found a single player who is consistent in knowing and explaining exactly what he [or she] does' (cited in Gladwell 2005). Ted Williams, for example, one of the most effective major league baseball hitters of all time has often been quoted as saying he was able to watch the bat hit the ball and encouraged his adherents to strive for the same. Malcolm Gladwell (2005) explains in his book, *Blink*, that this is functionally impossible. The ball travelling at speeds approaching 160 km per hour at a bat that is also in motion suggests that the player is 'effectively blind' at the moment when the bat meets the ball. William's explanations and his actions diverge.

Remarkably, elite athletes are routinely unable to catalogue what renders their movements efficient. Part of the reason for their shortfall stems from the fact that a significant part of our being-in-the-world even, or particularly, higher order functioning is pre-reflective and receives relatively little assistance or input from the conscious mind (Dreyfus and Dreyfus 1986). Turning on a familiar light or opening the door to one's home become pre-reflective. Until relatively recently, very few athletes have consciously reflected on the minutiae of their movement. Through practice they have developed bodies that are incredibly efficient and effortlessly move through space. During BJJ sparring sessions, the individual player is not only receiving stimulus from their own bodies, but their opponent is at the same time spinning, shifting their body weight, manipulating their gi and attempting to restrain their limbs.

Sparring bodies are moving far too fast to consciously reflect on and capture their nuances. As such, adept BJJ players rely not on their eyes and conscious reflections, but on the bodily schema they have forged through years of experience and practice. Experience bestows an elegant bounty – a capacity to pre-reflectively deliver the appropriate response when it is demanded. Habit is not pure biological instinct, it is not simply a reflex, but is rather won of diligence, patience and repeated encounters with the same.

World champion and author Saulo Ribeiro (2008, 11) maintains that 'the timing to make a decision is not based on what you think you should be doing. It is about your body recognizing the move and automatically doing it.' Developing such exquisite feel and sensibility comes with countless hours of training. Novice BJJ players with little or no experience rely almost fully on their conscious mind. 'Where do I put this hand?' 'Where should my centre of gravity be?' and 'What is this position?' Experts have long jettisoned this mechanical processing and nimbly respond to familiar stimuli. In a recent interview, champion grappler Ronaldo 'Jacare' Souza (2008) poignantly maintained that during a match he does not 'think of anything'. Instead, he says that: 'I see my opponent in front of me and I don't ever think of what I'm going to do. Things just pop up in the moment.' For masters like Souza and Ribeiro there is congruity between what is intended and the performance of the body to this end. Their bodies fully 'understand'.

The whole question of habits centres on corporeal means of dealing with sensorial prompts and, more importantly, how each perception associates itself with a motor response without there 'being any need to spell the word or specify the movement in detail in order to translate one into the other' (Merleau-Ponty 2002, 167). When I grab my opponent's collar I come in contact with the fulfilment of a scheme that was directed not at the collar as a particular object, a final end or object of thought, but as part of my corporeal being in the world. Like Merleau-Ponty's (2002) typist who 'performs the necessary movement on the typewriter', the practised grappler moves her/his body in ways that correspond to the right movement required by the particular instance as represented by their opponent's position, limb location and weight distribution. Responses have been incorporated into the grappler's bodily space and seemingly 'just pop up in the moment'. This 'popping up' or sudden realization may seem to imply that the practised body invents novel positions in the midst of combat. But this would be to miss the point entirely. Movements of the practised body are primarily pre-reflective. Novice grapplers clumsily plod along with a rather narrow gestalt compared to the adept who perceives the grappling arena as an expansive space.

While remaining open to future developments, the expert has many more techniques at their disposal than has the novice and is able to pre-reflectively and swiftly perceive the most effectual response to their opponent's positioning. Recently I was watching one of my newer students spar. She secured a dominant position on her partner's back when a perplexed look came about her. 'Now what?', she blurted at me. The appropriate response seemed obvious to me: 'Grab his collar and choke him', I replied. 'How do I do that?' she retorted. A few minutes before our exchange I had achieved a similar position on one of my more advanced students. Through experience he was well aware of my intention and predilection towards choking techniques and defended my attempts to grab his collar and apply the position. Although he had done well to thwart my initial attempts to submit him with a collar choke, I naturally swung my body to secure an arm lock that was opened by his defence.

Unlike the novice grappler, the habit body is geared with this space and efficiently perceives openings. It is equipped to deliver effectual responses from among a vast network of techniques at its disposal. It is not the case that I mentally scrolled through a list of techniques I have been taught over my years on the mats and selected what I deemed the best from among them. Rather, my body pre-reflectively understood what was required in and by that moment. Rickson Gracie (1999), widely acknowledged as the most proficient grappler in history, advises grapplers to 'allow yourself to go as an autopilot [...] You must allow yourself to be in a zero point, a neutral point and be relaxed and connected [...] This is a point beyond the knowledge.' Gracie's 'point beyond knowledge' is the product of blood, sweat and (often) tears that are spilled on the mats over years of training. Conscious reflection, deliberate thought and clumsy motility that is characteristic of the novice is supplanted through dedicated effort by 'knowledge in the hands' (Merleau-Ponty 2002, 166).

Experienced grapplers' bodies know both what is expected and when. Flawless technique courts impeccable timing. Correct timing buoys perfect technique. In the example just provided, it is only in the context of the choke defence that my well-timed transition to an arm lock was sagacious. Timing, Goodridge argues, is: 'the act of determining or regulating the order of occurrence of an action or event, to achieve desired results' (1999, 44, cited in Hockey and Allen-Collinson 2009). Hockey and Allen-Collinson (2009, 224) make the case that timing is an embodied 'sense of rhythm and timing requires a highly developed awareness of sensations emanating from organs (including the skin), ligaments, tendons and muscles as they move'. Ribeiro (2008, 11), for his part, claims that 'when someone is passing your guard you feel he is passing so you cannot wait to decide what to do. There is no time for thought – only reaction.' Movement unfettered by conscious thought is required in the immediate moment to prevent an opponent from establishing a dominant position. Exquisite timing is pivotal for grapplers because their world is one of unrelenting movement.

Drilling, practising and experiencing relevant timing and motility crafts a body that will move 'automatically' around and about the other who is often almost indistinguishable from the self. Gracie (1999), alludes to this state of being when he claims that: 'The most interesting aspect of Jiu-Jitsu [...] is the sensibility with your opponent – the sense of touch, the weight, the momentum, the transition from one movement to another – that's the amazing thing about it.' The other's body and my interaction with it is the instrument of my advancement. Through interaction with the other, my habit body has been honed. Feeling their weight, experiencing their strength and witnessing their movement in relation to my own enhance my timing and polishes my technique. During sparring sessions grapplers' bodies are continually connected and frequently entwined. When Sam Sheridan, author of the fine book *A Fighter's Heart* and a veteran fighter, first came face-to-face with BJJ, he was beguiled by this fusion. He recounted that 'to the uninformed observer it looks strange, slow, and [...] oddly intimate' (Sheridan 2007, 120). But it is this closeness that provides the feel and sensibility necessary to perform the many techniques that constitute BJJ.

Sweep without Sweeping

Acquiring the kind of perception evidenced and imagined by notable grapplers like Ribeiro and Gracie obliges dependence on the body of the other. Every grappler's body project is fused with others who are, at the same time, engaged in their own path. It is at this point that Merleau-Ponty's (2002) typist and organist depart company from the grappler, who interfaces with moving and resistant bodies. Whereas the organist and typist develop their body schema through static objects, the grappler's fighting habits are earned in interaction with dynamic subjects. After all, BJJ is a fighting art comprised of hundreds of nuanced corporeal articulations that athletes apply on bodies endeavouring to accomplish the same.

Cultivating my grappler's corporeality is enhanced when the other with whom I am grappling is more experienced, technically proficient and open to pointing out my errors and vulnerabilities rather than simply exploiting them and smashing me without explanation. Following a sparring session, or in the middle of one, generous and effective instructors explore the openings that fledgling grapplers left undefended and which allowed the teacher to gain advantage. Further, sparring with someone more adept compels the neophyte to feel and sense the smooth flow of the expert's almost magical motility as they advance almost effortlessly about their body.

Analogous to Wacquant's (2004a) DeeDee, someone much more accomplished than me has been my tutor. Along with being victorious at countless BJJ tournaments, she has won the Canadian championships and competed on the world stage. Sparring with a world-class athlete who generously devotes her time to her students has buoyed my progress. During our training sessions I am able to feel and sense the nuances of her movements as she manoeuvres to sweep, submit and control my body. I have assimilated the silent lessons taught by her body. The fighter's body is indeed the product of diligent practice, but even more, engendered in interaction. Each is transformed as they push contemporary limits of perception. My grappler's body scheme is above all else an expression of my training partners – experienced, world champions and novices alike.

Crafting a grappler's body schema commands committed training partners and dedicated teachers. Sparring is equally fundamental to this end. Rolling provides a space for students to practise and perfect their techniques against opponents of varying sizes and abilities. Brothers Renzo and Royler Gracie (2001) maintain that fighting to apply techniques under conditions approximating real combat is ideal for refinement of the body scheme. They suggest that '[t]he resulting familiarity with applying your techniques full power against a person doing everything in his power to defeat you is a great advantage in a real fight' (Gracie and Gracie 2001, 26) Although practising movements on a passive body goes some way towards adapting a body that knows what to do in the midst of the chaos of competition and fighting, it does very little to provide the acumen and timing to apply BJJ's many lessons. A body imbibed with knowledge bred of a familiarity that has been galvanized through sparring knows how. In the absence of intimately feeling the movement of a practised body, the nuances of BJJ motility can only be abstracted. The art is replete with invisible elements that are imperceptible to the uninitiated. It is a decidedly technical sport where novitiate spectators are often confused by who is winning and who is losing. Conventional wisdom to those whose education about fighting is primarily from Jackie Chan and Jean Claude Van Damme films, suggests that the fighter on their back is losing and should simply admit defeat to the athlete seemingly overwhelming them.

Much of the interaction between sparring BJJ players is visually imperceptible. Vectors of force and pressure underneath and between the bodies may be invisible to most, but it is these ingredients that engender efficiency. Rickson Gracie is convinced that the 'efficiency of vale tudo [no-holds-barred fighting] is invisible', that 'good jiu jitsu is invisible' and that 'there is something fundamental and invisible that sometimes takes time' (Alonso 2005). Although Rickson does not divulge exactly what this something is, his contemporary Braulio Estima, who is a world champion and impressive BJJ player in his own right, provides some insight when he says:

> the tiniest refinements of technique, timing and positioning are the things that make the difference between success and failure, gold and silver, the merely good and the perfect. If these details are frequently invisible to the observer, they are nonetheless the essential ingredients that allow for the flawless execution of submissions and the maintenance of position. Even if the crowd does not recognize the difference, your opponent will when he is unable to defend and is, therefore, forced to forfeit. (Estima in *Gracie Magazine* 130, 2008)

A few years ago a couple of novices recruited my services after they had entered a local tournament and performed less well than they expected from the volume and length of their training. Jim had purchased mats from a company he located on the Internet and invited Nick to his house to train at a minimum of three times per week.[6] Each diligently researched techniques online and dreamt about submitting their friend with their latest trick. When we met I asked the pair to perform a series of relatively basic positions (i.e. a triangle). Although each could show me how to place their legs to perform the choke hold, they were unable to manoeuvre their bodies in such a way as to properly execute the technique and force the other's submission. This scenario is repeated time and again as would-be fighters enter my academy trained only by watching the UFC on television. Novices are excited to perform the techniques they have seen their favourite fighters execute. When it comes time to spar they quickly become aware, however, that replaying an arm lock in one's head is considerably at odds with applying the technique to a resisting (and more experienced) opponent. In cases like these the novices' bodies are ill-prepared and unqualified.

A grappler's body programme is a way of being-in-the-world that has incorporated the nuances and intricacies of their art. Their bodies understand. Neophytes like Jim and Nick, by contrast, can emulate the macro and objective positions of the body, but without experiencing the feel and touch that is imperceptible in two dimensions their bodies cannot begin to comprehend. Newcomers may be able to replicate the objective elements of positions with their hands, feet and legs, but their bodies do not yet possess the mature sensibilities of the adept. Minute adjustments of the hands, or a reorientation of the grip, or a slight modification in weight distribution often makes the difference between securing a submission and the opponent's escape. Experienced bodies that can feel the novice's errors are functionally equipped to ascertain the gaps in technique and provide refining tutelage.

The master grappler's tendons, muscles and ligaments are finely tuned to the movements of the other. Coiled as if to strike they lie in wait for even the slightest error. When they feel their opponent's weight shift – which would likely be invisible to the eye – their bodies react and take advantage of the opening thus created. It is this body finely tuned to the nuances of movement that permits the expert to exploit ostensibly imperceptible errors.

My students often question me about positions they find ineffectual. For example, Brandon is an accomplished grappler who has won several local and provincial tournaments. Recently he came to me frustrated about his repeated inability to finish (to force an opponent to signal their submission) a triangle choke. In his most recent tournament he had 'caught' (secured the macro movement) triangles on two opponents who eventually escaped. I asked Brandon to perform the position on his training partner. Outwardly everything appeared solid – the objective elements were seemingly all in place. All that I saw had the appearance of being accurate so I asked him to apply the submission hold on my body. Once in place I immediately identified the problem. Proper administration of any choke hold requires that blood flow to the brain be restricted on both sides of the neck. Obstructing it on only one side, as Brandon was doing, is often uncomfortable but insufficient to force submission. A slight and inconspicuous modification in the inward pressure generated by his legs was all that was required to bridge the lacuna in Brandon's perception. His error was perceived through a body geared to the demands of grappling.

The grappler's body schema is ever evolving and is finely tuned to opponents' almost imperceptible shifts in body weight or comportment. As she/he refines technique and incorporates more into their schema, the grappler's body remains open to the unfamiliar. Even though I have spent a considerable amount of time developing grappler's bodily habits, there are depths that I have yet to probe. I do not only mean that there are techniques and holds with which my body is unacquainted – I'm sure that there are many. Rather, subtleties and shades of positions exist that my body has yet to fully incorporate into itself.

Throughout my time on the mats I have been instructed in countless positions, movements and holds. But this is not to imply that I have this knowledge fully in my hands. For certain I can show someone the position, but that, as we have seen, is not the same as knowing how to do the position. Some jiu-jitsu motility is difficult and my body often feels encumbered as it struggles to perform such movements. Such was the case with a particular sweep to which I have been exposed many times. Whenever my instructor would teach the position I would play along and topple my cooperative training partners. However, when those same grappling bodies provided even the slightest resistance my attempts would prove futile. I resigned myself to thinking that this assemblage of movements did not 'fit' my body schema.

This was before I travelled to Brazil and met Peachy who is a black-belt instructor under the inventor of the position. During one of the classes I attended, he instructed the class in the sweep's strictures. I languidly meandered through this training. Peachy sensed my discomfort and asked me to perform the move, which I did. His look of discontent confused me. I thought my body had performed as directed. Still Peachy was unimpressed. With an air of embarrassment about me ('I' should know this, after all) I shuffled into his guard whereupon he proceeded to grab my wrists and manipulate my legs and arms as if I were a marionette. He effortlessly dominated my body with motility that was seemingly foreign to it. Peachy then drew my attention to the tension in his legs and the push–pull of his arms that was initiated by my shifting centre of gravity. My body understood Peachy's tactile lesson. He and I became one without conveyance through speech or doctrinal pedagogy. My comprehension through the lesson imparted by Peachy's body goes outside of verbal and apparent instruction.

Grapplers observe with a body tuned to the subtleties of the other's body and feel the fine gradations that set apart efficient execution from the novice's awkward performance. Clearly, perception is not solely a function of the visual assimilation of stimulus, but the physical experience of the entire body in the milieu. The body that understands incorporates motility and feel into itself. Following from Peachy's bodily rubric, mine no longer fumbles in space searching for the proper hook, but experiences the motility that constitutes this sweep as part of itself. There is now harmony between my objective and the performance via my grappler's body. I have ceased to be stuck on the cognizance of my incompetence. Rather, the requisite feel and motility characteristic of this sweeping movement has become pre-reflectively my own – my body understands. When sparring, the sweep does not enter into consciousness specifically as an end to be achieved. It flows through my body instead of being the object on which my conscious mind abides. After months of practice my tendons spontaneously fire and I am able to sweep without sweeping. My body has overcome the halting force of intellectualism.

The practised grappler who has spent years on the mats extols pre-reflective action. When sparring – an activity where their body is at home – she/he moves from one position to another in such a manner that their ligaments and tendons are set to the task with maximum efficiency. They perceive with a body schema habituated to what has been repeatedly requested in this milieu. Although I aspire to constantly being in this manner of perceiving the world, there are many times while sparring when some unexpected movement or impediment activates my consciousness and it stops to consider the thing. Many times my mind has become affixed to a certain curious object or position that has interrupted the routine flow of things. For example, the BJJ belt often comes untied during sparring sessions. Most often when this occurs it melts into the environment. Nevertheless, there are other times when the belt or belts become entangled around grapplers' appendages and thus impede habitual movement. At such times sparring is typically halted temporarily so that belts may be retied or thrown to the side. When this occurs my consciousness inhabits the alien entry and my intuitive dealing with the world is interrupted. Instead of flowing on to the next movement the unfamiliar halts my body.

Conclusion

Reflections on how bodies, including my own, gain grapplers' dispositions has allowed me to highlight the relevancy of Merleau-Ponty's concept of habit, stress the cogency of corporeal knowledge and demonstrate the importance of a carnal sociology oriented to scrutinizing the 'active role of the body in social life' via a focus on '*what the body does*' (Crossley 1995, 43, emphasis in the original). Epistemic reflections on the intimate experience of my developing body has inclined my observations and buoyed my potential to comprehend the manufacture and generation of the grappler's perception that are held in common among much of the BJJ community. Acquiring grappling habits has pushed my body in new and (often) uncomfortable directions as it incorporated novel ways of being. By inhabiting and intersecting with the grappler's space my body acquired new ways of perceiving its environment. Over time and through diligent practice, my novice body began to understand – it discerned how to effectively gear with this space. It has assimilated fresh sensibilities, while at the same time modifying and tightening habits previously initiated. Forging my grappler's body is a constant process of back and forth between adaptation and inauguration, between acquisition and reinforcement.

Star of the long running sitcom, *Married with Children*, and the more recent half-hour comedy, *Modern Family*, Ed O'Neill has practised BJJ for many years. Speaking about his grappling experience and his instructor (Rorion Gracie), O'Neill (2011) says: 'They show you everything [...] and you learn the techniques that way. By repeating them over and over [...] the techniques become a part of you and you don't have to think about it'. This gets to the heart of the matter. Habits permit pre-reflective being. The body moves through space without calling to mind feet, ligaments or individual muscles. Repeated exposure to the same allow the body to 'catch-on' and understand what is required when confronted by familiar stimulus. Habit is not a reflex or zombie-like response. Familiar demands call forth the embodied 'habits' that have been drilled and practised into the body. Merleau-Ponty (2002, 166) claims that 'to know how to type is not, then, to know the place of each letter among the keys, nor even to have acquired a conditioned reflex for each one, which is set in motion by the letter as it comes before our eye'. He was convinced that habit colonizes the space between conscious thought and mere reflex.

Habits won of practice and dedication sanction pre-reflective being. As time passes and the days of rehearsal accumulate, neither the comportment of the body nor the manner of grasping the kimono enter conscious thought. While ligaments pull and muscle fibres contract, the grappler's opponent is swept from his feet to his back, but the expert's conscious mind does not abide there or anywhere. The expert grappler's body, forged ahead of present time, understands what is required and perceives each part in its relation with the others. It flows through space and time and, more importantly, it understands.

Notes

1 I leave this debate for others to engage more fully. Several scholars have explored the difference and similarities between these scholars. See for example, Marcoulatos (2001) and Kontos (2006).
2 I do not draw directly on these interviews here.
3 In recent years, the historical development of BJJ has been complicated as scholars (Green and Svinth 2003) and members of the Gracie family (Gracie 2006) turn their attention to this martial art's inauguration and development.
4 See for example, 'Brazilian Jiu-Jitsu: The Game of Human Chess' Online: http://www.youtube.com/watch?v=BRxrowcvOIw (last accessed 22 February 2013)
5 Significant differences exist between chokes and strangulation. However, grappler's parlance typically refers only to 'chokes'.
6 To protect their identities, all names have been changed.

Chapter 7

'DO YOU HIT GIRLS?': SOME STRIKING MOMENTS IN THE CAREER OF A MALE MARTIAL ARTIST

Alex Channon

Introduction: 'So... Do You Hit Girls?'

I am asked this question more times than any other when discussing the problems addressed by my research into mixed-sex martial arts.[1] Perhaps the most controversial aspect of the experience of mixed-sex training in combat sports, the ethical considerations and deliberations that surround the matter of *men hitting women* often present a personal conundrum for men involved in martial arts. For instance, is it wrong for a man to hit a woman while training? Or is it wrong for a man to think that hitting a woman while training is wrong? These questions are part of a broader study of the phenomenon of mixed-sex martial arts that I have been conducting over the past five years, and in this chapter I address these issues using a mix of auto-ethnographic storytelling, interview data and field notes, discussing how it is that training can affect the 'habitus' (that is, the 'embodied history, internalized as second nature' (Bourdieu 1990b, 56)) of participants in mixed-sex martial arts.

The rationale for asking such questions extends from an understanding of the 'subversive' significance of women's participation in martial arts and related combat sports, which has been well documented by feminist scholars researching this phenomenon over the past two decades (e.g. De Welde 2003; Guthrie 1995; Hollander 2004; McCaughey 1997, 1998). Consistently positioned as a 'masculine domain par excellence' (Mennesson 2000, 28), martial arts and related combat sports are widely considered in the research literature to have historically lent ideological support to patriarchal notions of essential male physical power (e.g. Messner 1988, 1990). Ironically though, because of their important symbolic link with dominant codes of masculinity, they can also be a powerful site through which to challenge binary, hierarchal conceptions of gender. This is an argument also made with regard to so-called 'masculine' sports more generally (e.g. Heywood and Dworkin 2003; Roth and Basow 2004). The subversive value of women's engagement in these activities is principally due to the fact that developing the ability to physically dominate an opponent is a key outcome of most (if not all) martial arts training cultures. And given that, ideologically, the physical domination of women by men is an essential element of hierarchal gender discourse, and more specifically of what feminists have termed 'rape culture' (McCaughey 1997, 28), then women's development of this supposedly 'masculine' ability to physically dominate others poses a direct challenge to a key ideological site of male power. In learning the techniques of physical domination, and developing a body suited to physical combat, women can come to embody the feminist denial of the passivity, fragility and violability of the female body (Dowling 2000; Lenskyj 1986; McCaughey 1997), whilst concurrently appropriating one of the most potent signifiers of male 'superiority'. By becoming accomplished fighters, it is suggested that female martial artists can be the living expression of feminist resistance (Guthrie 1995; McCaughey 1998).

Such an argument has long concerned social historians of women's sport. With particular reference to the UK, the site of my present research, scholars such as Hargreaves (1994, 1997) have pointed out that British women have been actively engaging with ostensibly 'masculine' combat sports, such as boxing and wrestling, throughout the past century. It is also known that women have practised Eastern martial arts since their introduction to Britain in the early 1900s (Looser 2011; Wolf 2005). However, to date there has been no explicit attempt among sports historians to chart the specific emergence and development of mixed-sex training in such activities in Britain. It is possible that integrated training, along with competition, has taken place for as long as women have been participating in modern combat sports and martial arts; for instance, Wolf (2005) describes early female jiu-jitsu practitioner Edith Garrud (1872–1971) as having choreographed and performed public demonstrations of the art's effectiveness against male opponents during the early twentieth century. However, it is only relatively recently that scholars have begun investigating formal mixed-sex sports training environments, leaving the sociohistorical context of sex-integrated martial arts in the UK, along with other Western contexts, somewhat unknown at this point.

This is surprising as, theoretically speaking, within mixed-sex training the subversive value of women's involvement in martial arts is amplified, given that they are learning to fight with, against and alongside men. This rests upon the fact that segregated training settings all too easily give rise to dismissive and trivializing responses among men towards female success; being 'good' among other women invites the argument that a woman is only good 'for a girl', rather than just plain good (McDonagh and Pappano 2008). Such segregations provide support for typical conceptions of female physical inferiority, which have long kept women separate from men in sports, or out of sports altogether (Dowling 2000; Hargreaves 1994; Lenskyj 1986). Conversely, mixed and undifferentiated training can give rise to mutual understandings of the shared physical possibilities of the sexed body in ways that segregated training cannot (Anderson 2008). It also broadens women's training opportunities in what female martial artists often describe as 'male dominated' gyms, wherein few other sufficiently talented women train (e.g. Lafferty and McKay 2004). Other ethnographers have previously argued that the intensely physical (and often painful) exchanges of sparring form the principle way in which martial abilities are developed, as well as one way in which belonging within martial subcultures is established (Abramson and Modzelewski 2011; Green 2011; McCaughey 1997; Wacquant 2004a). It therefore stands to reason that women's attainment of physical equality with men, as

Figure 7.1. Mixed training: Alex in light sparring with junior member 'Gianna'.

Photo © Mustanir Ali.

well as their enfranchisement among the groups that help them develop such physicality, rests upon their opportunity to engage in similarly intense bouts of sparring as do their male counterparts. And, given the typical over-representation of men in (most) mixed-sex martial arts clubs, this means that women's development of martial abilities is often dependent upon hitting and being hit by men. Yet as suggested at the outset, hitting women is rarely a straightforward, unproblematic proposition for men within martial arts, particularly as one's habituated sense of gender propriety, or 'honour', can come to conflict strongly with the practical demands of mixed-sex training (Guérandel and Mennesson 2007).

When discussing the ways in which martial artists work around typically gendered expectations about rough physical contact between the sexes, my own narrative thus leads to an explication of integrated, mixed-sex martial arts as the antithesis of physical segregation and the hierarchal sex difference this both implies and helps to produce (Channon 2012; see also McDonagh and Pappano 2008). As such, I claim that hitting one another, regardless of sex, is a normal and necessary aspect of a successful training career for both male and female fighters and is, from a pro-feminist point of view, *good*. This is because hitting is fundamental in the training regimes of virtually all striking-based combat disciplines, making it essential for the realization of combative ability as martial artists learn how to cope with physical attacks and as their bodies become tougher and more inured to pain (Spencer 2009). Therefore, *men hitting women* can be, contextually speaking, a good thing for sex equality and a potentially important moment in the 'subversion' of gender (Channon 2010).

So, in discussing such matters whilst in fact being a martial artist myself, the question is often posed to me: do I 'hit girls'? For it is one thing to take a philosophical position in advocating something that appears quite extraordinary, lying beyond the remit of everyday sexual propriety, but quite another to *actually do it*. In keeping with this volume's principle concern with addressing how social research can be done *from* the body, this contribution outlines how the embodied experiences of men within martial arts training (including myself) can lead them to be able to answer 'yes' to this question. In so doing I draw attention to the transformative potential that mixed-sex training holds for men's attitudes towards women's bodies, based on data drawn from field notes, personal reflections and interviews with numerous martial artists with whom I have trained and/ or met during my time 'on the mat'. In connecting the embodied realities of training with the broader social theme of gender relations, this work is intended to answer Crossley's (1995) call for a 'carnal sociology', positing that bodily practices are constitutive of social formations and play a key part in their ongoing reproduction and contestation.

The Research

As for the personal experiences that helped shaped my interest in (and form data for) this study, I originally began training in freestyle kickboxing in 2004, switching in 2006 to practising Shaolin kung fu, a discipline in which I have continued to train until the time of writing. I began researching the gendered phenomena involved with mixed-sex martial arts in 2007 as a postgraduate MSc student, continuing over the following years as I further developed both a scholarly interest and personal enthusiasm for martial arts. My work has been ethnographic in nature, involving a mixture of participant observation with formal, semi-structured interviewing of martial artists within and outside my own training environment.[2] These two approaches effectively facilitated each other as I became progressively more immersed in and familiar with the subculture of the club with which I trained, along with my growing appreciation of the wider identities, interests and experiences of martial artists in the UK today. In the course of my five years in kung fu, I have typically trained between 8 and 11 hours per week, whilst being involved at various different levels within the club and the wider institutional structure of the discipline. For instance, in addition to regular training, I attended several national-level competitions as competitor, coach and corner judge, and worked as assistant instructor at my gym until, upon earning my black belt, I began to work as a junior instructor, teaching full lessons in the absence of the club's *sifu* (head teacher). I also helped to organize and run free trial sessions and 'self-defence' courses for prospective members; I served for two years on the club's voluntary administrative committee; and during times of inactivity through injury I remained present as a passive observer in lessons. As mentioned by other martial arts ethnographers, this diverse engagement in the field enabled me to be both 'participant observer' and 'observant participant' (Abramson and Modzelewski 2011; Woodward 2008), which facilitated access to rich, 'insider' data through, on the one hand, buying credibility among my peers (who would later become my interviewees), but also through developing a deep, detailed insight through a wide and varied base of often personally felt experiences.

Throughout this process, and thanks to my ongoing education in sociology, I maintained a sociological consciousness as a lens through which to view these experiences. As Mills (1959) would suggest, I was using my 'sociological imagination' to make sense of what I saw, did and felt; not only was I an immersed and engaged participant, but also a scholar with an interest in '(grasping) what is going on in the world, and (understanding) what is happening (within myself) as minute points of the intersections of biography and history within society' (Mills 1959, 7). My degree of personal 'involvement' and scholarly 'detachment', to borrow Elias's (1987) terms, shifted at various stages of the research, as my immersion within the cultural milieu of mixed-sex martial arts fed this 'sociological imagination', while the rigorous demands of my academic engagements simultaneously drove me back to theory. This process enabled me to develop an ethnographic study rooted in the 'close-up', embodied experiences of the martial artist, yet firmly attached to the abstract narratives of social theory ('going native armed', as Wacquant (2011) suggests). I thus locate my work within the context of the simultaneously theoretical yet 'hands-on' tradition of recent combat sports ethnographers (e.g. Abramson and Modzelewski 2011; Butryn and deGaris 2008; Green 2011; Spencer 2009; Wacquant 2004a), being justified by the oft-cited assertion among ethnographers more generally that 'distance does not guarantee objectivity, it merely guarantees distance' (Scriven 1967, in Silk 2005, 73).

In this presentation of my research, the 'close-up' nature of participant observation becomes the focal point for understanding the experiences of men and women involved in mixed-sex training. While discussing the narratives and actions of others, I also foreground my own thoughts, feelings and ultimately, *transformations* as a method for discussing the embodied phenomenon of mixed-sex martial arts. This 'auto-ethnography' allows me to highlight what is in essence a personal journey of change, taking as evidence many of my own memories, formally recorded or not, of participating in this activity. As Butryn and deGaris (2008, 339–40) point out, 'this raises the question of when research begins and ends in any type of qualitative research', as scholars open up a space for informal, even 'accidental' discoveries in the social world to coexist alongside deliberately gathered 'scientific' data. Therefore, combined with excerpts from field notes and interview transcripts, aspects of my personal history (both in and out of martial arts) are offered in order to give a fairly typical, although in this case highly personalized, version of a specific transformative process that men may face when engaging in mixed-sex combat sports. Transformation through training is often a significant aspect of martial arts narratives, in both popular literature (e.g. Twigger 1999) and academic studies (e.g. Jennings 2010), and I propose that such transformations can be fruitfully examined through the deeply personal representational method of auto-ethnography.

Principle to the value of this method is its explicit emphasis on the location of the researcher within the research. Indeed, by its very nature such work cannot be divorced from the personality of its author, whose habitus neatly contextualizes interpretive data as specifically situated knowledge. For instance, in this case it is the very fact of my maleness that actually gives my account its relevance for debates over the transformative potential of martial arts training regarding the 'subversion' of gender. As Woodward (2008, 557) argues:

> Reflection upon the gender identity and positioning of the researcher helps to cast light on the representation of masculinities that emerge from the research process.

This is not to devalue the research, but to situate the knowledge so produced and acknowledge its partiality.

The work I present in this chapter is centred on producing such a partial view of martial arts training, which is principally concerned with the subjective transformations experienced by male martial artists as they train with and alongside women. In the following sections, I outline the specifics of the transformation, which I personally experienced, alongside the accounts of others,[3] to give a sense of how mixed-sex training can effect changes of this kind. This account begins with a brief personal history in order to better contextualize my story.

Refusing to Hit: Masculine Habitus, 'Holding Back' and Women's Frustration

Before I took up martial arts, my thoughts and expectations about fighting had been heavily structured by prevailing patriarchal discourses of gender, physicality and power. As a schoolboy attending a boys' school, I had frequently enjoyed bouts of play-fighting on the playing field, engaging my male friends in what were often chaotic and sometimes injurious wrestling free-for-alls. Having played rough contact sports throughout my life, I was enthused by the physical thrill of mock combat, and while I rarely fought 'for real' in aggressive confrontations, I nevertheless took great pleasure in these activities. In terms of the experiences of young boys in Western culture more generally, it is clear that I am not alone in having grown up with a taste for combative physicality (Connell 1995), and it is fair to say that my single-sex education had resulted in a more or less exclusive association in my mind between fighting, men and ideals of masculinity (see, for instance, Messner 1990).

In addition, and as was the case for several of my research participants, my only point of contact with female martial artists from the time before I began training revolved around the mass media; principally this involved television shows, movies, video games and professional wrestling. The surreal action sequences of Chinese cinema, along with the buxom, stilettoed heroines of Hollywood blockbusters and martial arts video games, failed to provided me with what I could consider a 'realistic' sense of women's physicality, as did the female personalities in pro-wrestling while they pouted, screeched and stripped one another in sexualized spectacles, performing, as Scambler and Jennings (1998) put it, 'on the periphery of the sex industry' (see also Hargreaves 1997). While there has nevertheless been a proliferation of images of physically 'empowered' women in the media since the 1990s, which has seen its share of celebration among feminist scholars over the past decade (e.g. Inness 2004; McCaughey and King 2001), such imagery had little impact on my own habituated association between 'real' combat, men and masculinity. My ideas about sex difference and fighting thus remained tied to prevailing, dominant representations of male action heroes, wrestlers and prizefighters – all far more visible and far more 'real', to my young male mind, than their (misrepresented) female equivalents.

My early engagement with mixed training was thus structured by the learned dispositions of a lifetime saturated with experiences and images of male physical prowess, with a concurrent, default belief in relative female 'frailty' (Dowling 2000). Further to this, a crucial aspect of my masculine habitus – that is, my socially conditioned, 'second nature' – was a strong sense of honour regarding the necessity of treating 'weak', feminine women 'correctly'. My earliest recollection of the importance of 'honourable' masculine conduct was from fighting with my younger sister as children, and the unforgettable reprimand my father once gave me after I had punched her during an argument. *Never, ever hit girls*, I was told, and this lesson had stayed with me from that point on. The underlying message of the code of honour implied in my father's lesson was simple: men's bodies are strong, women's are not, and so men hitting women is fundamentally unfair. This sentiment is echoed in the reasoning behind what McDonagh and Pappano (2008) call the 'coercive sex segregation' of mainstream, single-sex sports: boys and girls should not play together because boys are strong and girls are weak. In the course of my research, many male martial artists similarly recalled the moral importance of not hitting girls as having been taught from their early years onwards, whilst highlighting how this could make their martial arts training problematic:

> I know that I shouldn't [avoid hitting women during martial arts practice] but as we grow up that's how we're designed to act… It's part of the programming from when you're a kid. Being gentlemanly, that kind of thing. (Interview, Ed, 29)

The importance of treating women in such a 'gentlemanly' fashion, employing paternalistic conceptions of correct conduct as a standard against which to judge their gendered training behaviours, was a common theme amongst the men with whom I trained, and would frequently emerge as a problem in the context of mixed training. Such a standard was certainly something that I had held myself to when I first started martial arts; when I was eventually confronted with the unnerving prospect of physically hitting a woman, I had little idea about what exactly I ought to do. I recall the very first time I engaged with mixed-sex sparring, as a junior member of my kickboxing gym, completely bewildered and hesitant to the point of inaction. In this first exchange, I did as many inexperienced, supposedly 'chivalrous' young men do, keeping my fists to myself while my female opponent knocked me around the ring.

What was particularly pertinent about my own and other men's reluctance to hit women, however, was that it was felt as a *visceral* aversion – a deep-seated discomfort which can be felt at the level of one's body. As I became increasingly sensitized to the embodied anxiety that hitting women posed for such men as myself, I began to see this kind of hesitation surface time and again amongst others as well. I recorded the following account of a sparring bout at a kung fu training session, between Nico, a relatively inexperienced newcomer, and Beth, a more seasoned martial artist:

> Nico spars Beth. He can't get it. She says hit me, he says okay, does nothing. Been like this for the full two mins. I call time, they stop, he's not hit her once but she hits him good maybe five/six times. He bows and won't make eye contact.

Body language said it all, doesn't wanna fight, doesn't wanna be there. Everyone switches partners; he fights Steve, goes in hard and heavy like always. Must've seen this a hundred times now with these types of lads. (Field notes, kung fu training, 2009)

Talking with Nico after the session, I questioned him on why he approached sparring Beth and Steve so differently, and as he explained his actions he described being *physically unable*, let alone unwilling, to hit his female partner:

Nico: It's just not in me, man, to hit a woman, it's like I know I won't be able to do it even if I wanted to, like my hands just won't do it.
Alex: But your hands hit Steve fine.
Nico: I can do that 'cause he's a man. I can't hit Beth 'cause she's a woman, I can't do it. (Field notes, post-training, 2009)

Drawing on this recognition of the deep-seated nature of men's hesitations, I later asked my male interviewees to discuss their feelings and experiences of fighting women:

I feel really uncomfortable that I could hurt a woman in that way, even if she's asking me to do it I feel really uncomfortable, you know, physically uncomfortable with doing that. (Interview, Steve, 30)

When I was in the young categories… I had to fight a girl [at a tournament] and I just couldn't hit her, I just stood there and let her beat me. I was in tears afterwards. (Interview, Andy, 30)

That these men should describe feeling *physical* discomfort, or go so far as to experience an *inability* to hit women, is telling. For both Andy and Steve, as with Nico and indeed, myself, the habituated lessons of gender propriety affected them physically, evoking a sense of unease *at the level of the body*, which prevented them from engaging in effective training or competitive sparring with women.

The idea that men should approach sparring differently based on the sex of their partners has previously been reported by Guérandel and Mennesson (2007), who similarly discussed men's gendered sense of honour as structuring their approach to judo practice with female opponents.[4] While Guérandel and Mennesson's (2007) research was among relatively experienced practitioners, finding that men in fact employed a mix of *deliberate* gendered strategies as they negotiated their interactions with women, my findings suggest that men were adhering to an almost *involuntary*, habituated ideology of masculine honour. However, concurrent with my own experience, my findings also suggest that this tends to be principally a concern among younger, less experienced martial artists. As one of my female interviewees described it:

It's always the new guys, the ones who never saw a woman fighting before, they're the ones with the problem really… you sort of have to prove yourself to them before they'll spar you with any kind of commitment. (Interview, Marie, 30)

Locating this problem principally among inexperienced, younger male martial artists can be explained with recourse to men's gendered life histories, and the generation of habitus through the specific social formations of those histories (Bourdieu 1990b), as with my own example above. For men such as myself, and particularly prior to engaging in mixed-sex training, understandings of fighting, physicality and embodied sex differences are often firmly rooted in traditional, patriarchal notions of gender, which celebrate male physical prowess and overlook or trivialize women's abilities. As a multitude of sports scholars have attested, women's physical potential is too often lost among men (as well as among many women themselves), owing to the prevalence of essentialist beliefs about the sexual division of physical power, the trivializing of female athletes in the mass media and the tendency for women to be prevented from training to develop their strength to begin with (Hargreaves 1994; Heywood and Dworkin 2003; Lenskyj 1986; Theberge 2000). Combining this lack of appreciation of women's abilities with the moral imperative of gentlemanly honour, which is described as being habituated throughout one's lifetime and can affect men most profoundly, generates a masculine habitus that emphasizes the necessity of the special treatment of 'weak' women. This habitus then surfaces in mixed-sex training through men's refusal to hit their female sparring partners.

Whenever I broached the topic with my female interviewees, it quickly became clear that men's habitual unwillingness (or indeed, inability) to hit them was a source of significant frustration for women involved in martial arts, especially, although not exclusively, among those who had trained for long periods of time or were engaged in competitive participation. Indeed, many women interpreted men's excessive 'holding back' as unhelpful, patronizing and frustrating. In their own words:

> I get so annoyed when it gets to the point where they just won't spar with me properly, it's really annoying because they don't think I'm strong enough just because I'm a girl. (Interview, Keeley, 26)
>
> It gets so frustrating… Sometimes I just feel like saying, 'will you fucking hit me, for once?' Because otherwise it's pointless me being here. (Interview, Beth, 24)

Women typically described men's 'holding back' as being harmful to their development as competitive fighters, since for the majority of the women I spoke to, their gyms (including my own) had so few high-level female members that training with men was a practical necessity most of the time. According to competitive kickboxer Helen, being hit was central to her development as a fighter, which was stunted whenever a male partner refused to strike her:

> That's one thing that does annoy me when I spar with guys, that sometimes they'll hold back too much, because I need to get used to being hit, and especially when I'm preparing to fight [competitively]… I just need someone to be able to hit me, that's the only way you learn how to keep your defence tight, if you get hit in the face. (Interview, Helen, 29)

Figure 7.2. Mixed training: 'Ben' and 'Joanne' in a pushing exercise; 'Ben' dumps his partner head-first to the mat upon the instructor's command to 'take down'.

Photos © Mustanir Ali.

Kickboxing coach Sara asked how women could even be considered to be martial artists if they were never physically tested, suggesting that the legitimacy of one's identity as a fighter hinges on the 'authenticity' of one's training experiences:

> Sometimes [holding back] is good if you're just beginning, but for me, well I'm like, 'come on, hit me', you know? I can take it, it'll push me harder, and I'll learn more from it. There's no point in me calling myself a kickboxer if I've never been kicked! (Interview, Sara, 23)

For Sara and Helen, as with many other women like them, men's refusal to hit in training presents a roadblock for the development of their fighting abilities, whilst also threatening to cheapen and degrade their status as martial artists. And as Beth and Keeley both describe, men's hesitation is often experienced as a patronizing annoyance, reflecting what McCaughey (1997, 79) describes as the 'condescending or embarrassing atmosphere' of male-centred mixed training environments. As such, men's excessive 'holding back' could become a significant problem for women in mixed-sex martial arts.

Kick or be Kicked: How Women Force Men to Reckon with Them on the Mat

In order to address the problems posed by men's reluctance to hit, the women in my research invariably employed the most simple of strategies: when men continually held back, the women pushed forward. The following field journal excerpt describes a sparring bout between Jenny, a senior gym member, and Gavin, an intermediate member. Evelyn, one of the junior instructors, is trying to encourage them:

> Jenny's got the upper hand and, with everyone watching, Gavin's stepping it up a bit, but not enough. Evelyn shouts to Jenny to 'make him work, kick him in the chops', and she catches him neatly with a roundhouse. You can hear the slapping sound of her instep on his cheek as it echoes around the hall. Classic, everyone gasps, then laughs. He's alright but red faced in more ways than one. He steps up the level, can see he wants revenge. Evelyn applauds the change in pace. (Field notes, kung fu training, 2010)

In order for Gavin to engage in the sparring session at a satisfactory level for the instructor Evelyn, it was first necessary for Jenny to shock him into action by showing him her strength – and his own vulnerability. In a later interview, Evelyn described her own approach to sparring reluctant men:

> If [men have] seriously got a problem that they don't wanna hurt me then well that's their problem and not mine, I'm still gonna go at them… I've been kicked in the head and punched and stuff, like anyone. And I think they see that they can do it to me after I do it to them a few times. (Interview, Evelyn, 24)

In recognizing that the strategy of physically pushing men into action was the most successful, Evelyn neatly summarizes the feelings of the majority of experienced female martial artists with whom I have trained and spoken throughout the course of my research. Their example highlights the necessity of confronting men's *embodied* aversions to hitting at *the level of the body*. In this regard, my own experience is also telling, and reflecting upon it highlights how women's potential for violent physicality can destabilize the habituated 'chivalry' of inexperienced male martial artists. Expanding upon the earlier mention of my first experience of sparring against a woman, the following passage, written in 2010 for the opening section of my PhD thesis, demonstrates how I began to change my approach towards mixed-sex training, and is indicative of the centrality of hitting or, more accurately, being hit, which is shared in the narratives of other men in similar situations. This account is of a time from before I formally began researching martial arts, and so is presented as a vignette based on my best ability to recollect:[5]

> It was 2005, and I had been training for little under a year. Despite being relatively inexperienced, I was more or less obliged to accept when, during free practice, one of the senior girls asked me to demonstrate semi-contact sparring to some of the newer members. The outcome was to thrust my previous disquiet regarding the presence of girls in the gym into the forefront of my reckoning of women's participation in martial arts. While I had sparred seriously with other senior members before, I hadn't fought against any of the women, and had more or less successfully avoided practising with girls at my own level by sticking to a small number of male sparring partners. But now I had no option, and the prospect of fighting her immediately foregrounded the contradictions inherent in my understanding of gender and martial arts. I remember the trepidation well: I was stepping into the unknown as I squared up to what suddenly felt like my first 'real' fight with a girl. Typically, I found myself hesitating to attack, withholding all power and retreating rather than blocking and countering. Our sparring session eventually ended following a hit to my head which sent me to the floor. She had caught me on the ear with a roundhouse kick, and while not entirely powerful, it was at a sufficient angle and pace to snap my head to the side, dazing me and causing me to fall. I remember feeling stunned as she checked me, knowing that I would be unable to continue. I had just been 'knocked out' by a girl.

While it would be some time before I understood enough about social theory to adequately analyse the significance of the situation, this forceful, direct and undeniable demonstration of female power had rocked my assumptions about the sexes and would remain with me for the rest of my training career. Indeed, it eventually became apparent that I had experienced first-hand the kind of 'consciousness-raising' moment which, five years later, I would be discussing at length in my PhD thesis. And there was no better way for me to initially begin this intellectual journey than through a direct, physical exchange, forcing this transformative knowledge (quite literally) right into my head.

According to Roth and Basow (2004, 245), it is commonly thought that 'women are not just weaker [than men] but are just plain weak'. Yet female martial artists openly defy this patriarchal ideology with their fists and their feet, and by *physically* demonstrating their own strength they destabilize the grounds upon which men's paternalism is based, providing new embodied realities with which men must then contend. When Messner described the significance of male combat sports in supporting ideologies of masculine superiority, he commented on the 'dramatic symbolic proof' (1988, 200) that male athletes provided of men's inherent fighting advantages over women. I would suggest that in similar ways, men being punched, kicked, thrown and choked by female martial artists goes some way to providing the kind of 'dramatic symbolic proof' needed to challenge this idea and the sexual hierarchy it supports. A later example from my field notes indicates how my default approach to physically engaging with women had changed in the years since the above incident:

> Freestyle sparring, showing off our other styles. Evelyn's trying out jiu-jitsu moves. We're on the ground and she got me in a triangle hold, squeezed my neck so hard I thought my eyes would pop out. We reset and she tried it again but I countered, lifted and slammed her on the mat. Wouldn't have ever done that a few years ago, but I'm in a different place now, I do this stuff without even thinking about it. I know she'll try to get me back next week and I'm already looking forward to the challenge. (Field notes, kung fu training, 2010)

Similar transformations take place among other men, as illustrated through the concluding part of Andy's tale about his competitive engagements with female opponents. Recalling a more recent championship fight, this time in a mixed-sex grappling tournament, Andy described his behaviour as radically different from before:

> She was so good, if I'd taken the pressure off her for a second she would've submitted me, she was world class… I knew she's probably one of the best grapplers in the UK, if not Europe. And she submitted every guy in my category, so I had to go in and batter her, and I did! (Interview, Andy, 30)

Describing his opponent not as a 'girl' or a 'woman', but rather as a 'great athlete', Andy revealed that his experience had taught him to see his opponent as fellow competitor first and female second. In doing so, he could take pride in his victory, boasting about 'battering' one of the best grapplers in the UK. Jack, a senior instructor in kung fu, echoes this changing definition of the female sparring partner as he recalls the events of his earlier training career:

> Because of the context that we were in, doing martial arts, I just didn't see it as hitting a girl, you see it as hitting another martial artist… Once I'd learned about [women's] abilities it was different. I fought against a girl I knew and it didn't make any difference to me personally that she was female because I knew what she was capable of. If I didn't take her seriously, treat her the same, she'd kick me in the head, she'd hurt me… [This experience] forces you to look at women differently. (Interview, Jack, 34)

Ultimately, then, treating women as 'the same' as male opponents would result from men's exposure to the abilities of female training partners and competitors, and through a concurrent realization that 'even if women are not as strong as men in absolute terms, they can still be formidable opponents' (Roth and Basow 2004, 254). A signal moment in the 'subversive' value of mixed-sex sport, this replacement of the primary identifying label of 'female' with that of 'martial artist' signifies the disassociation of the exclusive links between masculinity, men and fighting prowess, showing that men are beginning to see women as potential physical equals in the context of physical combat

(McDonagh and Pappano 2008). Hitting women follows from this, and in light of these changing subjectivities and reworkings of gender propriety, it takes on a completely different set of meanings to those implied by male chivalry and paternalism. Hitting women, then, becomes the physical expression of men's reworked gender habitus, forged through the shared histories of men and women learning how to fight together, and therein learning to engage with one another outside of the bounds of typical, patriarchal gender norms.

Concluding Thoughts: Theorizing Habitus, Subversion and Reflexivity in Martial Arts

Given these examples, I would suggest that it is principally through the process of 'up-close' exposure to the abilities of female fighters that I, along with many of the men I have trained among and spoken to, have come to 'unlearn' the deeply ingrained lessons of masculine chivalry and come to practise gender differently in this respect. As female martial artists present their strength, toughness and fighting skills to men in direct and undeniable fashion, the essentialist, patriarchal logic at the root of this particular problem is challenged as men are simultaneously pressed to take action outside of the discursive bounds it once set them in. This ultimately improves women's chances to become ever tougher and more skilful martial artists through expanding their training opportunities among more willing male partners, whilst simultaneously opening up spaces within which men and women can better learn about the many shared potentials of one another's bodies, rather than remaining fixated on typical, socially constructed, binary and hierarchal differences (Halberstam 1998).

In theorizing such a change, the fact that this lesson must be learned *physically*, and not just visually or discursively, highlights the usefulness of the concept of habitus for making sense of the depth at which inequitable gender ideology is often held. As Wacquant deftly puts it, the habitus is 'a social competency that is an embodied competency, transmitted through a silent pedagogy of organisms in action' (2011, 5). This 'silent pedagogy' may at once also be a vocal one, yet the deep mechanisms through which it does its most effective work lie in the unwritten, unspoken logics taught to acting subjects as they move through their socially structured lives (Bourdieu 1990b), ultimately becoming written into their very bodies. Particularly, as they rehearse dominant codes of prevailing gender logic, the patriarchal discourses of masculine 'superiority' and feminine 'weakness' become embodied, being normalized and 'naturalized' through the disciplined, repeated bodily performances of their everyday lives, as suggested by Butler (1990). Bourdieu, writing of the paradoxical character of such 'naturalized' gender, suggested that to challenge this sexual inequity in its normalized, naturalized state, it would be necessary to '(dismantle) the processes responsible for this transformation of history into nature, of cultural arbitrariness into the *natural*' (2001, 2, original emphasis). That is to say that the subversion of gender, and of patriarchy in particular, requires finding ways for individuals to reflexively recognize the socially constructed nature of their 'sexually characterized habitus' (2001, 3), revealing the cultural – and not 'natural' – roots of sex difference more broadly.

To express these ideas in more explicitly feminist terms, Bourdieu's position here is remarkably similar to Butler's (1990) poststructural feminist analysis, wherein the subversion of the patriarchal system of gender is a key concern. For Butler, this subversion is said to occur when individuals bend existing codes of propriety within the discursive spaces available to them, exposing the faulty logic of essentialism supporting the ideologies which otherwise structure 'normal' gendered categories. This principally occurs when radical, new performances destabilize existing gender codes through their inherent shock value, whilst simultaneously revealing the constructed character of the default categories that are otherwise assumed to occur naturally. Central to this strategy for subversion is the recognition that:

> The strange, the incoherent, that which falls 'outside', gives us a way of understanding the taken-for-granted world of sexual categorization as a constructed one, indeed, as one that might well be constructed differently. (Butler 1990, 149)

I would certainly argue that the normalization of a practice that values men hitting women as a way to substantiate greater sexual equity 'falls outside' of this taken-for-granted world, making mixed-sex training a powerful arena for contesting the naturalization of hierarchal sex difference and concurrently producing different sexually characterized habitus (Bourdieu 2001). The pedagogical outcomes of such 'strange' and 'incoherent' gendered encounters, drawn from perhaps the 'dramatic symbolic proof' (Messner 1988, 200) of women's otherwise hidden combative abilities, are what drive (specifically male) martial artists to a point where they must reconsider and challenge their own previous patterns of behaviour. That is to say, it requires them to develop a certain degree of *reflexivity* about their ideological understanding of the world and of their gendered selves (Bourdieu 2001). The Bourdieusian reading of *habitus* offered by Wacquant (above) similarly leaves open the door for flexibility and change in our gendered selves, being a set of '*acquired* dispositions' (Wacquant 2011, 5, original emphasis) that a person picks up as they move through their life, and is thus inherently open to alteration as their life course changes direction. More specifically, 'the socially constituted conative and cognitive structures that make up habitus are malleable and transmissible because they result from *pedagogical work*' (2011, 6, original emphasis), the likes of which clearly takes place in mixed-sex sparring.

Commenting on such pedagogical work, male and female martial artists alike stressed the transformative nature of the lessons of sparring and hinted at the wider significance that they held for challenging conceptions of gender difference and encouraging reflexive examination of their own attitudes, past and present. When linking men's discovery of women's physical potential with wider social patterns of gender relations, one of my female interviewees stated that:

> I think it's quite important to do this as a mixed group, because one of the things it does do is it helps develop a certain amount of respect between men and women, and what men's and women's bodies can do… And so [the men] hopefully will start to realize that women aren't just the weaker sex, we can hold our own, and that's quite important. (Interview, Beth, 24)

Speaking personally, I can only reaffirm this statement, and suggest that my interest in researching this phenomenon came following such a reflexive turn, brought on via the embodied pedagogy of mixed-sex hitting. Of course, my own personal journey in this regard has clearly been aided by the theoretical insights gathered through an education in sociology, but this should not downplay the importance of the *physical* in shaping my subjectivity. Even without the help of such philosophical frameworks, men and women training at martial arts are becoming physically familiar with the abilities of either sex, coming to understand the shared potential for developing martial competencies that lie within both male and female bodies. The discourses that typically circulate within martial arts subcultures explain the body's developing aptitude for combat as being principally the product of training, rather than participants' (sexed) natures, and by drawing on these explanations, alternative gendered discourses can arise which in turn help to shape the bodies of those involved. As one consequence of this, we can see the emergence of a reworked habitus among men who have particularly profound experiences of training alongside women in martial arts. Whilst there are other ways in which the phenomenon of mixed-sex training can instigate 'subversive' gender behaviour (including, for instance, the emergence of 'female masculinities' (Halberstam 1998) and female martial artists' negotiation, retention and reinvention of both 'subversive' and traditional styles of femininity (e.g. De Welde 2003)), I would suggest that these changes in men's habitus provide a compelling point of departure for scholars interested in exploring such things.

Notes

1 Not to be confused with 'mixed martial arts' (MMA), I use this term to denote any and all practices of martial arts that are undertaken in sex-integrated, or 'co-ed' training environments.
2 I conducted formal semi-structured interviews with martial artists (n=34) drawn from several different disciplines (including kung fu, karate, kickboxing, MMA, tae kwon do and others) from around the English East Midlands, where my own training also took place. These interviews were in addition to the many informal conversations held with martial artists during training, at competitions, conventions, social events, etc.
3 Note that whenever names are used in conjunction with interview quotations or field notes, they are pseudonyms, self-selected by my research participants in order to protect their anonymity. Participants' ages are also provided to partly contextualize data.
4 Discourses based around male strength and female weakness have also been reported to structure players' conduct in other mixed-sex sports, such as softball (Wachs 2002) and soccer (Henry and Comeaux 1999).
5 As others with similar experiences will no doubt be able to attest, events such as this are not quickly forgotten!

Chapter 8

THE TEACHER'S BLESSING AND THE WITHHELD HAND: TWO VIGNETTES OF SOMATIC LEARNING IN SOUTH INDIA'S INDIGENOUS MARTIAL ART KALARIPPAYATTU

Sara K. Schneider

Introduction

By concentrating on the significance of two gestural vignettes that bookended my fieldwork on and study of the indigenous South Indian martial art kalarippayattu, this chapter surfaces both the gaps and the gains in undertaking study in another cultural setting, as well as the longing and the frustrations inherent in fieldwork. My experience as a Western female body-based researcher in South India underscores the complex ecologies of somatic learning. The very media of teaching and learning in this psychophysical form – attention; talk and silence; gesture, touch and stillness – show off Wacquant's notion of habitus as a 'methodological device' (2011, 7).

The focus of the present chapter is a cross-cultural, cross-gender guru–student relationship in kalarippayattu. I argue that both learning and the teacher–student relationship of the form are inevitably coloured by learner's and teacher's expectations, beliefs and common practices within embodied social structures surrounding appropriate gender, culture and class behaviour. Such a recounting of the complexities of cross-cultural, embodied learning and teaching bridges the literatures on the teacher–student relationship, international education and the anthropology of the body. It also asserts the centrality of embodiment in both international and American contexts of teaching and learning (Classen 1993; Cooks and LeBesco 2006; Freedman and Holmes 2003; Geurts 2002; Lave 1977; Light 2001; Ness 1992).

The data come from fieldwork notes, videotapes and photographs I took during two months of fieldwork in Calicut (Kozhikode), Kerala, India during the period May to September 2002, as well as from interviews I conducted with the kalarippayattu guru, T. Sudhakaran Gurukkal, his teenage daughter and student, Archana, and groups of his school-aged male and female students. They also come from my lived experience trying to learn kalarippayattu – blistered, clay-reddened bare feet and all – through

Figure 8.1. The gurukkal marks the movement as his young student practices one of the early exercises of kalarippayattu.

Photo courtesy of the author.

what Wacquant calls 'observing participation', a deepening and corporealizing of the concept of participant observation (2011, 7). As someone whose intentions changed over the course of fieldwork, as I pointedly deepened and grew down my role from that of participant observer to that of observing participant, I used my own 'suffering body' as a tool of analysis of the form and as an experiential guide to the questions I asked of the guru and his students (Wacquant 2011, 8).

With roots going back at least to the twelfth century, kalarippayattu is traditionally practised by the Nayar caste, though members of other groups in South India have also taken it up. In Malayalam, the language of Kerala, its name means exercises (*payattu*) performed in a practice space (*kalari*). Revived in the 1920s as part of Kerala's resistance to British colonial rule, kalarippayattu is closely associated with Malayali images of manhood (Zarrilli 2000). Ten school-age boys I interviewed in Sudhakaran's CVN Kalari in Calicut associated the practice with 'becoming strong and healthy', with excellence in sports and with the improvement of concentration (personal communication, September 2002). For those who associate martial arts with upright postures acting as grounding for sharp, angular strikes by the limbs, a first view of kalarippayattu can be startling. Its deep and wide preparatory squats, animal-inspired postures and weapons combat feathered with spectacular leaps and turns all offer to many Westerners a stylistically contrasting image of the Eastern martial arts with which they may be more familiar.

The complexities of the experience stemmed in part from my entering into, belonging to (to some degree) and then leaving a martial arts learning community as a person embodying the ambiguities of both high and low statuses. On the one hand, I was an upper-middle-class Western scholar, frequently treated with what felt like exaggerated deference as being of equal or higher status to many Indians in this profoundly hierarchical society (Osella and Osella 1998). There were also active lower-status valences attached to me, as, after all, I was a single childless woman of childbearing age in a culture that sees wife and mother as primary roles for women. I was electing to study a martial art that, though it attracts young girls to its study, has relatively few adult female practitioners, much less girls practising once puberty hits. My nearest companions in ability would be boys and girls in the primary grades. Even though I continued to ask many questions in the course of and after practice lessons, in making the transition from verbally and visually engaged scholar to embodied student, I suffered a palpable change in status, one that perplexed me at the time and that later revealed larger insights about the roles of touch and talk in an embodied subject of learning.

The Role of the Guru in the Transmission of Knowledge in Kalarippayattu

The word 'guru' is as readily bandied about in American speech as are such commercial monikers as 'Kleenex', 'Xerox' and 'Google'. For Westerners, the term can refer to a leading practitioner or taste-maker, even if the person doesn't actually teach, or it may be invoked disparagingly to designate a currently popular expert, one the radio stations go to for a sound bite. By contrast, in India the figure of the guru is defined through relationship and sacred responsibility. Originally, the guru was a teacher of the holy Vedic texts and he (for it certainly was a he) had to be a Brahmin, a member of India's highest caste; the term guru could also apply to a teacher of the traditional arts and crafts (Kale 1970). The guru's male disciples, who could be drawn from any part of Indian society, spent their adolescence living with the guru's family and receiving the tradition orally. The guru's teaching was priestly, made essentially as a gift to his students; it was only rewarded at the end of their years together, by whatever each student chose to give him.

With the rise of the devotional bhakti movement in Hinduism and its development through the Indian medieval period, as well as with the ascendancy of Buddhism and Jainism in India, the notion of the guru as an inspirational – even if not particularly learned – figure began to emerge. Rather than expecting that he would prove himself by his knowledge, the guru's students would invest him with faith. A form of guru worship, or guru yoga, dictated that the disciple submit himself without question, as a form of self-surrender or self-transcendence, to whatever requests the guru might make. It is perhaps this unquestioning submission embedded in the term guru that raises many Westerners' hackles; the uncritical acceptance of someone as an expert may reek of cultism. No less suspicious from this perspective is the person who would accept another's seemingly blind obedience. Even in India the unquestioning view of the guru eroded to a certain degree with British colonial rule, as Indians experienced a very different kind of teacher, one caught up in a wide bureaucratic net whose ultimate authority was the British government.

When I went to India in 2002 I was already somewhat familiar with the figure of the guru from two years of yoga study. In American ashrams I had seen disciples place in their gurus' hands full authority to make such weighty decisions as selecting a suitable marriage partner for them. In India I learned a new title common to kalarippayattu for the master, *gurukkal*, which indicated his representation and incarnation of a long line of teachers in his tradition. The gurukkal stood as that line's culmination and apex (Zarrilli 2000, 301).

While I spent some time observing martial arts practice at the southern kalari with which the Western expert on the form, Phillip B. Zarrilli, is best associated, I wanted to undertake study in a traditional village setting and travelled up the coast to spend the most time at a kalari in the north of Kerala. During my first trip to Calicut, Kerala's third largest city, I photographed and videotaped T. Sudhakaran Gurukkal's work with his students; observed the young people in training and practice; and sat in on rehearsals and demonstrations of the kalarippayattu performance troupe, which did shows for tourists staying at the higher-end hotels.

As threat of nuclear war with Pakistan arose in June 2002, foreigners were evacuated from South India. When I returned to Kerala that August, I had already adopted two relatively powerful roles with Sudhakaran Gurukkal, as researcher and as possible stage director, since I had expressed interest in creating an elaborate production showcasing the performance strengths of the martial art for national and international audiences.

To these roles I had decided, if Sudhakaran gave his permission, to add that of student – or as Sudhakaran put it, disciple – and adopting the mores of his kalari. In addition, in order to make it to early-morning and evening practice, in keeping with my teacher's suggestion I moved from a hotel in the centre of Calicut to the city's outskirts, where the kalari was located, and rented a bedroom in the home of Sudhakaran's brother and sister-in-law, his immediate neighbours on the family compound. In so doing, I would find it easier to make morning and evening practice sessions, to watch the performance troupe rehearse and to catch Sudhakaran or his students for an impromptu interview. I would also have my comings and goings scrutinized, and find it difficult to gain my accustomed privacy to compose field notes and organize images. Not merely my body but also my thinking process became far more public than I was accustomed to through my changed proximity to the surrounds of the kalari, where both togetherness and collective perception reigned more powerfully than the aloneness and individualized consciousness to which I was more accustomed. My body shape, hairstyle and manner of riding astride a motorcycle as a friend's passenger became the objects of discussion, comment and curiosity.

I knew that studying under Sudhakaran would mean altering my relationship to him. After he accepted me as his student, I struggled mightily with giving up my collegial status with him. I noticed that I resisted, with all my American commitment to egalitarianism, calling him by the honorific Gurukkal, which was now more appropriate than for me to continue to use his given name.

As a child and well into my thirties, I'd studied with ballet and other dance teachers. My relationship with them was generally impersonal, and I knew nothing of their lives outside the studio. I certainly did not look to them for guidance in matters of the spirit.

Figure 8.2. The stick is an extension of the gurukkal's hand, ready to administer (more or less) gentle corrections.

Photo courtesy of the author.

By contrast, during my years in graduate school, the dance teacher with whom I took weekly private lessons in the history of Western dance was the first who offered me critiques based on more than my technical attack of the choreography: he insisted I attend to the spirit dancer, with with which I danced and he was ruthless in his own close observation of my intentions as they may have been expressed through my dancing. Despite this attention to the soul of dance, I believe he saw himself as someone who could offer wisdom but not insist that his students accept it. Our relationship was of artistic mentor and protégée. The mentorship was also physical and egalitarian: when he taught me partner dances, he danced the male role alongside me, both teacher and partner.

More recently, however, I'd had yoga teachers who, even in America, carried some of the air of spiritual guide even as they were engaged in improving their students' practice of the postures. They were careful to speak constructively and were evidently mindful of their students' evaluative gaze at their daily habits. They also performed helpful physical 'adjustments' on students' bodies to help them move more deeply into a pose or experience the correct muscular action required. So it was with a long-time identity as a dancer, with its attendant body consciousness and an expectation of dispassionate technical correction as the recompense for paying the class fee, and a more recent bodily sedimentation as a student of yoga, with its clarity around teacher–student boundaries despite a more hands-on teaching approach, that I undertook the study of kalarippayattu.

Contemporary ethnographers such as Behar (1996) have written sensitively about the ethical, relational and procedural complexities of their fieldwork experiences. Behind their prefatory explications of how they built rapport with their subjects, dealt with unexpected relational developments and made freighted ethical and practical choices in the course of collecting data and writing up their studies, lies their evident desire to help their audiences understand the methodology and the filters that have shaped their data. Those filters are situated in the ethnographer's habitus as much as in any sort of filters that are, perhaps falsely, understood as residing only from the neck up.

As readers we are to understand that what the ethnographer 'got' was largely what he or she, as an unmistakably enculturated researcher, was able to 'get' – to see, to hear, to understand and to experience. There is no guarantee that what an ethnographer observes from the outside is what the data means in its own context; in part, the ethnographer's hope is that, by revealing their own biases, predispositions and history, the reader will be able to see through some of the necessarily partial interpretations to a clearer view of the data itself.

In sharing this ethnographic reflection, I hope to surface the role of a highly specific body – white, Western, female, unattached to husband or child – embarked on cross-cultural corporal learning. The following two vignettes, which bookended my time in the CVN Kalari, Calicut, demonstrate both my attraction to the teaching and learning world presented as well as my recognition of its limitations.

When and What the Teacher Teaches Through Touch: Two Bookending Vignettes

Vignette 1 – The teacher's blessing

Immediately after entering the kalari, the teacher, bare to the waist, begins to pray at each of the platforms placed around the periphery of the small, moist red clay-floored and clay-walled structure. His contemplative clockwise circuit reminds me of the Catholic stations of the cross, with time spent in prayer or reflection at a series of spatially demarcated centres, each with one or more of the Hindu deities associated with the martial art. As they continue in their warm-ups in the thatched kalari, the guru's 6- to 12-year-old students watch him with quiet peripheral awareness, mindful not to disturb him in his spiritual preparation for the morning's practice.

But just as soon as he completes his circuit of the platforms, the youngest students throng around him. As each student rapidly touches his fingers lightly to his teacher's feet and then to his own heart and reiterates the gesture, the guru drops his hand to the crown of the student's head and carries it first to his own heart and crown. However, this customary blessing of each student does not end with this gestural and energetic connection between the hearts and heads of teacher and student, via the guru's feet, but with a final gesture of the guru's hand. For, from the top of his student's and then his own head, this guru's hand carries up into space, as if to connect both the disciple's vulnerability and need to be blessed and the guru's power to confer that blessing with a greater source of power and learning that embraces them both.

As a teacher, this coda to the gesture of blessing touches me to the core. In it, I see the submission of both guru and disciple (*sisya*) to a larger tradition that embraces them both. I experience with an unprecedented depth the honour of being a teacher — the humility and respect of the student, the love and faith of the teacher, but the submission of both within the gifts of knowledge and understanding for which both strive.

Vignette 2 – The withheld hand

Some months later, I prepare to leave my guru, the CVN Kalari and the home of my hosts, my guru's brother and sister-in-law. I expect the goodbye to recall the simplicity and purity of the teacher's blessing that introduced me to the practice. Instead, real and perceived cultural and financial differentials of power dominate the scene.

My teacher instructs me to put on over my practice T-shirt and shorts a red, white and black *katcha*, a costume wrapped around the waist and through the legs for kalarippayattu demonstrations. His wife, Anitha, helps me. Sudhakaran doubtless knows that I am still years of practice away from being qualified to take part in any such demonstration. Yet I know from other experiences, both with him and elsewhere during my fieldwork in India, that Westerners with sustained interest in Indian cultural practices can be ambushed into surprise photo sessions, whose products can add cachet to a local institution. Photos of a Westerner in the CVN Kalari can serve the kalari's as well as the Kerala Tourism Commission's long-range interests of showing that white Euro-Americans, as much as locals, seek out its training.

It takes a certain paradigm shift to admit the body as an instrument of knowing in research as well as the subject of research. Having made that shift, it is a further disorientation to have one's learning body suddenly transformed into a static yet evidently profitable image of generalized whiteness or Euro-Americanness – especially with an ingrained sense of such a body as normative (at least along those dimensions). It's also, of course, a bumping up against the individualism-centred prohibition, so common in my home professional culture, against dual relationships between teacher and students.

Feeling uncomfortably objectified, I try to manage the photo-taking so as to yield photos that I might be able to use as learning references. I naively ask the guru to pose with me as if he were correcting my postures — something that clearly still needs doing. He pauses for a moment, then quite tentatively allows his hands to alight on my shoulders, in a fashion both uncharacteristic of any other training correction I have ever seen — and entirely ineffectual as a correction for the posture I am doing.

Suddenly, what has been slowly brewing in me over the training period comes to full consciousness: I realize that Sudhakaran has not corrected a posture once by hand: that in contrast to my male American counterpart, William, who trained for weeks beside me at the kalari, as a woman I have received what could be considered the illusion of training, for Sudhakaran has taught me largely through demonstration and discussion. Customarily, kalarippayattu is taught through a combination of verbal commands in Malayalam, rapid raps of the training stick on students' rumps or arms and occasional hands-on adjustments, as are done in some forms of yoga. As a yoga student, in coming to India I had been expecting such hands-on corrections; my experience two years prior of studying dance in Hindu Bali had instilled similar expectations.[1]

I suddenly flash back to a topic Sudhakaran had brought up seemingly out of the blue as he was driving me in his truck back into town shortly after having accepted me as a student. He had begun talking about gender relations in India as compared with in the United States and Europe. It is a fact, he said, that men and women are different. And unlike in Europe and America, when a man touches a woman in India it is always sexual. Even a pattern of talking together in public causes others to think something is going on. As we drove by, people on the streets of Calicut waved and called to him, perhaps curious about the strange woman in the passenger seat. He called back in Malayalam, perhaps explaining that I was a visiting student from America.

At the time his speech had truly confused me: why had the topic even come up? What was the subtext? Was he explaining why so many people were calling to him in the car? Or was he just trying to warn me not to touch him, as would be my custom in my own country and my own instinct?

Now I realize that on some level he was explaining to me why William would receive a very different form of training to mine. Already studying at the CVN Kalari when I arrived, William was at once my companion and a thorn in my side. On one hand, I was glad for William's presence, as we could share cultural observations and travails. He also helped to deflect the attention I was getting as a single, white woman travelling alone. Yet I also noticed the explosion of feelings that were very like sibling rivalry: I found myself continually astonished by how much credence Sudhakaran seemed to grant William, for example, asking for his evaluation of the quality of my digital camera.

At the same time as the shock of the realization of the gender-specific ground of my learning experience fills me, the photo shoot itself skyrockets in importance to me. I realize that it may stand as the finest, though most unconventional, training I have received while in Calicut – here, as I silently adjust my own poses, my teacher simply waits, the corrective touch I have been craving supplanted by his critical gaze and his silence till I get it right enough. I try to self-correct, to distil the essence of each motion into something that when photographed can capture the spirit of the full movement. His saying nothing means that my efforts are still 'cold'; a slight change in his energy might mean I am 'getting warmer'.

The scene throws into relief the replacement of an impossible touch in this cross-gender training environment, as well as the remaining class basis of the interaction between this research subject and fieldworker, guru and student, and South Indian male teacher belonging to the historic warrior caste and a female learner from a purportedly classless American society. In taking in the first vignette, I had been so profoundly moved by the submission of both guru and disciple in the act of conferring the blessing that I minimized any difficulties I would later have in accepting my role in the drama.

Ethnography as *The Marriage of Toby's Idea of Angela and Toby's Idea of Angela's Idea of Toby*

The title of Caryl Churchill's 1968 puppet play tells the story of this cultural encounter: it was in a sense *The Marriage of Toby's Idea of Angela and Toby's Idea of Angela's Idea of Toby*. As an American somatic anthropologist, I was both open to examining my experience in a new culture and horrified to have entered into this hierarchical society in which a specific and complicated social position had been assigned to rather than defined by me.

My own way of being in my body was very specific to the dance and yoga cultures that had constituted my prior training. Expecting to be working out in the heat and humidity, I had hoped to learn kalarippayattu alongside young boys (and girls) in the snug, sleeveless yoga tops that I had brought along for practice. Of course, these were immediately forbidden by the guru as being inappropriate to wear around young boys and I had been sent shopping for more modest (and much more uncomfortably insulating) T-shirts. In addition, there was no room for the open, body-conscious female athleticism I had been accustomed to either as a dancer or as a yoga student in Chicago.

As may have been evident to the reader for some time, I came to the encounter with my ethnocentrism quite intact. I clung fiercely to my very American belief in egalitarianism in practice. Thus, the projection of the two sides of the ethnic and gender pedestal onto which I was being placed was enormously disquieting.

I had at least three warring desires. One, as I have said, was to retain my collegial relationship with Sudhakaran, rather than surrender to him as guru. At one point in the training I found myself, perhaps laden with stories of corrupt gurus in the United States, obsessed with the worry (without any real foundation) that Sudhakaran may not have been the moral exemplar I 'needed' him to be. These ruminations were hardly the brainchildren of someone willingly submitting to a guru.

Second, there was a certain attraction to Sudhakaran, a handsome, athletic man five years my senior; perhaps this was generated in part by the forbiddenness and charged quality of both physical and verbal contact. (There is, of course, a long history of female protégées projecting such feelings onto their male mentors.) I was also well aware, during the two months overall that I spent in India, of being touch-deprived, used as I was to greeting friends, fellow yoga practitioners and occasionally students with a hug. At the kalari, even hugging between women was discouraged.

Finally, there was the much larger professional concern about usurping a cultural practice and profiting by it without offering an appropriate share of the benefits with the people whose tradition it is. I struggled with this issue, as I had gone into debt to fund my research there. Yet did I really want to be the sole exploiter, demanding that in a relatively short period of research Keralans yield up their techniques and secrets to me, only to have me go away and make something of them?

To the people with whom I worked in India, I believe I was many things – someone who dwelt in the somewhat less defined space of being neither Hindu, Christian nor Muslim, a single childless female travelling alone, a fair-skinned Euro-American. I felt oddly depersonalized as I was faced with identity categories with unaccustomed significances. Sudhakaran and his family had had little or no prior experience of Jews; those who were neither Hindu nor Muslim were by default honorary Christians.[2] In addition, as a woman in India I was someone whose skin and shape had to be concealed in public, who in addition – as Sudhakaran had tried to help me understand – could not be seen speaking alone with or be touched by a man without others assuming a sexual relationship in this publicly chaste society. Finally, as a Euro-American, I received in India a consistent projection as potential benefactor for international career opportunities for Indians.

Frequently I felt as if I were being spoken to out of two contrary codes: one that would be used for honorary high-caste persons, the other I associated with the disregard shown to native women in India, even in the relatively liberal state of Kerala. Neither projection was comfortable for me and I less than half-jokingly strove with one of Sudhakaran's friends, Prasad – who seemed somewhat more comfortable with Western customs than was my guru – to get him to think of and treat me not as a white female but as he might an Indian male! Letting alone its practicality, conceptually this ethnocentrically egalitarian suggestion appeared (naturally) ridiculous to him – though to me at the time it seemed a solution to the discomfort of being either socially elevated, treated as an ongoing sexual threat, or ignored.

Corporal Teaching in Kerala

In the language of Bourdieu and Shilling, the 'professional body' is a kind of 'physical capital', able to turn the physical cultivation of years into a form of communication and development of others (as cited in Light 2001). Lave (1977) highlighted the inductive basis of apprenticeship learning, which readily applies to training in Asian martial arts in general and specifically to kalarippayattu, as students practise with others of their own age and level, more experienced students participate in the training of the less advanced, and the guru serves as the ultimate exemplar and not just the arbiter of practice. In the CVN Kalari in Trivandrum in the south of Kerala, which I visited, as well as the CVN Kalari in Calicut, at which I studied, students practise alongside peers working at their own age and expertise level, which were generally linked. Thus, the students who were at my level were certainly not my age or size. Rather they were loincloth-wearing schoolboys or young girls in shorts and T-shirts who, in their off hours, could be found giggling and peeking out at me from behind bushes.

In kalarippayattu, students engage in rote repetition. They practise the movements as the guru calls them out and offers physical corrections. The movements' underlying meanings come with time. As Sudhakaran explained to me in an interview, young students are only given the spiritual context for what they are doing once the teacher feels they are ready. While he will give his youngest students the basic outline of the actions they are to perform as they circle the kalari in worship, he considers early religious training to be the parents' responsibility. Thus, he will not go into extravagant detail at first on the mental state that they should cultivate as they pray before each of the deities around the kalari's periphery: telling a person too early in life to channel the power of the gods for his or her practice will only distract them.

A good deal of teaching in kalarippayattu is achieved through the guru's verbal articulation of the movements in the time they are to be performed and through his touch, which is frequently mediated by one of the yard-long bamboo sticks that are also the student's first weapon. Sudhakaran would, for example, incline a squatting student's upper body further forward by leaning the bamboo stick across his back. Trainers of adult students of kalarippayattu in Trivandrum also use the stick as a guiding corrective.

One teacher I observed used his stick to correct the turnout of a student's leg or the position of his lower back, hips or chest. Sudhakaran characterized inferior teachers as noticing their students' mistakes but electing not to correct them (Sudhakaran, personal communication, September 2002).

India's Supreme Court outlawed the corporal punishment of students only in 2000, and the prohibition has been only laxly enforced. Still, in 2002, with young students in Kerala, corporal punishment appeared to be a regular teaching and disciplinary strategy. I saw Sudhakaran swiftly rap a student who hadn't put into practice a previous correction or was failing to pay attention. He told me that this is a way to help the students learn and remember. The boys in his kalari characterized the use of the bamboo pole in the kalari as far less than what their schoolteachers rapped their hands with when they misbehaved in school. Nevertheless, Sudhakaran's daughter, Archana, told me that whenever Westerners, with their typical horror of corporal punishment, came to the CVN Kalari, her father toned down the frequency and intensity of his more punishing corrections, so she believed I was being exposed to less physical correction than a Keralan might have been.

Young boys in particular can be subjected to quite serious corporal punishment. At the Kerala Kalamandalam in Cheruthuruthy, boys are moulded both manually and technically into performers of kathakali, the highly stylized dance-drama form that draws heavily on kalarippayattu (Zarrilli 2000, 3). At the Kalamandalam, tales of abuse of students are legendary. Two teenage students told me the story of providing emotional and medicinal salve to younger boys who suffered welts on their bodies from a guru's beatings.

In physical disciplines performed to music, such as kathakali and classical Indian dance, the gurus often have sticks handy for keeping time as the students practise. However, the sticks are obviously handy for more than beating time. I observed one kathakali teacher at the Kalamandalam travel along a line of boys standing against the wall in his classroom, chiding and smacking each of them in turn. As I watched, he turned his focus on one, whacking him several times on the back of the head as he spoke to him caustically. Reminiscent of Hollywood films depicting army boot camps, the boy of the moment would gaze stoically in front of him, never reacting openly, while the next boy in the line-up kept his eyes also focused straight ahead and would appear unconcerned until the teacher began to speak to him.

Beatings can be both condoned and subject to some rebuke, though it's unclear how firmly it stands. Kalamandalam master Ramadass told me about being suspended from the faculty after having been accused of having injured students with beatings. He was reinstated but is cautious and reported never beating students again.

Even the pedagogical strategies that are not physically violent can seem harsh to a Westerner. Ramadass related the story of teaching a Dutch student who questioned his instructional shouting upon seeing a mistake; the student argued that since he wasn't from Kerala, why should the teacher verbally abuse him in the Keralan fashion? Ramadass described this interaction as being profound for him, causing him to alter his teaching behaviour around foreign students – though he continued to yell at native ones.

During the final kathakali examinations that I saw, each student demonstrated 20 minutes' worth of material – a long time to be subjected to the judgement and close observation of two teachers, five classmates and a Euro-American female visitor. Like kalaripayyattu students, kathakali students at the Kalamandalam are believed to learn from watching each other. During the examinations, if the instructor Krishna Kumar saw the student making a mistake, he would stop the dancing and ask first the student and then his or her classmates what was wrong with the student's performance. The examination room was filled with the instructor's derisive laughter, ridicule and negative reinforcement, both physical and verbal. Later Ramadass told me that he never tells a student when they have actually done well. The students only learned the teacher's impression of them when their parents got their report card with a score and class rank.

Conclusion

In the first vignette, which took place on my first day at the CVN Kalari in Calicut, I was an observer, a witness to a customary Keralan scene of seeking and offering blessing and of demonstrating respect between guru and disciple, as well as for the tradition and practice that embraced them. I have no sense that anything was altered for my viewing, neither in Sudhakaran's behaviour towards his disciples nor in theirs towards him.

Many things had changed by the period of the second vignette, which closed my time at the CVN Kalari in Calicut. I was no longer a distanced videographer, photographer and interviewer staying at the tourist hotel in the city. I was now a disciple of my research subject, rooming with my teacher's brother's family. The qualities of my own gendered, ethnic body would alter his practice – how he would teach, what he would choose to correct, where he would take me in the practice. Nevertheless, I had not made a transition out of a role whose valence in Keralan culture made me uncomfortable: I was still fair-skinned, Euro-American, female, single and childless though of childbearing age. When I determined to get closer to the practice of kalarippayattu by way of my own kinaesthetic intelligence – a mode I was recognizing as the readiest path for my own understanding – I paradoxically limited how close I would or could get to the understanding I sought.

So many strains skeined the second vignette, among them the relative superficiality of the contact at the goodbye, even given the length of time we'd had together; the willingness of the gurukkal to portray an a less-than-fully-competent practitioner as a performer of the art for marketing purposes. Perhaps the greatest of the ironies, and the moment that provided the greatest insight of my time in Kerala, took place as Sudhakaran silently waited to reinforce me with the snap of the camera until I had sufficiently corrected myself – wrong still, so long as his photo machine remained silent. When he half-compliantly touched me on the shoulders without actually correcting me, I saw the utter absence of the teaching touch that I hadn't up to that point realized I'd been missing. In some sense, I was like the youngest children who would make the circuit of the kalari in the outward manifestations of prayer without full understanding of what they were to do at each station; I was practising my way into the form with diminished maturity. Unlike them, however, I might never advance, so long as I was attempting to learn kalarippayattu within a relatively traditional kalari, informed by local social norms as it was.

Much has been made of cross-cultural differences in direct and indirect communication as well as of the varied uses of speech and silence in teaching and learning (see, for example, Radford 2009; Stahl 1994; Tincani and Crozier 2007). So too has scholarly attention focused on cross-cultural differences in eye contact as they may impact teaching and learning (Chiang 1994; Pitton et al. 1994). Historically in Western cultures, the principal way in which touch has been discussed as a teaching strategy is of course in the role of corporal punishment in disciplining unruly pupils. More recently, authors mourn the loss of touch in the American classroom in the wake of political correctness, societal litigiousness and concerns about students' emergent sexuality. They also emphasize the gendered, indeed sexual, presence of the teacher (Cooks and LeBesco 2006; Freedman and Holmes 2003; Johnson 2006; Sapon-Shevin 2009).

Sapon-Shevin's (2009) treatment of the loss for students when touch is withheld provides a rare voice. Certainly, my own longing for teacherly touch – which magnified after I realized I hadn't had it – had many sources, only a limited number of which could be attributed to the specifically cultural clash I generated by coming into kalarippayattu training as an adult woman expecting the same training that a man would have got, just as I had in dance and yoga training in the States or to some extent in Hindu Bali. Nevertheless, this example displays the power of corrective touch given – and withheld – and highlights the qualities of the peculiarly intercultural form of training in which a traditional practice rests within traditional values, even in a globalizing society.

In a situation with a compelling mixture of power relations – the one of us distinguished, among other things, by territorial domain, maleness, established caste position, a guru identity and family status, the other perhaps by relative wealth, Western identity and educational level – Wacquant's notion of 'the body as a target, receptacle, and fount of asymmetric power relations' (2011, 82) is redoubled in significance, is doubly and asymmetrically asymmetrical.

As my experience was no doubt influenced in part by the relatively short period of my fieldwork and study of kalarippayattu, it would be worthwhile to compare it with that of longer-term students, both male and female. Perhaps even richer would be a study set within a more widely known and urban kalari such as the Trivandrum CVN Kalari, which has a much higher volume and longer history of adult, Western and female students. An examination of the experience of both gurus and students, as well as the manner of teaching and learning within such kalaris, might offer a later model of a negotiated somatic pedagogy and practice.

Notes

1 Indeed, I had gone to Indonesia to experience what dance training would be like when the student was like clay in a sculptor's hands; I'd hoped to contrast this learning experience with the far more verbal and modelling basis of teaching in ballet, the dance form in which I had grown up and from which training I still clench my buttocks at every turn.
2 And as someone born Jewish and travelling in the most literate part of India less than a year after 11 September 2001, I was shocked to hear the theory that Israeli and American Jews were responsible for the terrorist attacks on New York's World Trade Center towers, that they had warned all Jews who worked in the building ahead of time to evacuate so that none of

them would perish and that no Jews had. I later learned this theory is widespread in many parts of the world, including among many Muslims in Asia and the Middle East, and that it may be considered a twenty-first century instantiation of the nineteenth-century anti-Semitic document, *The Protocols of the Elders of Zion*, which posited that a secret, powerful group of Jews was striving to manipulate world events to serve Jewish interests (Anti-Defamation League 2003, 6–7; Neuman 2005).

Chapter 9

WHITE MEN DON'T FLOW: EMBODIED AESTHETICS OF THE FIFTY-TWO HAND BLOCKS

Thomas Green

Introduction

The following remarks focus on my efforts at researching an African American vernacular martial art (VMA) often known as the 52 hand blocks (also known as jailhouse, jailhouse boxing, jailhouse rock, or the 52s, among other regional labels)[1] via thick participation, 'cultural knowledge recorded first in the anthropologist's body and only later externalized as visual or textual data for purposes of analysis' (Samudra 2008, 667). In addition to training in the 52s per se, I made an effort to 'thicken' my participation by utilizing related African American vernacular genres as channels for transforming my martial habitus. Traditionally, the art is learned by doing, by an active pursuit of street fighting rather than through any structured pedagogy.[2] Body toughening is a product of the learning process. The teaching method exists at a corporeal rather than the cognitive level. As Loïc Wacquant characterizes his boxing apprenticeship: 'Apprenticeship is here the means of acquiring a practical mastery, a visceral knowledge of the universe' (2011, 7).

In linguistics, the term 'vernacular' denotes a local language or dialect, and in art criticism refers to creations flourishing in isolation from the schools and fads governing elite art. When applied to martial arts, vernacular denotes a local style developed to address local needs and is consistent with larger cultural traditions (for example music, dance, play and religion) of the groups in which these fighting systems arise. They respond to internal imperatives of the local group or practitioners without recourse to governing bodies, as is the case with codified systems. For example, informant Rudy Curry[3] remembers a New York City practitioner, Justice, who 'had his own style called the "dead arm" he learned from a 52 fighter who had one bad arm. The hanging arm was used for shoulder blocks from a seemingly awkward position, and the other arm came out of nowhere (to strike opponents)' (personal communication, 2003).

What are the 52s?

As noted above, the 52s is a popular contemporary catchword for a range of African American vernacular martial arts. Turning again to Rudy Curry, 'The real 52s fighters were just like martial artists. Good ones were rare. Back then (ca. 1970s) it was a neighbourhood thing just like regional differences in martial arts. Southerners and Midwestern visitors and people from other parts of the country had different prison styles' (personal communication, 2003).

The regional subtypes of the methods to which Curry refers are known by various labels, but early styles often are collectively called 'jailhouse rock' or simply 'jailhouse'. In New York, the fighting style that evolved, both within and outside the prison contexts, was the '52s'. The origin of the name has been the object of considerable speculation over the past decade when the 52s came to wide public attention via Douglas Century's account of thug life and hip-hop culture *Street Kingdom* (2000).[4]

Learning 52s Techniques 2003–2007

I began my efforts to better understand the 52s during a transitional stage between the 'old school' period when the art and its precursors were confined to the prison and gang world and the renaissance period following in the wake of growing public awareness of the 52s triggered by the work of Douglas Century (2000, 2001), the growing influence of YouTube in 2007, and the launching of the efforts to organize a martial and fitness system derived from a boxing-based variety of the 52s in 2007.[5] At this point, the 52s became more public, more codified, more accessible to the general public, and unfortunately imitated by entrepreneurs with little, if any, real knowledge. When I began my embodied research, information on the 52s and its close relatives – except for the material that Century includes in *Street Kingdom* – survived mostly as oral tradition. One exception to this was an article on African American prison fighting styles that appeared in the popular media 30 years earlier (Darling and Perryman 1974).

A decade later, Dennis Newsome who had already begun to gain recognition for his expertise at capoeira and an Eritrean fighting method called reisy (Bruster 1982), served as one of the fight choreographers for the 1987 film *Lethal Weapon*. Newsome incorporated a prison style he identified as jailhouse rock (JHR) into the film's fight scenes, and publicity generated by a popular article featuring photographs of the film's star, Mel Gibson, executing these techniques brought national attention to JHR (O'Neill, 1987). Although Newsome refused to teach the prison style publicly, he allowed himself to be photographed using the art for a survey of martial arts styles published in 2001 (Soet 2001, 115–22) and included information and photographs of JHR on his web page.[6] He also generously provided information on and photographs of capoeira, JHR and related topics for articles I published in 2003 (Green 2003a, 2003b). Eventually, he shared with me the technical elements of his variety of JHR as well as demonstrating on me (as distinct from *to* me) a JHR defence against a knife attack.

I began additional research on JHR/52s through these published and filmed resources, as well as interviews with practitioners, but my primary goal was to pursue fieldwork via embodied ethnography (i.e. acquainting oneself with a kinaesthetic form by practising it). Jaida Kim Samudra has labelled this 'thick participation', which she describes as: 'cultural knowledge recorded first in the anthropologist's body and only later externalized as visual or textual data for purposes of analysis' (2008, 667). On the surface, at least, this perspective resembles Wacquant's mode of 'observant participation' (2011, 7). As he advocates, I allowed myself to be immersed in the topic but resurfaced with the intent of interpreting from the body my object of study. In addition, I attempted to thicken my participation by the inclusion of seemingly unrelated activities (drumming, dancing, playing folk games) that reiterate aesthetic and kinesic patterns of the 52s in a conscious effort to transform my habitus to one more congenial to learning the style. I adopted as a conscious regimen activities that served as unwitting training for the 52s as they exist in their indigenous setting.

I recognized significant obstacles to my chosen methodology. I have never been a prison inmate nor do I commonly associate with violent career criminals. Fortunately, I had mentors who had sought out former inmates to build their own skills in African American VMAs. Ethnicity represented a second stumbling block. I am not African American and, like Dennis Newsome, many potential teachers with whom I came in contact were reluctant to teach anyone and particularly Caucasians. To a certain extent, I had begun to overcome this obstacle. For example, Dennis Newsome and Daniel Marks had read and offered valuable advice on the drafts of my earliest attempts at discussing African American VMAs (Green 2003a, 2003b). My consideration of their comments and incorporation of many of their suggestions into the final versions of these book chapters undoubtedly served to bridge some of the gaps separating us before my fieldwork began in earnest. In addition, as I persisted in my training, what teachers labelled 'sincerity' further diminished any lingering reticence on the part of my teachers. As Wacquant observes, 'the forging of the pugilistic habitus entails the gradual effacing of extraneous properties – such as skin tone' (2005a, 452).

Finally, I could not sign up for training in a gym as I could if my object of study had been boxing or Brazilian jiu-jitsu. While my informants (teachers and training partners included) agree that while there are adjunct activities to sharpen one's attributes, historically, prowess has been developed by fighting, either in prison or on the street, or by watching violent encounters. As one informant described his street education in Baltimore, Maryland in the 1980s, '(I) was always getting into fights with others and losing on a pretty regular basis. I just kept on picking up moves and styles though [...] And picking up moves, at least around here, is how you develop your hands' (Moses Dyell, 2003). Daniel Marks (2004) confirmed: 'Every skill in Jailhouse Rock is earned through sparring, which is why it's creative. You have to be creative to hit without being hit.'

This use of the street as a venue for martial education echoes the ways in which capoeira was learned prior to the establishment of academies in the first half of the twentieth century. Greg Downey writes: 'Prior to capoeira's treatment as physical education, most practitioners learned through one-on-one instruction, observation, and self-guided practice' (Downey 2008, 206). This is the most common pedagogy for VMAs in general.

As Downey suggests for capoeira, in some cases, a seasoned 52s fighter might take a novice aside and pass along techniques either by demonstration or by verbal description. This has been my experience, at least. The comments of poet, actor and playwright

Miguel Piñero, who was first incarcerated at the age of 11, describe a comparable process of learning the styles of the institutions in which he was imprisoned:

> The first thing I did in the joint [prison] was to check out the style and learn to fight with a home piece – somebody from my neighbourhood on the streets. I learned the Woodbourne shuffle, an evasion technique that first was used in the joint at Woodbourne and got passed around. Then I learned wall-fighting, and somebody taught me the Comstock style. (Darling and Perryman 1974, 21)[7]

Even when mentors are available, the regimented drills associated with codified martial arts are non-existent. As I began my efforts to develop the level of 52s skills needed to understand it corporeally rather than simply cognitively, I was encouraged to get partners and develop impromptu training scenarios. Daniel Marks provided the following advice:

> Agree that you both are going to fight bare knuckle, full contact to the body. No hits to the face, and every target, except the groin of course, are game. Then, go at it. First, you get on a wall and play 'defence'; you are not allowed to throw any punches back; you must defend only. You can use the wall to duck, slip, throw him into, but you can't punch back. Doing this exercise will sharpen your defensive skills, and also teach you to absorb punishment. Few people realize how important this skill is. You will probably in a real fight 'get' as much as you 'give'. So you must take the fear out of getting hit by going at it in this way. Start off slow and moderate at first, and gradually increase the pressure. The dude who taught me beat the living crud out of me for months until I learned (and I did learn) to not flinch, and to block and fight back. (Personal communication, 2004)

This training is often scenario-based by utilizing subway cars, elevators, stairwells and similar confined and/or moving spaces to emulate settings in which genuine assaults might occur.

I engaged in this training with several partners (all of whom were 20–30 years my junior) I had met through my study of the Filipino stick-and-knife fighting arts of kali and arnis, and silat, a martial art native to Indonesia, Malaysia and Brunei. Our mutually agreed level of contact was very low, and we concentrated mainly on blocking, evading and 'hemming' (trapping punches through a technique in which an opponent's own clothing is used as a means of entanglement and manipulation). As a result, we absorbed relatively low levels of physical punishment, but did learn to avoid strikes and overcome the tendency to flinch.

Beyond adding a realistic dimension to the training, in Dale Spencer's terminology these methods add the element of 'callusing' (2009). Bro Sha, while explaining his own training strategy, emphasized that contact between bodies is indispensable for developing the 52s: '[There is a] big difference between hitting a bag, cement, sand, trees and hitting a person. The human body has a solid yet springy feel […] because of this springy solidness […] even if you trained hitting cinderblocks […] you can still easily break your wrists [by striking an opponent] if you're not used to training without gloves' (personal communication, 2005). Therefore, an obvious physical goal is to callus, 'to harden the body and turn it into a weapon' (Spencer 2009, 127). Even blocking hardens the body. For example, the repeated striking of the elbows when they are used to block punches to the mid-section (and in the real world to break an opponent's knuckles) hardens them, makes them less sensitive to pain.

I discovered that these controlled fights harden the psyche as well as the body. They train the mind, the emotions and the will, by engaging in relatively managed violent actions regularly enough to callus instinctual reflexes such as flinching, blinking or turning one's back, spontaneous responses that prove dysfunctional in the real world of a street or prison fight. This is accomplished not by instruction (i.e. at the cognitive level), but by educating – scarring – the body at a corporeal level through repeatedly subjecting it to the shock of physical punishment.

Despite its realistic goals, 52s training incorporates 'scaffolding' (Downey 2008). Techniques are slightly altered in order to assist learning and control injury. As Daniel Marks attests above in his comments on bare-knuckle sham fights with limited targets, when 'sparring' exists, what are considered the most vulnerable areas of the body are not targeted. Partners also refrain from using some of their most destructive, and effective, tools such as overhand punches with the forefinger bent at the second knuckle and directed at the opponent's eye. In genuine fights, the technique intends to burst an eyeball.

As a general rule, slap-boxing, a game played on the streets and in schools by African American adolescents,[8] occupies the same ecological niche as the 52s. The game most often targets the face and head with the players' open hands. Slap-boxing strikes draw on the model of sport boxing rather than the striking methods of arts such as karate. Beyond the use of the open hand, these contests may vary from standard boxing techniques by throwing slaps from unorthodox angles (from extremely low, bent over stances, for example). Slap boxing is not formally used as a training method among African American youth, nor was it by my mentors (although all talked about it), but I sought out opportunities to play the game whenever possible in order to learn basic attributes passed along informally in the traditional cultural milieu. The reasons for my self-imposed training are obvious. These contests teach evasion by means of footwork, body and head movement. They teach how to throw combinations, to keep one's hands in appropriate defensive attitudes unencumbered by boxing gloves and, one of the major attributes of the style, how to develop and maintain rhythm. From personal experience, a stinging slap to the face delivered by means of a full hooking strike combines pain and humiliation, which in turn produce physical and mental callusing.

I obtained instruction where and from whom I could. My mentors were accomplished teachers of more codified martial arts; consequently, much of the instruction came in the context of martial arts workshops as private asides to me during breaks and in short intervals before or after instruction in these other arts ended for the day. Sometimes, they came as subtexts embedded in the instruction in silat, kali or other arts given to public classes. For example, my teacher Thomas Lomax had been emphasizing to me the necessity of 'changing an attacker's mind the first time you touch him' and of the utility of attacking any target that the attacker offers.[9] As an example of the latter, he mentioned the 52s technique called the 'dead arm',[10] striking the opponent's arm in such a way that it goes 'dead' momentarily, providing the opportunity for another strike.

The next day during a class in pencak silat, he went through a list of vulnerable points, one of which is known in traditional Chinese medicine as 'heart 3'. Then, he turned to me and said quietly, 'Remember what I told you last night?' I nodded, and he carried on (field notes 2007). From time to time, I was able to get blocks of time dedicated exclusively to 52s, but this was rare. As a result, my education was best characterized as 'piecemeal'. As far as I can determine, this is close to the authentic pedagogy not only of the 52s, but other vernacular martial arts in general.

In spite of what is best described as creative idiosyncrasy, a tendency to 'martial bricolage' characterizes the 52s. In an analogy introduced to the discipline of anthropology by Claude Lévi-Strauss (1968), the 'bricoleur' is like the handyman, an expert at do-it-yourself building or jury-rigged repairs with the tools and materials on hand. A bricoleur is adept at improvisation using a finite stock of randomly accumulated materials and tools. The universe of the bricoleur is closed by opportunity, and he often is forced to make do with whatever is at hand. As applied to martial culture, this describes street fighters, such as 52s adepts. The 52s fighter is rarely given the option to procure a specialized tool kit or develop a unique strategy for a particular encounter with a given opponent, as in boxing or mixed martial arts matches. The street fighter must be capable of freely applying a random accumulation of tools in an unpredictable situation.

The tool kits are assembled opportunistically, but they are not disorganized. Each 52s fighter bases his style on a 'foundation art' that operates in tandem with the cultural aesthetic (discussed below). This combination produces a habitus that, as Hilgers (drawing on Pierre Bourdieu) argues, operates like a generative grammar (2009, 730–31). In this case, habitus is a generative grammar of movement from which individual expressions of the 52s are derived.[11]

As the precursors of the 52s emerged in the early decades of the twentieth century, the most accessible martial art in the USA was boxing. This was particularly true for inner-city African Americans. In the 1930s in New York City, for example, formal instruction became available by the Police Athletic League to African American and other inner-city youth at no cost. Both youth and adult detention facilities maintained boxing programmes where many professional fighters got their starts. Archie Moore, Floyd Patterson and Mike Tyson are among the better-known boxers who learned their crafts as a result of incarceration, and all have been looked to for displaying 52s techniques at one time or another.

Informants confirm the importance of boxing as a foundation system. Most of them claim that 'jailhouse' and its regional variants such as the 52s peaked in the 1970s and 1980s, and began to decline as gang culture became gun culture. According to Ben Hill, who grew up in the Bronx borough of New York City: 'In the Bronx around 1976, this [foundation] was most often boxing, and the same energy that was there in break dancing and in rap and in DJing came out in the fight... came out of that same creative flow' (personal communication, 2009). Thus, from Hill's perspective, the VMA is characterized by a creative aesthetic 'like the disk jockey's freestyle and the jazz musician's improvisation; essentially, it is a riff, a variation on an established theme' (Green 2012).

Military training also contributed to the 52s arsenal: '(A) lot of former G.I.s in the joint had learned hand-to-hand combat – they came home, styled it, made it hip, and gave it

Figure 9.1. "Switching the L" demonstrated by Kawaun Akhenoten VII.

Photo courtesy of Kamau Hunter.

soul' (Darling and Perryman 1974, 21). In the 1970s, Chinese martial arts (kung fu) were added to the mix. Jim Kelly and Bruce Lee are commonly cited as major influences on practitioners (Daniel Marks, personal communication, 2003). Gordon Liu – particularly his film *36th Chamber of Shaolin*, also released as *The Master Killer* (1978) – has been cited as another role model,[12] some informants present convincing arguments that most of the 52s techniques from some boroughs of New York City from the late 1970s through the 1980s were influenced by Hong Kong action films (Novell Bell, personal communication, 2004). 'The closest thing you'll see to it [techniques resembling genuine 52s on film] is the last fight scene in Jackie Chan's *Drunk Monkey in the Tiger's Eye* (1978, released in the USA as *Drunken Master*)' (Rudy Curry, personal communication, 2004).

My own teachers consciously drew on boxing and the Asian martial arts in which they had trained, primarily jiu-jitsu, kali, kung fu and silat. For example, during this period Daniel Marks compared the 52s' movement structures to kali:

> We did a knife drill in kali class yesterday... Catch and roll. The blade was in reverse grip, which for some is the primary fighting grip. We proceeded to attack and defend the four corners of the body. When adding the centreline. You had your male and female triangles on the torso. The reason I bring this up because in tape one with

Saladeen [interview with King Saladeen], he shows me this exact movement before he goes into the blocking. The attacks were the same, the movement to counter and attack are the same… even switching leads. (Personal communication, 2004)

Although techniques are fortuitously acquired and grounded in an individually chosen foundation system, cutting across all the variants appears to be what elsewhere I analyse as the distinctly African-descended aesthetic of the 'sick' balanced with the 'sweet' (Green, 2012). This balancing of the effective (sick) with the display of flamboyant style (sweet) yields moves such as the trap and kiss, a signature move of the 52s in which as a defence against a straight punch the defender claps the forearms together to trap the punch, kisses the trapped fist, and then throws back the attacking fist. The action stops the punch, disrupts the rhythm of the attacker, and shows disdain for the opponent, simultaneously. Consistent with this aesthetic are the recurrent themes stressed by all my teachers and the ones I attempted to introduce into my own training: attitude, rhythm and the '52s body'.

Thomas Lomax, a major source of my 52s knowledge, held a weekend seminar on pencak silat in 2006. On the Saturday night after dinner, he decided it was time to add to my understanding. After a few of my tries at imitating the techniques he demonstrated, he said, 'You did it, but you still didn't get it.' When I asked for clarification, he told me, 'It's all about the attitude.' I tried the moves again, making the movements more forceful and aggressive. 'You still ain't got it. Get out of your head. Attitude. Watch.' This time I focused my attention not on bodily movements, but on what I considered the markers of 'attitude': facial expressions and body language. Impressionistically, his face wore a mask of contempt, and the gross physical movements and postures, while remaining smooth and effective, were executed in a fashion that I could only characterize as disdainful. This turned my efforts to 'pure' imitation of his movements as distinct from analysis, to learning in the body without mediation by the brain.

'Get out of your head' became in my studies with Thomas Lomax almost a mantra in his efforts to pass along both the 52s and silat. It is a directive to get out of my 'intellectual self' and into an 'emotional self' that registers its presence proprioceptively. That is, the attitude cannot intentionally be placed on the body (from the outside in), it must be felt and allowed to emanate as visceral expression (from the inside out). Similarly, Samudra reports that the trainers in the silat style she studied were prone to treat those students who attempted to learn silat intellectually rather than corporeally in a similar fashion. Echoing Lomax, students were told, 'Don't think, do' until the knowledge enters your body directly, unmediated by language (Samudra 2008, 668). According to Lomax, this took from 300–500 repetitions to be absorbed (his term) by the body.[13]

Daniel Marks made regular references to attitude, especially 'dissing' (disrespecting, showing contempt for) the opponent in the 52s as in the following comments: the 52 hand blocks is from Brooklyn; at best it's like a dance. Break-dancing pulled some of its dis moves (disrespect, when a dancer executes a move that 'shows up' another dancer) from the way the hard rocks (gangsters) used to slap box in the streets (personal communication, 2002).[14] Clearly then, some techniques are designed to inflict psychological as well as physical damage. The 'kiss move' described above is one such technique that gained popularity in the New York penal system. Other manoeuvres have a more general distribution.

The 'pants leg flip' has been around since at least the 1970s, and in the urban north-eastern USA is also known as hemming, cuffing and tossing. Bro Sha identifies the symbolic importance of the trick in commenting, 'In New York, we call it Tossin' a cat... It was a major disrespect to have that happen to you, because it was like [throwing out] garbage' (personal communication, 2005). The flip is known down the east coast of the United States as far south as urban Richmond, Virginia, where the stunt is called the 'upset'. In fact, my best descriptions of the flip and demonstrations of its practical application come from Michael Hume from whom I studied arnis in 2005. As he describes it: 'The technique focused on coming straight into your opponent for an upper body charge, then shift at the last instant to grab him under the cuffs of his pants. The object being to throw him onto his back or either side or even to toss him over your head and behind you' (personal communication, 2005). I discovered Hume's knowledge of the upset in particular and 'rough and tumble'[15] in general when, in the closing minutes of a class in modern arnis, he decided to pass along something that he had learned while growing up in Richmond, Virginia. After asking the senior student in the class to assume a defensive grappling posture, he performed the manoeuvre described in the preceding paragraph. I recognized this as the pants leg flip, and he generously shared his knowledge of the upset and other details of rough and tumble, including the following statement on the use of the upset (also known as 'cuffing' because the trouser cuffs are used to lift and toss an opponent):

> To get cuffed [thrown] was a sign of complete disrespect. A good fighter would never allow himself to be cuffed. If you were lucky enough to cuff a guy, you would either slam him to the ground immediately with much energy or (the ultimate embarrassment) you would pause a moment at the height of the lift, just to allow others to admire your strength, technique, skill, and bravery, before slamming the guy on his head. (Personal communication, 2005)

The attitude and commitment to humiliate an opponent are obvious in this description.

After discovering my interest in the 52s and interest in developing skill in the art, Michael Hume set aside time in several classes for the sorts of informal skill training and callusing that I had begun to learn from Daniel Marks and others. This provided access to training partners on a regular basis for several months, both during and outside of arnis classes.

A more covert expression of the '52s attitude' appears in the Comstock-style defensive posture.[16] When assuming this posture, the fighter stands in profile with the lead fist on the hip, the lead elbow pointed at the opponent, and the chin shielded behind the lead shoulder. The rear arm is across the chest with the hand held open or in a fist. The posture has important utilitarian functions, as taught by both Earl White and Daniel Marks. As the former explains it, 'You make your body small and protect your chin' (personal communication, 2006). The latter teacher emphasized, 'You give them bone (the hardest part of the skull and the elbow) to hit' (2003, personal communication). The posture may also symbolically play out an attitude. Robert Farris Thompson reports that his informant Fu-Kiau describes a kongo pose called *fútika nkome* ('tie the thumb') in

Figure 9.2. "King Saladin" (left) teaching 52s techniques to Daniel Marks in New York park.

Photo courtesy of Daniel Marks.

which the right closed fist is held over the heart and the left fist is on the hip. Among other meanings, this is a sign of power, a signal that one has heart (1990, 301). It is also a good description of the left-facing Comstock cover. Connerton, in addition to his important concept of the 'sedimentation' (i.e. the importance of corporeal habitus) of culture in the body, writes: 'The importance of posture for communal memory is evident. Power and rank are commonly expressed through certain postures relevant to others' (1989, 73). Thus, the Comstock cover (if it is in fact an assertion of dominance), like the kiss move and the flip attacks, operates on both psychological and physical levels.

In one of many attempts to help me develop the proper 52s movement patterns, Daniel Marks shared the following about his own training with King Saladeen:

> The most important thing? Rhythm! With my teacher right now, the hardest thing for me to do is get into his rhythm! It's like his is based on 3 (beats to the measure), whereas mine is based on 2 or 4. He's got these stutter steps in his technique, too. The only way I have found out how to get around it is by using (a) 1 (beat pattern) and just straight blast. If it don't work, then another straight blast. (Personal communication 2003)

As fist fighting (like drumming, dancing and stick fighting) is a percussive activity, a feel for rhythm becomes imperative as striking evolves from blind swinging to a 'sweet science'. Predicting the opponent's rhythm allows for both evasive activity and efficient penetration of the other's defences. Along with the corporeal feel, another, aesthetic, dimension of the 52s emerges with the development of rhythm. Or, as Thomas Lomax – who is both a martial artist and jazz saxophonist – put it: 'When I was growing up in Memphis [TN] the most important thing about fighting was to look good while you were doing it (personal communication, 2011).

Rhythm, in fact, is often regarded as a primary marker of authenticity for the 52s and other vernacular African American martial arts. For example, Daniel Marks dismissed 52s' claims of jailhouse rock expertise by reporting: 'I saw a little demo of his rock. So he has seen it, but I wasn't impressed. He just didn't have the flow. Without the rhythm you look a little a cat ('man') smacking his elbows' (personal communication, 2004). In essence, 52s displayed one of the common elements of JHR, elbow strikes, without the coherent rhythmic structure, 'the flow' of the art; this constituted incontrovertible evidence against his claim. Marks's sense of flow in 'jailhouse', along with his observation that urban dance 'pulled some of its diss moves' from slap boxing, suggests a primary means of training for the correct rhythm in the African-descended martial arts in the Americas. Robert Farris Thompson asserts that West African and African-descended dance is percussive music made visible (Thompson 1999, 75), and dance is an important means of developing correct rhythm for the 52s.

Ethnomusicologist Alan Lomax characterizes dance as 'the most repetitious, synchronic of all expressive behaviours, it has turned out to be a kind of touchstone for human adaptation' (Bishop 2002, 1). For our purposes, dance is a template (or perhaps a mirror) of the group's cultural kinesics, and whether it imitates combat or both combat and dance draw on a common physical vocabulary, in much indigenous dance the similarities between the expressive and the martial are palpable. While obvious to the careful observer, the similarities between vernacular movement genres are not cognitively mediated. They are literally etched into the body via repetition in diverse contexts. As Paul Connerton points out, 'In the cultivation of habit it is our body which "understands"' (1989, 95).

In the absence of the drills common to codified martial arts, urban dance genres such as up-rocking, break-dancing and top-rocking provide a kind of 'scaffolding' for the fighting techniques of the 52s, although dance is not commonly practised for this express purpose. Daniel Marks points out that up-rocking[17] and the 52s embody the same footwork patterns (back and forth and side to side): 'The most significant difference is in level changes' (personal communication, 2010). These level changes allow the use of 52s techniques to attack the lower body with fists, forearms and elbows. Daniel Marks observes: 'The 52 is all about rhythm. It may look wild and untamed, but that's deliberate. The up-rock (pattern of movement) is a huge part of the deception. At best, it's like a dance' (personal communication 2005).

I did not perform well at this aspect of training. Daniel Marks attempted to help me incorporate the dance pattern described above by comparing it to the Filipino martial arts that I had studied: 'The up-rocking movement is a modified box step in FMA [Filipino martial arts]. Draw a square on the ground [with the corners] shoulder length apart. Stand on the base and cross step to the opposite point. Then step back. Do the same for the other foot. That's your Toprock basic' (personal communication, 2007).

I practised this and similar stepping patterns while listening to hip-hop, capoeira and similar recorded music as an adjunct to internalizing the appropriate rhythms, but with only moderate success.

Another means of training rhythm employed the standard boxing speed bag, a piece of equipment with which I was familiar from both 'conventional' boxing and from other martial arts. Daniel Marks introduced two bag concepts from his 52s training. Typically, the percussive rhythm one can hear when punching the speed bag is a three-count. The initial strike is beat 1; the double rebound when the bag strikes the platform from which it hangs are beats 2 and 3 that follow each other in rapid succession. I was urged to transfer this rhythm from the hands to the feet. The simplest way in which this can be done is: 1) step with lead foot, 2) back foot slides up to follow, and 3) step with lead foot. In addition, Daniel emphasized that the speed bag is ideal training for catching a punch. The speed bag is struck with horizontal fists in a rolling motion, with the bottom of the fists coming into contact with the bag, and the forearms kept parallel to the floor. I most often practised this without bag gloves, so along with training timing and developing some ability at diverting (and occasionally catching) punches I found that this is an effective way to toughen the hands and forearms. In essence, I came to understand in the body concepts that do not lend themselves to verbal transmission.

Earl White advocated drumming on the djembe (an African drum played by slapping the drumhead with the open hand) to develop rhythm. This also serves to toughen the palms for catching punches, blocking and striking. Thomas Lomax demonstrated the ways in which drumming translated to fighting, by striking me on the chest with the palm slaps used for playing the djembe. Each had a different sound and type of effect that could be felt, but not described intellectually.

Along with movement training, Daniel Marks emphasized the need to develop a '52s body', a sort of corporeal habitus that allows and eventually predisposes one to a particular set of martial behaviours. The forearms are given particular attention. They are integral to 'Switching the L', a defensive posture in which one arm is held horizontally across the body with the other held vertically, with the elbow touching the horizontal fist at a right angle. Rather than remaining static, the arms alternate (switch) positions, attempting to trap punches and deliver hammer-fist strikes when possible. Daniel explains: 'This is how you pound on a cat, and when your arms look like tree trunks you can get off a serious beat down' (personal communication, 2005). Other informants in the New York area confirm this: 'I'm feeling you on the use of the forearm in 52… [C]lotheslinin', tossin', and bumrushin' with your guns [arms]. Kind of like a train… running him down… while you're percussively breaking him down at the same time' (Bro Sha, personal communication, 2005).

Following my teacher's advice, I trained the forearms for strength and size via squeezing tennis balls, lifting and carrying heavy objects in a pinch grip, and conventional weight-training exercises such as wrist curls. Specific strikes (for example, 'clotheslining', strikes using the forward edge of the arm), as well as strengthening and callusing (both mental and physical) were trained by pounding the forearms against solid targets: the heavy punching bag, lightly padded posts, and trees. More exotic methods of training circulate among practitioners, such as training one's hands by numbing the arms in buckets of ice water. Rudy Curry, who told me about this method said, 'Don't try it. It is bad for the heart' (personal communication, 2004).

Many 52s fighters are avid weight trainers (especially in prison) and perform pushups, pull-ups and similar calisthenics in the hundreds; however, roadwork – a staple of boxing – is conspicuously absent. My previous training for combat sports (freestyle wrestling, judo and boxing) and traditional Asian martial arts (karate and kung fu) had treated aerobic conditioning through running as imperative. Therefore, the absence of this component troubled me throughout the traditional (i.e. the regimen that was most directly descended from the prison art) phase of my 52s training. There are, however, logical reasons for the training regimen.

There is no roadwork because of the context in which 'jailhouse' and later the 52s developed. The limited activities dictated by the institutional control and the confined space of the prison do not make distance running a viable conditioning option. Instead, cardiovascular fitness can be generated by practising 'prison push-ups' (burpees) by performing one repetition of the exercise, then walking to the other end of the workout area to perform two, walking back to perform three and so forth until one has attained a predetermined number of repetitions. A final set of 20 was proposed as a respectable goal. On reaching this number, the repetitions are decreased with each set until the trainee works back down to one repetition.

Also, the nature of the 52s, especially in prison settings, negates the need for the level of cardiovascular conditioning required by boxers or wrestlers. Unlike the bouts of combat sports there are no rounds, rest periods, rules or protective equipment. These factors contribute to making real street fights brief affairs requiring aggression and brutality as distinct from endurance and patience. Moreover, prison fights take place in confined quarters. Turning again to Bro Sha, 'Jailhouse is like fighting in a phone booth or like fighting inside a small circle' (personal communication, 2005).

Close quarters fighting has 'the person doing 52s slamming his body against his opponent as in a body strike to break limbs, collar bone, hip bone, knees, ribs' (Bro Sha, personal communication, 2005). To facilitate this, 'everyone I know had to train push-ups, dips and pull-ups (or just lifting weights) because you realize that to finish quickly you have to use your body as part of the pounding' (Daniel Marks, personal communication, 2005).

Because of this, Marks taught that the ideal '52s body' had all development from the waist up and as much muscle mass as possible.[18] As a consequence, running, which reduces the overall bulk that is desirable for 52s tactics, is not merely unnecessary – it is dysfunctional. Instead, we built muscle via conventional calisthenics. Practitioners developed unconventional variations on a limited number of bodyweight exercises to work the muscles in as many ways as possible. There are a variety of motives: to increase demands on the body despite a finite load of resistance, to develop a wider range of physical attributes, to 'randomize' (make the body react more spontaneously to the unexpected) physical demands, and to conform to the African-descended aesthetic of the 52s through performing spectacular athletic feats.

The training incorporates no sense of periodization or even days off, principles that are part of the common wisdom in contemporary bodybuilding. Daniel held up as an example one practitioner who 'didn't have an ounce of fat' because he kept a towel with him that he twisted and pulled constantly to work muscles isometrically. The prisoners who developed the 52s and its precursors worked out at every opportunity during the day, at least during confinement (Daniel Marks, personal communication, 2005).

Diet was also an element of my training. At one point I asked Daniel: 'I was just thinking about K's workout. What does he eat to maintain 260 lbs and put in a couple of hours a day in the weight room plus all those push-ups and pull-ups?' He responded: 'Plenty of peanut butter and fish. Oatmeal and water, orange juice. I heard that peanut butter and squid and protein shakes are used to give them bulk' (Daniel Marks, personal communication, 2004).

After following a modified version of the diet, I reported back that at a recent physical exam I had developed a high cholesterol count. Daniel responded:

> Yeah that's the downside to it. I would say keep more salmon and sardines. Tuna without the oil. Lean beef, turkey and chicken barbecue-style. But unless you have like all day to work and all day to recover, I don't think it's [religiously following the diet and workout 'programme'] worth it. (Daniel Marks, personal communication, 2005)

Conclusion

In character, if not precisely in kind, my training in the 52s closely follows the model provided by Downey (2008). Ultimately, this method allowed me to emulate a few of the 52s techniques. I continue, however, to feel like Daniel's 'cat slapping his elbows'. Having seen both jailhouse and the 52s, I can recognize the flow, but I still do not have it. Perhaps, as Connerton wrote, '[I]t is the body that understands.' The understanding body is both the receptor and the medium of what Downey (2008) has labelled 'microsocial processes of cultural learning', processes 'that are behavioural, neurological, and even physiological but no less "cultural"' (2008, 210).

To join this with a concept introduced early in this article, the 52s (like traditional capoeira) are vernacular martial arts, physical disciplines woven into the fabric of culture rather than existing as discrete activities. Overtly non-martial pastimes provide opportunities to acquire and refine martial skills at a visceral level where they become 'sedimented in the body'. As noted above, the 52s are aesthetically consistent with African American musical and movement genres – rap, jazz, break-dancing – and adapt sport such as basketball, boxing and calisthenics within the same kinaesthetic framework. These activities provide venues for microsocial learning that meet on the dance floor, in the court, in the ring and on the street.

In the final analysis, it is less a matter of 'white guys can't flow' than it is that in general at the microsocial level of culture they do not flow.[19] The art must be embodied in the authentic cultural context. Anything else is a modification and adaptation. In terms of my own subdiscipline of folklore, the context of performance (or, in this case, learning) was not natural, rather it was induced (i.e. inauthentic by virtue of simulation). Vernacular martial practices continue to flourish in restricted local and/or ethnic environments not only as fighting systems per se, but also as grounded in 'larger' indigenous cultural traditions (e.g. festival, dance, games, posture and so on). A VMA bears the marks of the culture's built-in qualities. To master the elements of the culture's fight, one must have been mastered by the elements of the culture at the visceral level. This does not contradict Chris Shilling's assertion that, through training, athletes not only acquire skills and habits but 'becom(e) different people' (44–5). It does, however, suggest another reading of Wacquant's argument that 'practical mastery operates beneath the level of consciousness and discourse' (2001, 230). In certain cultural contexts and for some ethnographers, mastery resides not only in the body of the practitioner but also in the social body, in cultural practices and predispositions. In spite of personal limitations, I dug deeper than the usual relatively detached participant observer could. I learned from the body by subjecting the ethnographer's body to as much of the 52s discipline as I could reasonably simulate. Therefore, while not resulting in a perfect model of the 52s practitioner, I did come to understand beneath the level of consciousness and discourse. In the last analysis, however, while learning from the body, I did not embody. Unless I ever manage to dig that deep, I must remain 'a cat slapping his elbows'.

Notes

1. For economy, the term the 52s is used to refer to all of these cognate fighting styles.
2. The 52s are a VMA developed in prison and nurtured in the streets.
3. The names of informants are used with permission. In some cases, street or prison names (King Saladeen, for example) are employed because of informant preferences.
4. Because of references to the 52s by the hip-hop artists the Wu-Tang Clan, many of whom were members of the Nation of Gods and Earths (NGE), also known as the Five Per Cent Nation of Islam, established in the mid-1960s by Clarence 13X (Clarence Smith), a former member of the Nation of Islam, street history maintains that '52' alludes to the 'divine mathematics', a mnemonic device for the NGE theology in which each number represents a particular attribute. These attributes may be combined as in the case of the 52s: 5 plus 2 equals 7, the number of God (or perfection). For more detail on the system, see Swedenburg 1997. Daniel Marks offers an explanation based in the geometry reflected in the various blocking and striking angles of the VMA (email, 2011). Another folk etymology associates the name with the prank '52 Card Pick-Up', in which the butt of the joke is invited to play a game of 52 Card Pick-Up. An affirmative answer results in the prankster scattering a deck of 52 playing cards on the floor and directing the dupe to pick them up. In any case, 'the style is as fluid as a pack of cards flying up in the air' in Douglas Century's apt phrase (personal communication, 2005).
5. Daniel Marks and Kawaun Akhenoten VII led the efforts to use the 52s as a heritage art and tool for community pride and empowerment. In 2012, they combined their efforts with Hasaan Yasin to form 52 blocks constellation.
6. http://www.malandros-touro.com/ (last accessed 22 February 2012).
7. The Woodbourne reference is to Woodbourne Correctional Facility in Woodbourne, NY. Comstock refers to Great Meadow Correctional Facility a maximum-security prison located in Comstock, NY.
8. Slap boxing is not exclusive to African Americans, of course.
9. Lomax also notes that this sort of attack is a common tactic of both Southeast Asian and African martial arts. (personal communication, 2012)
10. This differs from the dead arm fighting style discussed by Rudy Curry (2004).
11. Compare this to Chris Shilling's assertion that habit (i.e. mechanical repetition) and creativity are not opposites, but habit that leads to competence is the means to creatively assimilate oneself to new forms of experience (2008, 52–4).

12 The title of the classic 1993 debut album of hip-hop innovators the Wu-Tang Clan, *Enter the Wu-Tang (36 Chambers)* (RCA Records) attests to the impact of Hong Kong films on hip-hop culture in general.
13 It is worth noting the fact that students never questioned the source of these numbers. When I asked him after several years of hearing the figures quoted, he cited an academic source (Richard Schmidt, *Motor Learning*). Masters of VMAs are not limited to folk sources of knowledge.
14 Again, there are individual exceptions to this general rule: 'the only time you saw his (Everlasting) skills was when someone felt to push an issue. The fight was too short to gain anything from watching. He would duck and block once, and one to three blows later his opponent would be out cold in the first volley. Most of the time no one knowing what hit the poor fella […] He didn't feel the need to test his skills and never showed them except in real fights.' (Rudy Curry, personal communication, 2004).
15 A regional VMA in the southeastern USA.
16 'Comstock' seems to have made extensive use of elbow strikes, strikes to the groin and low kicks. However, I have yet to see the style demonstrated by a reliable practitioner.
17 A challenge dance form that evolved as an element of gang culture in which competing dancers mime attacks on opponents.
18 My two primary teachers, Thomas Lomax and Daniel Marks, weigh 250 and 270 lbs respectively at heights of well over 6 ft. Kawaun Akhenoten VII, who ultimately became Daniel's mentor weighed 260 lbs in prison and approached 300 lbs on the outside. At 170 lbs and 5 ft 10 in, I was at a profound disadvantage.
19 This addresses collective cultural aesthetics. The success of performers such as white US hip-hop artist Eminem (Marshall Bruce Mathers III) demonstrates that 'race' is not a factor in mastering cultural idioms outside one's own. Constellation 52, in fact, has trained many non–African American students to attain a high level of competence in boxing-based 52s.

Chapter 10

JAPANESE RELIGIONS AND KYUDO (JAPANESE ARCHERY): AN ANTHROPOLOGICAL PERSPECTIVE

Einat Bar-On Cohen

Introduction

Yawatashi is performed by the highest-ranking teachers at the opening of each public kyudo (Japanese archery) event such as grade (dan) tests, tournaments and seminars. This highly prestigious ceremony is intended to ensure the well-being of the participants and the auspicious progress of the events. Yawatashi sets into motion a complex cosmos in which the archers will act in the course of the ensuing event. In two separate interviews I conducted in Tokyo, I asked two senior teachers, Sakamoto-sense and Ishigawa-sense, about the meaning of yawatashi. Sakamoto, a senior teacher in the Honda school of kyudo, gave me a detailed and informed answer, explaining how the ceremony calls on the Shinto *kami* to give the arrows over for the event and thereby ensure its safe unfolding.[1] The other interview was with Ishigawa-sense, a central figure in the 'All Nippon Kyudo Federation', senior teacher at the Shiseikan – the main kyudojo in Tokyo situated at the Meiji Jingu Shinto shrine complex – who is also head of the Tachikawa school and served as leader of the Japanese delegation to the European kyudo federation's summer seminars in 2009. I have watched him perform yawatashi to perfection several times, at the most important kyudo events in Tokyo; he registered slight surprise at my question about the meaning of the ceremony, replying only, 'That's how we always do it!'[2]

Both teachers do agree that the rite is crucial for the successful unfolding of the event, but whereas one explains the auspicious affect in religious terms, the other situates its affects in the practical domain, in practice in its own right. Whereas Sakamoto positions the ritual in a more general cultural phenomena than the yawatashi itself, i.e. in Shinto, Ishigawa provides a radical theory of practice by stating that the rite generates its meaning as it is done. Nonetheless, looking closely at the yawatashi ritual reveals that the two replies are in fact quite close to each other. Furthermore, the apparent discrepancy between the two answers discloses a central trait of the world of kyudo, of Japanese martial arts, and of other Japanese cultural and social logics. All these cultural constructs have little or no exegesis, so that ritualistic practice and religion are all but interchangeable. Japanese religions are not situated on a meta-level in relation to practice; rather, like martial arts, they come to be through practice alone, and thus performing yawatashi does not open up a gap between plan and practice, between abstract and concrete, between religion and practice; rather, practice and habitus become inseparable through it.

Yawatashi opens a space made up of intensities in which the body of the archer has no tendencies or dispositions; the performer is attuned to practice alone, accumulated over years and years of more practice, and through this exactness the world of kyudo comes into being, transforming the social context as it is done, from within itself, and including all participants in it. Yawatashi is based on non-dual cultural logics drawn from Japanese traditions, such as the double negation *mu* and *homology*, which are incompatible with the notion of habitus. At the end of the chapter I will briefly suggest replacing the dyad practice/habitus with the Deleuzian actuality/virtuality.

Yawatashi

At the outset of an event at the central kyudojo in Tokyo held in 2008,[3] all the participants gathered on the lawn between the shooting gallery and the targets for a short purification ritual in which a Shinto priest dressed in a white kimono wafted a wand to which white paper knots were attached. Everyone clapped hands and bowed,[4] and then the announcer invited the participants to watch the yawatashi. The archers sat on the right-hand side of the shooting gallery – the 'honourable' place where the judges will later sit, in front of the *kamiza* (shelf of the kami) holding important objects, such as calligraphy and the Japanese flag.[5]

Although yawatashi is not the most difficult ritualistic archery sequence,[6] it is the most prestigious. It includes three distinct roles performed by the three most advanced kyudo experts attending it: one archer and two helpers. At this event the archer was the most advanced teacher, Ishigawa-sense. The role of the first helper, who for the most part waits behind the archer, is to help the shooter arrange his kimono when taking off and putting back on one of its sleeves. He will take care of any untoward event and will also return the arrows to the archer before the three leave the gallery. The second helper formally retrieves each arrow as it is shot and brings them back to the shooting gallery, handing them to the first helper.

The Japanese bow is long and asymmetrical, with a grip two-thirds of the way up its bare bamboo and wooden shaft, which has no aiming or balancing devices; the string is made of linen. The bow is so light that it swivels around the arm after the shot. The arrow shafts are also made of bamboo, and the feathers, which are taken from the tail of a bird of prey, are cut lengthwise so as to create two sorts of arrows, one that will turn towards the right when shot and the other towards the left. And since kyudo halls face south, one arrow will rotate in the direction of the turning world, while the other will oscillate opposite the movement of the world. Dressed in formal men's kimonos, the kyudo practitioners lower one sleeve to keep the arrow from getting entangled with their clothes as it leaves the bow; without putting down either bow or arrows, they tuck the sleeves into their belts before shooting (women archers tie the sleeves with a string called *taski*).

The shooting technique consists of rendering the archer's body so stable, calm and finely tuned that it becomes an anchor. The act of drawing the bow serves to aim the shot at the target, and virtually no corrections are required once the bow has been drawn. The archers enter the gallery, take their places facing the targets, and follow the eight steps of *hassetsu*, which includes fixing the body and the hands in the correct position, drawing the bow, aiming and shooting. They then linger in this final position for an instant before leaving the gallery in formal stride. The Japanese archers follow this pre-set series of steps without altering their rhythm, performing this sequence slowly, solemnly and ceremoniously. Despite the strain involved in drawing the bow, they do not so much as change their expression, having been taught that even the colour of their faces must remain constant.

The yawatashi sequence is always simple; in the event I observed, after a series of bows the second helper left the stage for the lawn, where wooden slippers awaited him, and moved towards the target space. Meanwhile Ishigawa prepared himself, dropping one sleeve and shooting the first arrow. After the shot, the second helper took the arrow, cleaned it with a small piece of cloth stuck in his belt, and put it on a special rack, while the archer moved away from the shooting line and sat down on the floor. Then Ishigawa came back to the shooting line and shot the second arrow. After he put back the sleeve of his kimono, the first helper moved to the edge of the stage to meet the second helper, bowing to each other as the second helper handed the arrows to the first helper. The first helper then sat down behind the archer and, in two crouching steps, moved to the archer's side. The first helper then gave the arrows back to the unmoving archer, who held them at the same angle as he carried them when he first entered the gallery. After a second series of bows, the three left the stage and all participants clapped hands. Once outside the gallery, the three again sat in a circle and bowed to one another.

Each senior archer performs this sequence in a slightly different and personalized style. Satake-sense is a high-ranking female teacher who was also a member of the Japanese delegation to the European seminars. Her yawatashi style is very smooth and feminine, passing elegantly from one movement to the next, whereas Ishigawa performs in a more determined and masculine style.

Interpretation of Yawatashi

Like many Shinto rites, yawatashi is a ritual of purification and invocation. The bows in Shinto rites act 'as conductors along which deity enters into the bodies of the initiated, while the arrows apprise the kami that the rite is taking place' (Ben-Ari 1991,139; on the role of the catalpa bow in Japanese shamanism, see Blacker 1975). Yawatashi means 'hand over the arrow': the kami hand over the arrows to the participants. The ritual sets an event into motion and delineates it from everyday life to yield its special, auspicious cosmos. Sakamoto, my teacher in Japan, told me that such rituals are sometimes also performed at the end of an event, to hand the arrows back to the gods. However, since yawatashi is performed only at the outset of the kyudo federation's events, I never saw one.

Yawatashi differs from other ceremonial archery sequences in several major ways. First, it is the only ceremony in which the arrows are retrieved before the participants leave the gallery; in other sequences, the arrows are retrieved later. Second, in formal events there is a non-participating steward who calls the archers as their turn arrives and who restrings the bow if it breaks; in yawatashi, the helpers are part and parcel of the ritual itself. This means that the archer should not perform any movement other than what is relevant to the perfect shot: he cannot correct his posture nor make any extraneous movement to tuck the sleeve into his belt. His movements are completely dedicated, concentrated and nearly sacred. Some archers prepare themselves for the ritual by refraining from certain foods or from talking for several days before the rite in order to ensure a heightened state of purity and concentration. Lastly, whereas in usual practice and events, a performance is carried out by juniors for seniors to judge, yawatashi reverses the roles; the juniors are seated in the place of honour, their backs to the kamiza, and the most senior teachers bow to them and perform.

An archery event is launched with the perfect performance of two arrows shot at a target; the best archer shows the participants (and the kami) how to shoot, and concomitantly performs the transformation enabled by shooting in this manner. Not only yawatashi but also every launch of arrows in kyudo holds a spiritual–transformative potentiality. Sakamoto insists that hitting the target is not the goal of kyudo, that the target is part of the archer, and that nonetheless the target is there and taking aim at it is the proper way to shoot. This is because by aiming at the target while disregarding it, the aim of the archery is to energize and renew the cosmos, and so it may yield transformation. The exact implementation of the hassetsu, the eight steps of the shot, permits the archer's body to generate homological connections with the turning of the world, with the weather, and with the flight of the bird out of whose tail the feathers for the arrow were taken, and thus to invoke the kami. Connecting humans, the world at large and the kami through the flight of the arrow permits passage between these worlds and, in particular, permits auspicious forces to be drawn from the kami. The perfect shots of yawatashi fill the event with these potentialities.

Yawatashi sets into motion an all-inclusive cosmos; the arrows that have been shot return to the place where they were held before being launched, the archer is protected and insulated from unplanned occurrences by his helpers, and all the archers who will be participating in the later event and who watch the ritual become part of it. During the subsequent event they too will do exactly as Ishigawa did, going through the eight steps to become a perfect bowman who can bring the goodwill of the kami to the gallery through perfect praxis.

Habitus, Practice and the Internal Paradox[7]

Bourdieu, faced with the mismatch between anthropological ethnographies and social norms, posits as paradoxical the relation between the phenomenological 'subjective' experience of praxis and the 'objective' social reality governed by doxa, habitus and symbols (for example, see Bourdieu 1990b, 26). Nevertheless, both the profound antinomy between subjective consciousness and the objective world, and the paradoxical solution to the simultaneity of this opposition, are foreign to the world of yawatashi (and, I venture to add, to any cultural attempt to overcome duality). The relations between aiming at a target and ignoring it, for example, suggest two logically opposed ways of doing, yet they are not paradoxical but, rather, they generate resonance.

In more general terms, Kitarō Nishida – considered the most original modern Japanese philosopher – rejected the idea of consciousness as subject/substance, positing it rather in spatial terms as place or field. Nishida's view is determined by the ambiguity inherent in the Japanese language concerning the identity of speaker and subject in any given sentence (Saski 2010, 10). In other words, although consciousness and the world are not one, they are not binary opposites either; they are both situated within the same field, both are that field, as they also generate it, and the relations between them do not cultivate complete separation but instead entertain a variety of relations. These non-dual relations can be organized according to different logics, such as the double negative mu and homology – which I will go into in detail below – yin-yang relations, resonance and more. The concomitant twofold attitude toward the target is therefore not an artefact of the rift between the two opposed propositions of the 'real' target out in the world and the 'imagined' target as part of the archer's body. The relation between the archer's subjective consciousness and the objective world is not one of opposition at all; the twofold attitude toward the target is planned and intended to form the archer's specific type of consciousness, to enhance a somatic split mode of attention. By shooting perfectly, the distance between the archer and the world can be overcome to enable transformation.

Scholars have criticized Bourdieu's view of the paradoxical relations between the objective and the subjective from other points of view. Looking at Bourdieu from within his own theory, King (2000) observes a mismatch between Bourdieu's theory of practice and of habitus. Whereas practice is a form of intersubjective, creative and unpredictable virtuosity, emanating from social action in and of itself and which cannot be defined by rules, habitus is thoroughly determined and defines human choices and actions in strict parameters. Social agents act through approximation and adjustment to the emerging social context; from somewhere above, habitus imposes its norms on the societal level. While social interaction is based on negotiation of relations and meanings, habitus offers a correct answer to each situation, imposing its constraints through violence.

Therefore, King concludes, the theory of habitus cannot explain external influence, creativity, or any other form of social change; it states social structure as fixed and non-processual. Moreover, whereas practice generates its own social reality in and of itself – or, as so beautifully put by Terry Evens, 'there is no key to the grammar of human practice, for the grammar is a question of self-fashioning in the face of otherness and therefore entails creative or gifted as well as pragmatic choices' (1999, 29) – habitus is comparative and it follows social categories. Habitus is intended to set genders, races, ethnicities and social classes one against the other, yet these categories of identity are more often than not external to practice itself. According to Evens (1999), Bourdieu fails to overcome the objective–subjective divide and remains in the 'mind-lock' of dualism. Practice on the material level generates its opposition, namely, habitus, on the abstract level; and thus, so Evens claims, dualism returns (1999, 5).[8] What is more, because habitus is situated on a meta-level, the relations between practice and habitus are paradoxical, as paradoxes are designed specifically to permit passage from one level to another (see Bateson 1972). In yawatashi no meta-level exists; the archer does not stand for anything transcendental to himself; he generates transformation through a meticulous set of actions, thus excluding the necessity for a paradoxical solution. In other words, identity and its categories are at the forefront of Bourdieu's proposal, whereas the non-dual world of yawatashi is based on difference and intensities in the Deleuzian sense (Deleuze 1994).

Bourdieu transposes the relations between object and subject to the body; as the most material and practical as well as the most regimented of tools, the body is the intimate site of the durable, transposable dispositions, which are the constraints of habitus. For Bourdieu, habitus and its choices inform the body paradoxically, violently and practically (Evens 1999, 9), and this conceptualization also becomes one point of departure for 'carnal sociology'.[9] In yawatashi, however, the body as a tool of perception and movement and as the site of understanding are one, while meaning unfolds as it is done without generating any gap; the violence of the arrow, splitting whatever it encounters on its flight, is culturally harnessed to enable the breaking of boundaries between different aspects of the world.

Mu

Japanese practices – religious rituals, martial arts training and other practices – follow a common attempt to break down dualisms. Japanese philosopher Yasuo Yuasa (1987) explains that Japanese non-duality does not stem from an axiom of unity between the physical body and the mind, or between what is natural and what is man-made; rather, Japanese culture promotes practices that are designed to coax non-duality into existence. These ways are devised to force passage between parts of the body and of the world so that they may work together. The two contraries do not become one but remain perpetually in the process of becoming one, at the same time also constantly disintegrating into two. Continuous and strenuous effort is invested in order to prevent them from falling apart, and this man-made perpetual processuality embedded in practice is central to Japanese cosmologies. Here I would like to foreground two tools or cultural logics that permit this perpetual effort: mu – nothingness or somethinglessness – and homology as a non-linear alternative to causality.

The word of negation, mu 無 (*wu* in Chinese, indicating the principle *wu wei* – 'effortless action' or 'the action of nonaction; see Loy 1985; Duyvendak 1947; see also De Prycker 2011), is central to martial arts, as summarized in the Tao principle of *mushin* – 'no mind'. In the Tokugawa era of peace (1600–1868) the samurai did not have to fight and many held instead administrative positions as clerks. Martial arts then were refashioned, as some took an esoteric turn and included this negation in their name, e.g. *mugen* ('no eyes') – fighting with one's eyes closed; *muteki* ('no enemy') – fighting as if there was no enemy; and the well-known *mushin* ('no mind') (Hurst 1998, 74), which, simply put, urges the participants in martial arts training to relinquish their mindful control over the body, to stop attempting to understand what they are doing and to act directly through the body. The apprentice is exhorted to seek a way that will allow them to forego reliance on a reflecting 'self' as an autonomous entity and to encourage instead a missing self, a negation of self, for example, by extending the body-self to the target in kyudo. This is a complicated process, since it involves discovering within the body direct access to its capacities to sense and act, while contrasting with the well-embedded habit of discipline over both mind and body. Whereas we try, more often than not, to control our behaviour and translate logical decisions into social interaction, in martial arts training the student must trust their masters and the traditions they transmit, following strict orders with their body alone, letting the body decide on its own when and how to attack or defend, when to release the arrow, and so forth.

Mushin follows the lines of the Chinese Taoist practical principle of wu wei as adapted in Japan. Wu wei is a state of 'harmony in which action flows freely and instantly from one's spontaneous inclinations – without the need for extended deliberation or inner struggle – and yet nonetheless accords perfectly with the dictates of the situation at hand' (Slingerland 2003, 7). In wu wei, a system – be it the human body, a family or the entire state – is set into motion so perfectly that it demands no further effort because it flows in the 'right' way, as does the rarified yawatashi. In order to generate effortless action, to be able to withdraw from action, many meticulous preparations must be set in place; only then can the system flow perfectly of its own accord. *Mushin* invokes precisely such a system; after painstaking preparations over years of practice, the martial artist can perform his art with no conscious effort, without correction, and without a 'self' to monitor the action. The arrow seems to leave the bow of its own accord rather than having been shot by the archer.

Loy calls the ambiguity of the action-less action wu wei 'paradoxical' (Loy 1985, 73); but paradox assumes the coexistence of two incompatible truths, such as action and non-action or effort and effortlessness. The logic of wu wei, however, does not concern static truths, but rather two different dynamics of practice that are simultaneously and ambiguously present within one action: the dynamic of meticulous planning and endless, tedious training within cultural wisdom polished to perfection, and the dynamic of letting go, of forgoing will and of trusting the body, the social event and the situation at hand to act as they are set into motion, of their own accord. The opposition of the two dynamics relates only to exertion of effort versus letting go, action as opposed to non-action, while sharing the common goal of attaining a harmony; the dynamic in which there is no gap between plan and execution I call elsewhere 'perfect praxis' (Bar-On Cohen forthcoming).

Mu is a specific sort of negation, which Ohnuki-Tierney (1994) calls, in semiotic terms, a zero signifier, 'a signifier without materiality of linguistic label or objects' (1994, 59). In other words, mu signifies negation, the hollow centre of nothingness that predicates all its surrounding (1994, 67) and therefore bears great transformative potentialities. By virtue of the 'absence of' something – sensory perception in *mugen* and conscious effort in *mushin* – everything works as it should. The understanding of mu, which derives from Taoism, was ardently adopted in Zen and is also a central feature of Shinto. Both the Shinto shrine and the Shinto palanquin transporting the kami from one place to another during festivals are empty. It is forbidden to look at the emperor in his guise as living god, and he can therefore be considered an empty centre of the entire Japanese society (Crump 1991; Bar-On Cohen 2012).

Mu is an empty something that, if (re)filled, could become too powerful, too sacred or too defiled, and must therefore be handled with care. It may still hold remnants or traces of what it negates, of what is lacking or lost, or it can be a complete void, like the eye of a hurricane. The mu negation is like a hole in topology: what is it made of? Is it the matter that was retracted from the hole, or is it the air that fills it? And what are the contours of the hole? Are they the contours of the object in which the hole is lodged, or instead the interior contours of that object (Casati and Varzi 1994)?

On the other hand, mu may also be bare negation, neither negating anything nor empty or lacking something specific. Instead, it can be a double negation fundamental to non-duality, because mu cannot be equated to something else nor can it negate something else. Thus mu dissolves binaries as absolutely exclusive (just as yin is not yang, being its opposition, and not not-yang, because it constantly holds the potentiality of becoming its opposition). This kind of emptiness is intuited within Zen meditation and similar practices, including martial arts (Bar-On Cohen 2007). The twofold negation leaves porous borders through which correct practice can create a passage or can dissolve altogether. According to Nishida Keiji, absolute nothingness is a field of emptiness where all living beings exist in 'circumferential interpenetration' (Kawamura 1994, 72). Since the centre is empty, all activity takes place on the circumference of this emptiness, and this deformation, or thinning out, also enables a better and larger adhesion surface and smooth passage through borders.

The aim of practice according to the logic of *mushin* is to turn oneself into a mirror, into water without waves that can reflect, without distortion, a modest non-egoistic life in harmony with others. In contrast to existentialist emptiness, mu as a meditative goal is not a frightening, alienated, dark emptiness, but rather an emptiness that makes you smile. It is an emptiness that is not void of things; rather, the void is seen against the landscape of ordinary, mundane life (Hyers 1974). Emptiness can generate different intensities relative to the objects that are separated by the void and to the potentialities of energies that may be released by their coming together. Thus the empty space between the archer and the target generates a whirl of potential intensities, which if carefully assembled by the eight steps leading up to the shot, may animate potential connections.

Homology

Mu concerns the relations animated by the empty centre, and homology determines what these potential connections are, what can be activated through what else. Unlike mu, homology is not an explicit emic notion but rather a logic underlying ways of doing, ways of connecting planes in the world, ways of encouraging a causal result. The relations between shooting an arrow and cosmological transformation are achieved by activating the forces of homology. The transformative dimension of kyudo does not operate or affect through representational semiotics, nor does it move along the parameters of simple causality. Instead, this dimension of kyudo, and of Japanese religious rituals, depends on another logic: they engage the forces of homology, a cultural logic that does not generate a gap between deed and meaning. Semiotic understanding can only provide meaning, while the forces of homology, when activated, immediately enter into process, concomitantly providing meaning as they act in the world. Homology can set into motion pre-existing relations between different phenomena, which are connected in a way that holds a potentiality to initiate change. Through homology as a cultural tool of sense-making, and as a way to activate a desired effect, the powers of one plane can be harnessed to exert a change in the other.

French thinker Gilles Deleuze's philosophy of 'difference' can contribute to an understanding of these cultural logics.[10] In Deleuzian terms, while mu can be understood as a form of 'pure difference', a difference internal to the object or event that determines its potential dynamics and intensities (Deleuze 1994), homology can be seen as a 'line of flight' (Deleuze and Guatarri 2005). It is a 'path of mutuation precipitated though the actualization of connections among bodies that were previously only implicit (or "virtual") that releases new powers in the capacity of those bodies to act and respond' (Lorraine 2005, 145). In other words, a line of flight can connect completely separate planes of consistency. The connection between the planes precedes activation as a virtual or implicit potential, ready to be set into action; and when the connection is actualized, it is generative and multidirectional, awakening something that cannot be found on either one plane or the other alone. Unlike the usual unidirectional understanding of causality, it is multidirectional and the direction from cause to effect can be reversed within homological relations. Handelman summarizes the effects of homology as follows:

> Relationships of homology are akin to ones of cause and effect, or perhaps more accurately to a mutuality of relationship, in which cause turns into effect, effect into cause [...] X and Y (whatever their content) were bound in webs of mutuality, such that a change in one effects a change in the other and vice-versa. (1995, 268)[11]

Activating a line of flight or homology opens up new connections, relationships and potentialities, and thus is an immanent way to augment the whole.

Elsewhere (Bar-On Cohen 2009a) I describe how participants in an excruciatingly taxing and painful karate exercise called kibadachi employ the forces of homology in order to accomplish their feat. All participants assume the same squatting position for an hour and a half; by transferring energy from one participant to another this similarity enables them all to remain crouched, and to squat even lower and increase the pain they feel. Kibadachi cannot be performed alone and is possible only within a group because the members of the group draw energy from one another, and this energy enhances everybody's endurance and makes it possible to sustain and even increase the pain and effort. Performing the exercise activates the homological relations between the participants. Trapped in the same somatic duress, they open their bodies to one another and thus permit a flow between parts of their own body selves and among one another. In kibadachi, the forces of homology challenge the boundedness of each individual within his or her skin; the design of the exercise stipulates that it is possible to overcome such boundedness and that a continuum exists between disparate individuals. Moreover, movement – in this case arrested movement – and volition also lose their separateness, as the will to continue squatting overcomes physical limitations and vice versa. Thus the directionality of cause and effect is blurred as the squatting enables passage within and between the participants, and also concomitantly the other way around: the breaching of boundaries is a condition that permits this feat to be accomplished. The sameness of the human body, the homology of human bodies and their potentialities to open up through kibadachi, is harnessed to create a loop of feed and feedback that renders the whole greater than its constitutive parts.

Within Japanese culture three planes are situated in homological relations, called by Kawamura 'nature, humanity and transcendence' (Kawamura 1994, 75), harmoniously unified through 'nothingness' or mu. Yawatashi as transformative (religious) ritual does precisely that. Through the perfect arrow shot, homology is instilled and all other potentialities and uncertainties are excluded. The archer's human body–mind is connected to the turning world – the bird of prey, the bamboo – and to the kami. The connection or line of flight between these planes is the trajectory of the arrow whirling through the air. Indeed, potential connections exist between planes of the world within such understanding, and they are made to operate harmoniously through the forces of homology embedded within double negation. But Kawamura's choice of words is problematic; 'transcendence' cannot coexist with homological relations because homologous connections must be continuous and nothing can transcend them.

Japanese religions do not include external forces found exclusively outside our world; rather, the Shinto kami, and a fortiori the Buddhist gods, are integral parts of the world. The gods do not transcend it but are part of a continuum that includes sentient beings and natural phenomena, and they can be connected through correct practice. The gods subsist on a different plane, but a line of flight can be created ritually so that the homology between them and other sentient beings, and the world itself, can be coaxed into transformative action. In other words, the Japanese gods are immanent. Homology depends on a cosmology that views the world as continuous, namely, a world in which no absolute separations or unreachable distances are posited. Such a world is holistic (Handelman and Lindquist 2011). Monotheistic worlds, by contrast, stipulate absolute boundaries between god and man, between man and nature, between the human and the animal world, between individuated selves, and so forth. In Japanese religions, as well as Indian and Chinese ones, such impenetrable obstacles do not exist. Moreover, it is precisely the connections between these planes that are set into motion through homology to engender transformation.

Between Doing and Meaning – Semiotics of the Non-dual

Mu and homology generate relations between aspects of the world that, in contrast to other conceptualizations, obliterate the gap between objective and subjective, between practice and habitus, and between a word and its signified. Meaning emerges as it is performed and, recursively, practice follows the understanding that it shapes. Casalis (1983a) shows the mechanism within Sino-Japanese culture that challenges semiotics through the juxtaposition of non-representative connections between different semiotic planes belonging to the same field of meaning. Different planes of signification such as Japanese ideographic letters (*kanji*), the world at large, and cultural events or objects become mutually interchangeable. In such a framework an object is not randomly assigned a sign; rather the sign, which may be a kanji or another cultural object or event, has a relation of content to something in the world that is imitated by the cultural event and which refers to it.

Both the thing in the world and the cultural event may be further repeated in yet another cultural event or object, and so on, reciprocally giving and drawing meaning from one another. Because these relations are not unidirectional, the kanji may imitate the cultural object or event in some cases, while in other cases it is the object or event in the world that simulates the kanji. These relations are engaged with to create a variety of mutual connections, yielding increasing complexity. Casalis refers particularly to the hassetsu, the eight steps of kyudo, and to the most famous *karesansui* (Japanese rock garden) at the Ryōan-ji temple in Kyoto. Unlike the semiotic interpretation, which stipulates that man-made cultural artefacts − word, event, object, or symbol − imitate and refer to something natural in the world, no such order is posited in Japanese cultural logic. It is never clear which plane is a reflection or imitation of which other, since they recursively feed one another's existence and are nourished by it, generating both meaning and life processes concomitantly. Both kyudo and the rock garden thus become 'multidimensional in [their] semiotic organizing principles and communicative purpose' (McGovern 2004, 347).

Both kyudo and the rock garden are austere, minimalistic and meditative, and both depend on the moving body, since the meditative effect of the rock garden is best achieved when contemplated in the course of a slow walk along the viewing platform. Moreover, the rock garden is oriented in the same directions as are kyudo shooting galleries, namely, both the archer and garden observer move on the northern end of a platform from east to west, looking or shooting southward. These directions improve vision by reducing the sun's glare at different times of the day (and in kyudo they also ensure that the turning of the earth does not divert the shot), but they are also auspicious according to Chinese cosmology, which is an additional dimension connected to both cultural events by homology.[12]

The rock garden as an image is confusing; the clusters of rocks, isolated from each other by raked gravel, look like islands surrounded by the ocean. The rock garden employs the loose watery metaphor to 'convey nonverbally, quietly, irrefutably, this feeling of fluidity of emptiness' (Casalis 1983b, 361). It creates a play between movement and non-movement, as the eye of the viewer oscillates between rock and raked gravel, between object and background (McGovern 2004, 350; see also Onishi 1993).

A contentless (zero) signifier closely related to mu (無) is ma (間), designating the empty space or interval that gives sense to the objects around it, such as the white paper in calligraphy or the empty space in a picture. Ma as the dynamic distance between opponents in Japanese martial arts is a crucial factor in a bout, determining how the opponents move and who has the advantage (Bar-On Cohen 2006). It is also one of the most important components of the Japanese rock garden, where it is the raked gravel that gives sense to the clusters of rocks. The theme of the garden invites interpretation − perhaps it is a tiger and its cubs crossing a river, or mountain tops emerging from clouds, or possibly an altogether abstract image. Ambiguously formulated Japanese meditative gardens 'are designed to depict the way the natural elements of rock, water and plant life actually appear in nature' (Wright and Katsuhiko 2008).

Here is a conundrum: the Ryōan-ji temple rock garden has 15 rocks, yet only 14 can be seen from any point on the viewing gallery. Its mind-boggling ambiguity or multiplicity − the empty and the full, the seen and the unseen, the various potential meanings immanent in it – is essential to the meditative role it fulfils, just as the challenge faced by the kyudo archer as he takes aim at the target, oscillating between object and background, between the various images floating in the viewer's mind, between the movement of the body and that of the mind, produces the meditative effect.

Casalis shows how the same kind of relations between different semiotic planes are also at work in the body movements of kyudo's eight-step shot. The steps are named after kanji, a mnemonic technique in which the form of the kanji can be traced within the form of the archer with bow and arrow, and simultaneously the sense of the kanji takes the body form. As 'the archer traces harmonious characters in space using his body, and his bow and arrow' (Casalis 1983a, 321), the kanji and the archer's movements become interchangeable. Both the kanji and the movements, he adds, are also identified as 'manifestations of the flow of the Tao' (1983a, 321). The kanji for the seventh step of the hassetsu, the *hanare* (release) – when the arrow leaves the bow and the archer stands with both hands extended to the side – is called *dai*. It is a clear example of the multidirectional relations between movement and kanji since dai (大), which means big, imitates the archer. So there are at least three reasons for and consequences of this identification of body movements with the corresponding kanji: to help remember the steps, to provide layers of meaning for both the movements and the kanji, and to actually lead to the transformative force of a shot through homology. The homology between the planes (which Casalis calls semiotic) – the human body and man-made objects and events, the world at large and non-human beings such as the kami, and the Buddha – are placed in relation culturally and, through correct practice, can be coaxed to work together in order to activate greater forces.

Practice/Habitus, Actuality/Virtuality

Yawatashi follows both Japanese cultural experience and the archer's personal one, to purposefully blur distinctions between the archer, the arrow, the world, the kami and the other participants watching it, producing transformation through its own ordering. While the arrow pierces the distance between the shooting gallery and the target, it brings to life a continuous cosmos, and both the social and physical environment are forcefully shaped. As noted, this cultural design challenges the distinction between practice and habitus, and I offer a brief proposal to replace these two concepts by the Deleuzian 'virtuality' and 'actuality'. Following the Japanese cultural logics, however, simply replacing the notions of practice with actuality, and habitus with virtuality, will reproduce the same problems; therefore I propose that the relations between the dyad practice/habitus be replaced with the relations between the dyad virtual/actual.

Actuality and virtuality are mutually exclusive, joint and sufficient characteristics of the real (Boundas 2004, 296–7). Yet, like many of Deleuze's idiosyncratic concepts, actuality and virtuality are purposefully fuzzy and elusive and cannot be defined in a comprehensive way. From the variety of usages Deleuze proposes in his books, the relations between actuality and virtuality for our purposes here can be regarded as following the lines of problems and solutions, respectively.

The main split between habitus/practice and actuality/virtuality consists of the former being based on identity and the latter founded on difference. Virtuality is the ever-proliferating becoming of perpetual differentiation, the multiplicity of potential solutions to every problem. This is why habitus clarifies the determinate aspect of the social, while the virtual brings indeterminate processes to life. Habitus is related to the past, as an accumulation of tendencies and inclinations; virtually has a more complex relation to time: it is a past that was never the present; a pure past or an eternal future. Habitus can be deduced only by the approximation of actual practice, while the relations between actuality and virtuality are never unequivocal: the part of the virtual that is not actualized continues to live in the form of potentiality (Colebrook 2004, 10), just as solutions that are not actualized continue to yield more potential solutions, only a few of which will be actualized, and so on. Actuality can help intuit what the potentialities of virtuality are, but the potentialities of virtuality have a life of their own, unrelated to actuality.

Habitus is situated on a higher, more abstract level than practice; actuality and virtuality are part of the empirical world, both appearing together, and thus no meta-level is formed, neither concept transcending the other. Consequently, the relations of causality between the two pairs also differ. Habitus is defined as the cause of practical choices, paradoxically also made up of empirical reality; no direct causal relations exist between actuality and virtuality, where causality is mediated and reversible. Such conceptualization makes the relations between practice and habitus one specific case within the multiplicity of potential relations between virtuality and actuality – one that is intimately connected to the striated world of Deleuze and Guattari's (2005) State.

In these terms, yawatashi is intended to capture a certain virtuality and actualize it in the archery hall, excluding, by prefect praxis, all potential solutions, uncertainties and haphazard occurrences in order to coerce transformation. Yet the effort can yield only a fleeting result, which will have to be constantly reified through more shooting of arrows.

Notes

1 *Kami* are usually translated as 'gods', but a better translation would be 'mysterious numena' (Blacker 1975).
2 Sachiko, the interpreter who helped me on both occasions, was intrigued by my having posed the same informational questions to the two teachers and was impressed by the discrepancy between their answers.
3 In this particular event all three participants were men. For opening and closing rituals in other Japanese martial arts see Bar-On Cohen 2009b.
4 The *kami* are summoned by the clapping of hands.
5 At Shiseikan the *kamiza* also holds a small Shinto shrine in the form of a straw hut behind which water and rice stalks provide food and drink for the kami.
6 The one said to be the most difficult is *hitotsu mato share*, in which three archers must stand and shoot at a single target, with only one archer situated exactly opposite the target while the other two stand at a slight angle.
7 Due to lack of space, Bourdieu's theory is presented here in an extremely simplified manner, glossing over changes Bourdieu himself introduced over time. For a more nuanced view, see King 2000; Evens 1999; Robbins 2007; Myles 2004; Verter 2008; Throop and Keith 2002.
8 Evens (1999) proposes that Bourdieu's dualistic view be replaced by a basic ambiguity and that the role of violence in imposing behaviours be exchanged for ethics that are inherently two-sided and ambiguous. Yet he also bases his solution on the workings of paradox.

9 Sociologists such as Wacquant and Crossley have encountered these inherent difficulties through their ethnographies and have proposed other solutions; in this chapter, however, I wish to take another route.
10 My study of the relations between violence, anthropology and Deleuzian thought was supported by Israeli Science Foundation Grant No. 393/10.
11 Handelman discusses homology as a method of legal reasoning used to create taxonomy in ancient China. The homology of doing, and not only of classification, has a similar effect.
12 There are, of course, exceptions, such as the *kyudojo* at Waseda University, where the shooting gallery faces north.

Chapter 11

TAMING THE HABITUS: THE GYM AND THE DOJO AS 'CIVILIZING WORKSHOPS'

Raúl Sánchez García

Introduction

In this chapter I bring in Norbert Elias's notion of habitus applied to ethnographic settings (the boxing gym and aikido dojo). Complemented by other conceptual tools such as 'tension balance', 'thresholds of violence' or 'double-bind process', I try to contribute in the advance towards the possibility of a real 'carnal sociology' (Wacquant 2005a, 2011). Even though Elias's usage of habitus is less well known than Bourdieu's, I argue that it is as important as a topic of research (especially when dealing with martial arts and combat sports) and as a tool for conducting ethnographic studies. In both Bourdieu and Elias, the notion of habitus refers to some kind of tacit disposition, a kind of 'second nature' that allows a pre-reflective relation to the world affected by the social conditions of its production. Nonetheless, there are some differences. Whereas in Bourdieu (1990b, 2000; Bourdieu and Wacquant 1992), the notion of habitus implies a whole common sense, a way of perceiving and acting,[1] in Elias, the notion of habitus is restricted to the balance between spontaneity and constriction in the expression of affects and emotions.[2] This difference does not prevent both notions from being complementary. On the contrary: as we can see in Wacquant's study of boxing in Chicago (Wacquant 2004a), the specific conditions of being/learning in the gym affects the whole common sense of boxers but also the way they express and control their affections, especially (but not only) those related to violence. But, before going any further, I shall elucidate a bit more the notion of habitus used by Elias and the reason why I have applied it to the ethnographic study of boxing and aikido.

The original usage of habitus by Elias in German was translated into English as 'personality structure', 'personality make-up' or 'social make-up'. Later, in revised versions of *The Civilizing Process*, the term remained in the text. We could define habitus as emotional or affective management (*Affekthaushalt*) or 'modelling of urges' (*Triebmodellierung*), in the balance between external controls and internal self-controls. This is normally attached to what Elias termed 'psychogenesis' of individuals taking part of specific figurations, developed in dynamic processes in what is identified as 'sociogenesis'. Elias always stressed the close relation between the individual and the social. That is why habitus is named also as 'second nature', interiorizing social controls. This is to stress that the habitus of individuals are developed within a social milieu, a figuration.[3] Elias's most famous oeuvre, *The Civilizing Process* (2000), connected changes in habitus (towards more self-control) with the long-term changes happening in European societies since the Middle Ages.[4] Figurational sociologists have dealt with the issue of combat sports in a sociohistorical manner, relating the development of activities such as boxing (Sheard 1997; Sheard and Murphy 2006) or mixed martial arts (MMA) (Sánchez García and Malcolm 2010) to changes in habitus within civilizing/decivilizing processes.

Although belonging to the figurational scope, the present chapter is innovative in the sense that it applies Eliasian tools to ethnographic settings. The figuration to which Elias referred normally was very big (a society, a nation state) but he also offered figuration as a conceptual tool applicable to different sizes of human chains of interdependence (Elias 1978). My claim in this chapter is that we can focus on the figuration constituted by participants in the gym and in the dojo. These settings constitute 'civilizing workshops' where participants learn their craft but also learn how to deal with human conflict in a more detached way. The figurations in the gym and the dojo are the social milieu where participants' habitus dynamically changes towards a more controlled way of dealing with conflict and violence. These statements are based upon my ethnographic research, consisting in a four-year period of observant participation in a boxing gym (three years) and an aikido dojo (three years) (Sánchez García 2006). Semi-structured interviewing, informal chatting and attendance to courses and seminars of these activities were also part of the methodological techniques employed to carry out the study. Further engagement in these activities after the research period also helped me to test and critically assess these findings.[5] During the period of research I began to acquire a boxing habitus and an aikido habitus. My own participation implied gaining not only some mastery of the skills, but a better embodied understanding of the 'violence negotiation' within the activities and also of the feelings, values and behaviours of the participants. Several examples taken from my fieldnotes (including some self-observations) will illustrate the analysis presented.

The Gym and the Dojo as 'Civilizing Workshops'

I argue that the boxing gym and the aikido dojo can be conceived as kind of 'civilizing workshops' where a more controlled and detached way of dealing with violence and human conflict is acquired. As immersion in the activity grows, a developmental pattern can be observed in almost all the participants: transition from the pole of 'affective violence' (due to emotional discharge facing danger or as a pleasurable end in itself) towards 'rational' or 'instrumental' violence (attending to the achievement of a goal or aim). This does not mean automatically less dangerous or less harmful (imagine the potential threat posed by an expert in these crafts); just a more detached, calm and controlled way of dealing with violence.[6] This is precisely the meaning conveyed by the term civilized in Elias. Referring to the habitus, this means a greater self-control in emotional discharge facing conflict. Aggressive urges are more controlled, expressed within the specific forms of the crafts; they can be harmful, even lethal, but under the subject's control. But, how does this process happen? How do the activities in the gym and the dojo affect participants' habitus in this way?

This process is possible because each subject is part of the social milieu of the setting where he/she engages in a learning/teaching experience. Within this repetitive interaction the subjects acquire little by little a sense of what is the normal–desired–legitimated pattern of behaving in this interactional context. This is not to say an automatic compliance to social norms in a Parsonian sense. This just refers to the acquisition of a sense of the normal pattern of occurrence in social interactions in a Garfinkelian view.[7] The habitus of the individual is always linked to a social figuration. It does not make any sense to think of the habitus as a thing, a passive acquisition inside the individual once and for all. It just makes sense to talk of the habitus related to the dynamic notion of practice. The habitus is progressively generated in the interaction between subjects and is always linked to the 'normal pattern of behaviour' in the social situation where we can observe the degree of self-control exerted by the subject. Thus, the social and the personal are inextricably intertwined in the practice. Martial arts and combat sports imply practices dealing with human physical conflict, a kind of 'institutionalized violence'. Therefore, during the training some degree of pain and harm is expected. But, how far are the participants willing to take and give punishment? Where are the limits, the permissible and banned actions?

As Elias and Dunning (1966) suggest, in every sport there is a tension balance between emotional decontrolling and emotional controlling. We find some points where this tension balance is optimum and the situation is lived as pleasurable.[8] But we can find other points where the tension balance is not good and the situation is lived either as boring or very frightening. I argue that the pleasurable area of practising martial arts and combat sports is encapsulated between two thresholds of violence,[9] one upper and one lower. This area comprises what we could call the normal/acceptable ways (in mode and intensity) of interacting within the activity. However, if the activity falls under the lower threshold of violence, it will be experienced as something boring; if it falls over the upper threshold, it will be experienced as scary and frightening. As we are talking about interactions between individuals, such thresholds of violence must be embodied in specific actions, as we will see later in the examples from my field notes. 'Having' a certain habitus implies to live as normal certain interaction patterns (about the negotiation of violence) that fall within a zone of adequate tension balance between the two thresholds of violence. Nonetheless, the acquisition of the just sense of where these thresholds are is neither easy nor automatic. It takes a very long time and it is a crucial part of the development of the specific habitus: at the same time that technical skill is being acquired, this ethical component on 'how far to go' is also embodied in the participants. This is why within the same gym there is a progression, a development both in skill acquisition and ethics linked to the activity.[10] This is to pinpoint that within a setting of practice there are different participants with different levels affecting the thresholds of violence (from the instructor or sensei to the newcomer) and it implies different interactions and negotiations in relation to the thresholds of violence. What is scary for a newcomer can be very boring for an expert. As we see, the thresholds of violence are related to the individual pole of every participant but also to the social pole of the whole group as a reference. This does not imply just plain relativism. In fact, there is a clear-cut progression of what is expected from you as your level of expertise increases. There are some actions allowed between experts that are not allowed between expert–novice interactions. The figure of the instructor is paramount in the establishment of this social dynamic order, constituting the gym or the dojo as a certain kind of 'civilizing workshop'.

Negotiating Violence: A 'Double-Bind Process'

> That is a well-nigh universal regularity of a double bind: violence engenders counter-violence, counter-violence heightens the violence on the other side, and so on. (Elias 1996, 200)

We have seen how the acquisition of habitus in the practice is linked to interactions whose reference is the normal way of behaving, delimited by the thresholds of violence. But, how exactly are these interactions carried out? These interactions must be seen as negotiations on violence occurring in double-bind processes (*Doppelbinder-Prozess*). This Eliasian concept applies to two different but interrelated issues concerning violence and conflict. Elias (1996, 200) uses the concept of double-bind process when talking about human conflict to talk about escalation and de-escalation of violence between parties. But he also uses the term referring to his theory of knowledge (Elias 1991, 2007): the more involved and emotionally driven is the subject, the less capacity he has to control the situation, the more involved he gets. Thus, when talking about conflict, if the subjects lose control over the situation, escalation of violence between parties is likely to occur. On the contrary, the more detached is the subject from the emotional arousal due to the situation, the more control he or she gains over it. Thus, when talking about conflict, subjects are able to gain more control and so de-escalation of violence between parties is likely to occur. This fact is extraordinarily important in activities such as martial arts and combat sports where several emotional traits such as pain, fear, shame and pride powerfully influence these negotiations of violence. It is argued that as expertise increases, such emotional traits are experienced in a more detached and calmed way, with less anxiety.[11] This allows expertise to develop even further, continuing the looping effect. As a result, the long-term engagement in the activity brings a more controlled manner to face a potentially physical conflict.

Before presenting the examples that give flesh and bones to the interactions of boxing and aikido, let me briefly say something about the contextual influence on the negotiation of violence within these activities.

I take into account two main factors: (a) sociohistorical development of Spanish combat sports/martial arts and (b) material characteristics of the site of practice.

Sociohistorical development of Spanish combat sports/martial arts

The development of combat sports and martial arts models in the Spanish society is to be conceived within the general development of Spanish physical culture (endogenous games, sports, gymnastics, etc.). Before the nineteenth century, a strong fencing tradition and some different local wrestling styles (lucha canaria, aluche) were already practised and organized in specific regions. Nonetheless, it is during the spread of British sport as

Figure 11.1. Techniques executed among the crowd. Aikido seminar in San Sebastián, July 2006.

Photo courtesy of Fátima Núñez Delgado.

an international phenomenon and the reception of such practices in Spain during the last third of the nineteenth century (Rivero Herraiz and Sánchez García 2011) that the discipline of boxing started to be known, evolving from a predominantly amateur practice of upper and professional middle classes towards a progressive proletarization, linked to a successful professionalization of the activity; during the 1920s and 30s boxing was (with football and cycling) a big spectator sport, with several titles obtained by Spanish boxers (e.g. Bantam Weight World Championship by Baltasar Belenguer Sangchili in 1935). Nonetheless, at the end of the 1970s, professional boxing in Spain suffered powerful opposition from Spanish public opinion in a society undergoing a democratization process after Franco's dictatorship (Sánchez García 2008). During the 1980s, recreational amateur boxing started to spread among different gyms, out of the professional circuit approach that had been predominating until then. The spread of martial arts in Spanish society is clearly bounded to one main discipline: judo. Jigoro Kano's judo (known as jiu-jitsu at that time) arrived to Spain at the beginning of the twentieth century, first as a fighting spectacle linked to professional wrestling and music hall. Soon, it started to be practised also as a kind of 'scientific self-defence method' for the middle classes (Gutiérrez García 2004). Judo's national federation was created in 1965 and acted as a core activity around which other martial arts (such as karate) were organized. During the second half of the twentieth century judo organization was both focused on the competitive side (being an Olympic discipline since 1964) and on educational grounds. Aikido arrived in Spain in the 1960s. Within the federative system, it always remained (and still is) under the tutelage of judo. Nonetheless, it was mainly organized in a myriad of different small organizations, apart from the federation, linked to foreign masters (mainly Japanese or French), keeping a strong position in a traditional approach of budo, focused mainly on self-defence and spiritual development and against any kind of competition.

I researched recreational amateur boxing and traditional aikido. Both congregated participants who were not focused mainly on their competitive career and/or on the efficacy of techniques and where security in the practice for the participants was a paramount issue. Thus, the main concern was focused on the upper threshold of violence: the excess of intensity that could trespass this threshold deriving in non-acceptable violence. The lower threshold of violence was not so controversial and did not raise as much 'problematic cases' as the upper one.[12] A good example of this argument can be found in the content of this field note about aikido:

> It all happened too fast. Around the middle of the class it comes the time to do ykkio[13] technique and sensei signalled Roberto,[14] who bows and goes to the centre of the mat to perform as uke.[15] The first two times are going well. Next time sensei says 'strong' and when the two of them meet at the centre, sensei turns and make a sudden movement over the shoulder of Roberto who is hanging in the air, pinned by the grip of sensei. The action appeared to be stronger than usual and Roberto has fallen to the ground with the other arm and the chest, lying down without turning his head up. Everybody thought that he's hit in the head and sensei's face is full of surprise, almost in panic. He's really altered – I have never seen him like that – and tries to talk to Roberto and the class but he just repeats again and again: 'What has happened?! What has happened?!' Roberto kneels and holds his elbow with the other hand, making gestures of excruciating pain. People stood up and took him to the dressing room […] Almost at the end of the session, sensei says (in a saddened pitch): 'At the end of the day we all are tired and these things can happen. Besides, I had been thinking about the fact that aikido must be considered as a budo and for this reason, sometimes, some stupid things happen. Uke must not be treated as a potato bag, he must be treated with respect.' (Aikido field notes, 12 February 2004)

The sensei, the person in charge of the group, the one who provides the direction of the activity, seems so sorry and worried because of what happened: a rare and disgraceful event indeed. He states that this thing happened because he tried to conceive aikido as a budo;[16] so to say, to stir the model towards a more 'hard', 'effective' approach. He regrets deeply this change of orientation, linking it to the happening of 'stupid things'. The last sentence about 'respect' places the special interest in the security of participants, and the biggest worry about the upper threshold of violence in the activity.

Material characteristics of the site of practice

Talking about the material characteristics of the site of practice, there are different factors affecting the intensity and the degree of danger: available space per participant, columns or other architectural accidents. In the case of boxing, there was a central column that impaired some movements but the ratio of available space/participants was high. Thus, there was not a great influence of material characteristics in the boxing practice. On the contrary, the aikido that I researched was overcrowded sometimes. This circumstance affected the intensity of the techniques, with participants quite often withholding. Besides, due to the noise and disturbance that affected the neighbours in the building, high ukemi (high falls) were not practised. Thus, there was some influence of material characteristics in aikido practice, diminishing the intensity of practice as an overall effect.

Breaking Thresholds of Violence

In this section I present different scenes of boxing and aikido from my field notes. They are interesting because they make visible the established thresholds of violence by breaking them. Two scenes are related to the upper threshold (much more common in the activities I researched) and two to the lower threshold. Moral reaction against threshold breaking will be observed, as normal patterns of negotiation have been violated. I have named each of these scenes as a way of giving a sense of the main events happening there.

Guard like Ali

> Paco is a novice boxer. He had spent just one month attending the gym before I arrived. When we were exercising, the trainer got very angry with him because he had the bad habit of keeping the front hand very low, as if he was some kind of Muhammad Ali. He was new in the trade but when he sparred with veterans, it was commented that he went really hard. Trainer always shouted at him: '[...] up this hand, put up the guard, fuck... you can't do this to people because they think you are kidding them and then they got wound up.' At the end of the class we all started sparring. As we were odd numbers, the trainer sparred as well, something that he usually does. Suddenly, at the middle of the round more or less, the sense of something wrong fills the air: louder noises, excessive breathing. When my partner and I look at the scene, I see that José is cornering Paco with several serious punches that ended up in a combination with a cross impacting in Paco's left cheek. In the meantime, the trainer has realized what was going on and rushed towards them, taking José to a side. Paco has gone directly to the dressing room, mumbling something like 'I don't come here to get hit'. The trainer is talking to José: 'No mate, this is not the way to do it.' And José: 'Fuck, he wanted to take me. He can't act like that, no way.' After some more chatting José admits that he went over the limit, that this is not the way to do things and that he lost his mind. Paco does not come again to the gym. (Boxing field notes, 17 October 2002)

This case is a clear influence of pain and pride/shame factors in the breaking of the upper threshold of violence as a consequence of a double-bind process of escalation in violence. Paco, a novice boxer, was doing the worst thing to keep the situation under control: very little respect to veterans (showing this challenging low guard) and hard hitting (high level of intensity). On the other side of the encounter was José, a veteran boxer who felt an obligation to put this novice 'in his place'. So, Paco, a newcomer, an outsider to the group, was not colluding with the established norms of the gym,[17] mainly represented by the old members, veterans such as José. Acting out of pride, José decided to add more 'fire' to the action, increasing the intensity of the exchange. A third actor, the trainer, was missing and was responsible too for this ascending cycle of violence: the trainer was otherwise engaged in sparring during the time that these events were unfolding. Thus, he was unable to stop this spiralling cycle before it got out of control and broke the upper threshold of violence. When this threshold was broken, moral reactions from all of these agents appeared. Paco stated that he was not there 'to get hit' and never came back. The trainer reproached José that this was not a suitable 'way to do it' but José excuses himself arguing that 'he [Paco] can't act like that'. The three of them acknowledged that the normal pattern of negotiation had been broken due to excess of intensity. The upper threshold of violence materializes before our eyes, becoming visible only at the moment it is broken , as we have witnessed in the event presented in this field note.

High falls

> I'm performing a technique with two black belts, Javier and Pablo, both strong, heavy and with high level of expertise. Javier is doing the technique with great intensity, even with me, acting very tough on Pablo. In the final moment of irimi nage,[18] Javier put in so much verve that Pablo makes an awkward movement and falls to the ground heavily, hitting it with his arm. Then Javier says to Pablo, 'There's a lot of fear to fly, uh?' When Pablo performs the technique on the next occasion he does it in a much more powerful manner and Javi, giving himself up, has made a perfect high fall, with great elegance. When they change turns again and Javi was doing the last movement again, Pablo steps out of the tracing, going to the side, avoiding in some degree the action of Javi and falling to the ground in a soft way. Next turn, Pablo has made the technique with 100 per cent energy and Javi responds with a high fall that booms all over the hall. Then the sensei approaches and says 'More carefully' and stays to keep them under surveillance. From then on, both diminish the degree of intensity in their actions. (Aikido field notes, 12 February 2005)

In this scene we can observe an increasing double-bind process of violence due to certain 'status anxiety' linked to shame/pride. Nonetheless, the upper threshold is not broken; the normal pattern of negotiation is maintained. Javi and Pablo were equal-level practitioners and they were pushing each other in order to establish their position in the hierarchy of the group. Different to sparring in boxing, in aikido there is no free interaction between participants. Normally, aikido practice is carried out through kata (prearranged forms). It implies that participants take turns to perform as tori (the one performing the technique) and uke (the one receiving the technique). But this is not to say that there is no negotiation of violence between them; it is just that this negotiation is often exerted in an indirect way. As we can see from the present scene, Javi increases intensity, adding a pejorative comment towards Pablo about his 'fear to fly in high falls'. This is a very disrespectful and dishonouring statement for an aikidoka with the level of expertise supposedly held by Pablo. Pablo responded with the same coin, augmenting the intensity, but Javi, far from stepping backwards, responds with a graceful high fall. This is a direct account of difference in levels between them and a reinforcement of the fact that Pablo was really 'afraid to fly'. Spiralling negotiation of violence is escalating high in this 'status anxiety' confrontation, presenting growing intensity and elements affecting shame/pride. This double-bind process threatens the normal pattern of negotiation, going to the extreme, almost breaking the upper threshold of violence. Then, the figure of the sensei appears in the scene. Acting as a mediator and regulator of the negotiation of violence, he prevented the situation getting out of control, forcing both participants to cool down and remain within the adequate mode of practice.

I already commented that the main preoccupation in the activities I analysed was focused on the excess of intensity, on the breaking of the upper threshold of violence. In fact, these events are provided as 'typical' and several other examples could be extracted from my field notes to show this phenomenon. In addition, transgression of the lower threshold of violence occurs as well, although with lesser frequency. I present just two of these cases to exemplify this phenomenon.

Asking pardon

A new girl, Lucía, has been training with us for some weeks already. She has been training boxing for some years and knows the trainer. She is good at performing techniques but a bit weak in combat. At the end of the session she is sparring with Pedro and the trainer is observing. At some point, Lucía hits Pedro and says 'sorry' and then stops. The trainer exclaimed: 'But, why pardon? You are paying for that, we come here for that, to learn how to box, come on, come on', moving his hands, indicating them to resume sparring.

Later, in the dressing room, Pedro and the trainer are commenting on the incident.

Pedro: Fuck, after sparring with Ricardo [high intensity], the punches of Lucía were like nothing but even so, she stops and… well, I don't know …

Trainer: Don't worry… It's just that Lucía is afraid of punches, of giving them back, but you don't have to pay attention, you have to keep on going as usual, working, marking some punches for her to get the feeling of it. She does it very well indeed but she chickens out in combat, she has to get that thing. She thinks that combat is technique and a bit more and it is not so, it is not so. (Boxing field notes, 6 April 2005)

On this occasion, we can observe precisely a downward spiral in the double-bind process of violence. Lucía does not want the intensity of the practice to escalate over certain limits that are not so pleasurable for her. Either because she does not like to hit opponents hard,[19] and/or she is not so confident about boxing against a supposed stronger opponent, she is trying to keep the intensity low. That is why when she hits Pedro she asks for pardon and stops the action, avoiding retaliation and freezing the escalating spiral of violence. In this way she is precisely breaking the threshold of violence in the activity, but in this case, the lower one. Instantaneously, the trainer scolded her and told her to avoid such kind of actions and keep focused on the sparring. Later, in the dressing room chat, we can account as well the moral reprobation of Lucía's action by Pedro ('her punches were like nothing but even so, she stops') and the answer of the trainer, suggesting to avoid reinforcing the downward pattern of double-bind processes when sparring with Lucía. He states that Lucía is stuck in a level of intensity that is not suitable for the activity ('she is afraid of punches, of giving them back') so we must help her to improve and get close to the accepted patterns of violence negotiation within the class. Sparring implies certain intensity to be appropriate; good technique or looking good does not suffice ('she thinks that combat is technique and a bit more and it is not so, it is not so').

Enduring pain

> During the explanation of a luxation technique, Nikkyo, the sensei, picks a white belt. He's a beginner and it must be one of the first times he receives this technique from the sensei. He is going to catch the wrist of the pupil but, before (or so it seems) a proper pressure is applied, the pupil crumbles down to the ground. The sensei tightens the grip again, twisting the wrist in a sudden but controlled way, the pupil palming the ground repeatedly [to indicate stop]. The sensei seems surprised and says in a loud voice 'This should not hurt yet' and leads the pupil to the ground, applying another twist. This time the pupil resists a bit more before palming the ground. The sensei looses pressure and indicates him to stand up in order to repeat the same technique again. (Aikido field notes, 14 December 2004)

This scene exemplifies the 'socialization of pain' that a newcomer experiences in the process of becoming an aikidoka. I commented already that the acquisition of a proper habitus implies the acquisition of a certain sense of what is included between two thresholds of violence. This sensitivity towards pain is necessary for you to harden enough in order to receive technique and for you to apply a proper intensity when applying techniques on your partners. Naturally, the degree of pain and intensity increases successively as the level of expertise increases and the aikido habitus is settled more and more solidly.

Appearances of Danger: Protective Gear versus Self-Control

A permanent feature in the activities I researched was the little protective gear used, both in boxing and aikido. Controversial as it may seem at first glance, I argue that, far from being always a civilizing booster, protective gear may act sometimes just as 'civilizing make-up', resulting in a more risky or harmful practice. Yet lack of protective gear does not always represent a more savage or barbarizing practice. In the activities I researched,

Figure 11.2. Basic protective gear: First set of bandages, gloves and mouth guard used in my boxing activity.

Photo courtesy of Fátima Núñez Delgado.

the use of little protective gear was a reminder of the reality and possibility of harm. This circumstance boosted greater self-control over the participants, resulting in a civilizing trend: a greater control of risk and a greater care for the security of participants. This is particularly so because the activities focused on in my research placed special attention on the upper threshold of violence.

The controversial development of protective gear in combat sports was first expounded in the influential figurational study carried out by Kenneth Sheard (1992, 1997) on boxing. Sheard argues that, even though some changes in the regulation and equipment of prizefighting/boxing made the practice safer, the main reason fuelling this process was to make it more suitable for highly civilized audiences.[20] Less blood and fewer bruises were needed in the activity if it was to be accepted publicly. From the introduction of mufflers by Jack Broughton in the gentlemen's practice in the nineteenth century until the development of modern gloves for professional boxers, the civilized appearance of the activity was the main issue. Sheard's convincing argument is that the introduction of protective gear, such as gloves or helmet, could be conceived as kinds of 'cosmetic changes', making the activity more dangerous for boxers but more bearable for public sensitivities and opinion. According to Sheard, gloves are mainly to protect the hands of the hitter not the head of the opponent. More powerful punches, repeated more times can be delivered without suffering a broken finger or a sprained wrist (the head/face being a more robust block than the hand). In addition, circular blows instead of just straight punches can be delivered efficiently and with the added weight of the glove. All of those factors mean that the punched opponent is more prone to suffer brain damage even though he or she is less 'gory' in appearance. Furthermore, the head guard or helmet does not make things much better. Used in sparring, it is true that it avoids cuts (maybe this is its main function for a boxer before a match) but it adds further factors to the brain damage equation: more sweating (means the brain shrinks and collides more violently with the skull), less vision (the punches are more difficult to see and therefore avoid), more weight in the head (adding spinning momentum to the head, precisely what makes the brain hit the skull). In the boxing activity I researched, no head guard was ever worn, just a mouth guard and gloves.

The basic principle spoken often by the trainer was 'not to go for the K.O.' when hitting your opponent, especially when punching in the head. Body checks were much harder but the face was an area for hitting with caution. There was a main focus on 'going loose, gentle', placing the weight on the punches with no extra effort. The trainer usually remarked: 'We are not here to train and compete as professionals. We just want to make some sport.' That was a clear strategy (amongst others) to stress the care for the partner. In the years I was practising, I did not see a clear K.O. or a gory scene. Of course some accidents happened: momentary dizziness; a broken rib, wrist or finger; a busted nose and some blood. All of that was due to isolated actions and there was always special attention to this issue. An example from my field notes on boxing is telling in this respect:

> Ricardo and Nacho were sparring at the end of the class. Nacho was much more experienced than Ricardo but the latter was heavier and stronger and also becomes considerably anxious when sparring. In an escalating double bind of violence things went over the limit and Ricardo ended up with a bloody cut in the nose and lips. He started complaining angrily about this fact and the intensity exerted by Nacho. The latter responded he was just responding to Ricardo with the same coin. About the cut, Nacho says that it was accidental, not on purpose. He stated: 'I saw you weren't protecting yourself and I hit you once but the cut is due to the Velcro (signalling the glove). I did not want to make a K.O. or something like this.' The trainer intervened and warned: 'Alright, if a bad mood starts to spread, we just quit sparring and that's it.' (Boxing field notes, 21 March 2005)

In aikido, ukemi is the basic tool of protection. The concept of ukemi is normally referred to as 'falls' but it also encompasses a broader idea. Ukemi refers to the 'taking of the technique', ending normally in a fall that allows the person to regain balance in order to continue the attack and/or avoid getting injured due to the applied technique. The art of ukemi is difficult to develop and it takes a very long time. It evolves with overall aikido skill and is highly influential in the double-bind process embedded in the practical negotiation of violence. As ukemi evolves, you feel more secure in your response to the technique applied on you and have more control over your actions and your opponent's actions. More control means less anxiety, so your skill in ukemi evolves as well. Gaining more control and a relaxed attitude and movement in ukemi also affects the way that you apply techniques to partners, becoming more relaxed and more effective as well. This virtuous looping allows an aikido expert to perform at very high level of intensity with low level of risk. Generally speaking, they perform more stable, more secure, more relaxed moves and with more control. In a nutshell, they really gain insight into the way that aikido works: through organic movement of the whole person (expressed in concepts such as ki or hara) instead of muscular force. As observed in the field notes of high falls (see above), Javier was not getting worried about the intense technique applied by Pablo. He was just taking elegant ukemi and landing without any harm. On the other hand, Pablo was not so confident to fly and that was a potential risk factor of the practice. This lack of confidence was one of the triggering factors of an ascending double-bind process of violence (apart from the shame/pride element acting there).

As we have observed in this section, the kind of protective equipment used in both activities was mainly an internalized one: an increased degree of self-control oriented to protect yourself and your partner. What I try to convey here is that such kinds of protection evolves in a civilizing trend as part of the participant's habitus. Elias's characterization of 'civilizing process' implied that the balance between external and internal control shifted towards the internal control of the individuals. This is the process taking place in the activities in which I took part. Avoiding relying strongly on external control (expressed for instance in the protective gear), participants were learning how to rely on their internal self-control to avoid excessive levels of violence, risk and harm. Besides, in relation to the issue of appearances and 'cosmetic changes' discussed earlier, external protective gear usually offers 'a false sense of security' that often translates to less attention/care to actions and the taking of risks that could be either higher than they appear to be and/or unadjusted to the level of expertise of the participant.

Promises of a 'Carnal Sociology': Habitus as a Tool of Research

So far I have analysed some examples from my ethnographic research in order to show the progressive acquisition of a boxing habitus and aikido habitus amongst the participants in these activities. But the question of methodology remains unsettled: how my 'observant participation' in the activity helped me to conduct a more informative and adequate research of the activities under study when compared to other research techniques such as non-participant observation?[21] That is crucial if we are to develop a real proposal on the approach of a 'carnal sociology' (Wacquant 2005a, 2011). I argue that my direct participation was paramount for the research all along. The self-acquisition of the boxing and aikido habitus as the time of my participation increased was paramount: I was as implicated in the negotiation of violence as any other member of the group; I was part of several of the revealing examples about the breaking of thresholds of violence; I could feel the pain, fear, risk and the sense of inferiority/superiority of rank linked to shame/pride. Without these experiences I would have been impaired not only to understand but to write and show appropriate accounts of what was going on in these specific settings of practice. I include some field notes of self-observation during the research period on boxing to show how my habitus – and thus, my understanding of the activities – was changing. Before illustrating these data, it is worth noting that my previous experience in combat sport had been just a bit of judo and fencing. I had no previous 'socialization in street fighting' either, just kids' hard play with friends and brothers. Even though I had a developed sporting habitus (having practised different sports all my life and completed a degree in sport science) I had no real connection with combat experience. Thus, during my first year of research – dedicated to boxing – a lot of inferences to fear and anxiety appear in these notes:

> Too much fear about contact. I try to keep the distance to avoid being hit and to hit strong. I'm very stiff, I can't move my feet, just dodge and block sometimes. (3 October 2002)
>
> I can hit the body but not the face. I prefer to dodge and block and stay out of distance but I avoid interchange of punches. (20 November 2002)
>
> I'm feeling bad. After sparring with Javi and receiving some hard punches in the face I noticed the idea of: why should I risk my face for research? (6 March 2003)

Nonetheless, as my second year of boxing advanced, there were much less statements about fear (if they appear it is to say I am overcoming it) and more discussion on the acquisition of technique:

> I love it. I feel very comfortable. I'm looser when sparring; I do not mind engaging in contact, even though two or three clear punches have impacted my face. (9 February 2005)
>
> Now I see less danger but I see it is very difficult to do the thing right. However, I start to see more lines of attack. I have less reservations when hitting someone, even though always aiming right, knowing what I'm doing. (21 February 2005)
>
> Well done! At the end of the session I have sparred with the trainer and I have moved well, loose, dodging, with good timing. (20 June 2005)

As my habitus was changing I was moving along the path that every participant has to tread. I was able to get a sense of the changing feelings of fear and anxiety, of the changing negotiation of violence, the evolving 'tension balance' as my level of expertise increased and the changes in the expected behaviour when dealing with different participants of lower, equal or higher level than me. As I was acquiring such habitus I was acquiring also a more adjusted sense of the circumstances happening around me in the activities.

Before concluding, it should be remarked that practising two combat disciplines at the same time was both troublesome and insightful. In the first year (2002/2003) I studied just boxing and in the second year (2003/2004) I practised just aikido. But during the third and fourth year (2004/2005; 2005/2006), the research was conducted while alternating in the same period between boxing and aikido practice during the week. Sometimes I suffered a kind of 'habitus short circuit', especially when practising aikido, the less intense activity. Being used to punches, anxiety and pain in boxing often generated a feeling of disdain when practising aikido afterwards. This fact can be acknowledged in my notes of self-observation during the first year of aikido, after having practised boxing the year before:

> I have not got very tired and have doubts about the efficacy of the techniques, even though I believe they can be efficient if applied with energy. Maybe it is because I don't know much about it. The only danger I see is that someone can fall over you or apply the technique wrongly and you get a twisted wrist but I do not fear for my integrity. (1 October 2003)
>
> During a technique against a punch, uke has slightly hit my eyebrow and says 'sorry' and I have thought to myself: 'Holy Mary, if you knew. This is nothing compared to boxing.' (20 February 2004)

This fact is very telling about the concept of 'tension balance' in the acquisition of habitus. My boxing habitus was adapted to a certain tension balance, a certain negotiation between thresholds of violence that was more intense than the aikido habitus that I was exposed to. It took me a while to succeed (and never in a complete manner) in separating both activities, switching my habitus mode depending on what I was practising. Thus, on the one hand my boxing habitus was contaminating my observation of aikido, not treating the practice on its own terms. But, on the other hand, such a comparative framework was elucidating even further the differences in the negotiation of violence, of thresholds, of habitus depending on the activity I was analysing specifically.

Notes

1. For a detailed analysis of the term see Wacquant (2004d).
2. Nonetheless, on some occasions, Elias (1996, 111) uses habitus as in the Bourdieuian manner, as synonymous of world view or cosmovision. On other occasions, Elias (2006) uses the term *ethos* as synonymous of Bourdieu's habitus.
3. In fact, Elias (2001, 182) talked about the *individual habitus* emerging from the *social habitus*.
4. Changes in habitus linked to the emergence of sport were also studied from a figurational standpoint. See Elias and Dunning (1986) for the connection of these changes with the sportization/parliamentarization processes in England.
5. After some time of combining both activities I focused on aikido, currently holding a black belt first dan (*shodan*).
6. On affective and rational violence see Dunning (2011). A more controlled, instrumental, rational violence does not imply always a less harmful type of violence. This is to avoid an idealization of martial arts or combat sports as a school of virtue for human conflict. Even though my research activities responded to a civilizing trend I am aware of the potential decivilizing consequences of martial schools as used for instance in pre–World War II Japanese budo (Sanchez García, 2013).
7. See Sánchez García (2008) for an ethnomethodological reading of the habitus in physical activities.
8. Sport psychologist John Kerr (2005, 148) talks about 'security zone' precisely referring to the area with an adequate tension balance; a pleasurable area to practise the sporting activity.
9. Elias (1986) used the term 'threshold of violence' (in singular) related to the development of sport in the civilizing process.
10. This is also why even under the same name – e.g. boxing – we can find different habitus in different gyms (compare a recreational and a professional boxing gym), depending on the interactions that are being carried out in these settings.

11 A research by Williams and Elliot (1999) on karatekas showed how novices were more sensitive than experts towards increases in the levels of anxiety, performing worse as a result.
12 Compare it with activities centred on a professional career or on very realistic combat training. The latter ones are much more worried at not trespassing the lower threshold, a thing that would indicate a non-realistic training or training with little intensity (non-suitable for a competitor).
13 A basic but paramount technique, literally translated as 'the first one'.
14 In order to preserve anonymity of participants I have used invented names.
15 Uke is the one who receives the technique. Ideally, he or she represents the adversary, the contrary.
16 Semantically differences between 'bujutsu' (linked to efficacy) and 'budo' (self-perfection) are ideally placed and they are not always straightforwardly clear in real language use. In this case, sensei uses the term 'budo' (instead of 'bujutsu', an old term) to refer to 'martial way', expressing the idea of fighting efficacy in aikido.
17 On the power relations within groups between established outsiders see Elias and Scotson (1994).
18 A powerful aikido technique that consists in 'entering' by the side until at the back of the opponent, turning the body and then throwing him.
19 This kind of feeling was encountered on more occasions by those engaged in the negotiation of violence. For example, Sebastián, an aikidoka who I interviewed, commented that he was 'more concerned about hurting others than getting hurt'. Also, see Alex Channon's chapter in this volume, about the gendered issue of hitting and getting hit in mixed groups of practice.
20 The same controversy can be observed in the recent development of mixed martial arts (MMA), adding regulation to the practice in order to avoid public rejection as a consequence of the gore and the guts (Sánchez García and Malcolm 2010).
21 For a joint research technique between observant participation and non-participant observation in a two-people ethnography see Delamont and Stephens's chapter in this volume.

Chapter 12

'AUTHENTICITY', MUAY THAI AND HABITUS

Dale C. Spencer

Introduction

Many authors have commented on the introduction and diffusion of Asian martial arts into the English-speaking cultures and its impact on the philosophical and spiritual elements of martial arts (Chan 2000; Krug 2001; Villamon et al. 2004). Krug (2001) asserts that post–World War II, the cultural appropriation of Okinawan karate and the integration of this martial art into American culture had the effect of removing many of the knowledges and meanings systems of karate and replacing them with American meaning systems. Karate became converted into a sport, free of its original *bunkai* (explanations) of kata and a considerable portion of its esoteric philosophies. Also, the underlying sciences of chi, healing and health-enhancing aspects were removed and replaced with the individualized competitive sport form of karate, more closely aligned with the American ethos (Krug 2001, 403). According to Villamon et al. (2004), judo has undergone a similar translation in its ascendancy into an Olympic sport. Drawing from Anthony Giddens's concept of reflexive modernization, these authors show the disembedding of the philosophic and moral aspects of mutual prosperity integral to traditional forms of judo developed by Jigaro Kano, and a re-embedding of a philosophy of meritocratic individualism central to Western sports. The effect is the conversion of judo as a way of life into an efficiency-based, winner-take-all mentality sport (Villamon et al. 2004, 146). In the main, these authors hold that in the diffusion of Eastern martial arts into the West, there is a disembedding of the philosophical and moral aspects of these martial arts and a re-embedding of a philosophy of meritocratic individualism. Resultant of this process is the cultural appropriation of martial art styles and conversion of them into 'winner-takes-all' combat sports.

At the epicentre of this 'Westernization thesis' is an underlying assumption regarding what judo and karate would be if not for the Westernization of these respective styles. The claim is that there was 'authentic' martial arts that have been ruined or modified in less than desirable ways through the translation of these martial arts for Western consumption. The East is again the object of the processes of Orientalism (see Said 1978). This chapter interrogates the notion of the 'authentic' based on ethnography of muay thai in northern Thailand. I document the ways in which muay thai practitioners, qua tourists from the so-called developed Western world, travel to rural and urban areas of northern Thailand seeking 'authentic' Thai boxing. Drawing on field notes and photographs taken at muay thai events, including the author as an observant participant (see Wacquant 2004a) in a muay thai fight, I document the ways in which Western fighters understand and embody the philosophical and religious aspects of muay thai in the search of the 'authentic' muay thai style and experience. Utilizing Bourdieu's discussion of culture and habitus (see Bourdieu 1984; 1990a; 1990b), I show the interconnections between Thai culture and muay thai. I analyse the spiritual rituals (*ram muay*, *wai kru*, etc.) and training practices associated with muay thai to show the production of a muay thai habitus. Here I delve into how the 'authentic' muay thai habitus as embodied and experienced serves as a goal of 'Western' practitioners; that is, an axiom that is strived for. The muay thai habitus is the site of Thai nationalism, defined against the West. Lastly, habitus is the site of emergence, where bodies challenge conceptions of what a muay thai body should be.

Cultural sociology is wrapped up with bringing the social unconscious into view. That is, to reveal to women and men the myths they believe in, so that they can in turn make new myths (Alexander 2003). Muay thai is Thailand's national sport and serves as a prime, albeit contradictory, signifier of Thai culture. Here I engage with the myths surrounding muay thai and what it means to be a muay thai practitioner, but with the tools that are afforded through carnal sociology (see Crossley 1995; Wacquant 2005a). Carnal sociology is concerned with the active role of the body in social life; that is, what the body does, and it stresses and 'examines the necessarily embodied bases of the praxical-symbolic constituents of social formations' (Crossley 1995, 43). Here I connect what the performing body actually does and the body that produces it, with aspects of representation such as symbolism that emerges from these performances (cf. Brown, Jennings and Leledaki 2008). I utilize habitus both as a topic and as a tool (see Wacquant, this volume) for understanding the embodiment of muay thai habitus and challenging existing notions of 'authenticity' and Westernization. I contend that 'authentic' muay thai is a fluid object continually changing and modifying through the collision of different cultures and bodies taking up the sport.

In this chapter I triangulate data gathered on a two-month sojourn to the town of San Kampang in north Thailand to train in muay thai; data gathered on a four-year ethnography of mixed martial arts (MMA), of which muay thai training was one part of the observant participation; and, lastly, muay thai films produced in Thailand. While in previous work emerging from this project (see Spencer 2009, 2011) I have been somewhat critical of Bourdieu's work, here I embrace Bourdieu for his discussion of culture and habitus. I have always conceded that I think with and against the work of Pierre Bourdieu; here I approach muay thai with him.

This chapter is structured in three main sections. In the first section I offer a brief discussion of Pierre Bourdieu's explication of the relationship between culture and habitus. In the subsequent section I offer a brief commentary on Thai culture and the notion of 'authentic Thai-ness'. In the third section, I explicate the combat sport of muay thai. In this section I reflect on my embodied experience of muay thai and observations made over the course of my sojourn to northern Thailand to train in a muay thai club, and reflect on the notion of body qua habitus as a site of 'authenticity'. I also analyse the case of the 'Beautiful Boxer' Parinya Charoenphol, a habitus that challenges the notion of a static, 'authentic' muay thai.

Culture and Habitus

Pierre Bourdieu razes the distinction between 'Culture' (high culture) and 'culture', treating the distinction between the two as arbitrary and as a manifestation of class relations.[1] Bourdieu is interested in struggles and competition over status (see Bourdieu 1984, 1990a). Here status can be viewed as synonymous with lifestyle. It is the sum total of cultural practices including dress, speech, perception and bodily dispositions. Status confers political entitlement and legal status for Bourdieu, but it also involves style (see Turner 1988). He was continuously fixated on the struggles for recognition as a fundamental dimension of social life (Bourdieu 1990a).

Bourdieu also connected his thinking on culture and practices to consumption. Consumption, here, is a process whereby agents engage in appropriation and appreciation, whether for utilitarian, expressive or contemplative purposes, of goods, services, performances, information or ambience, whether purchased or not, over which the agent has some degree of discretion. Furthermore, in this view, consumption is not itself a practice but is, rather, a moment in almost every practice (Warde 2005). Bourdieu's (1984) concern was with the internal differentiation of practices, focused on their social classification, the processes of access and assimilation to them, and the external rewards going to different positions in fields.

Bourdieu (1984) presents a tripartite, or three-zone, model of cultural tastes, consisting of 'legitimate tastes', 'middlebrow taste' and 'popular taste'. These tastes and preferences coincide with education level and class. Bourdieu (1984, 56) states that 'like any sort of taste, it unites and separates'. The working-class aesthetic is a dominated aesthetic, incessantly defining itself in relation to the dominant aesthetic. While the working class possesses limited resources (forms of capital) to define itself against the dominant aesthetic, the upper classes possesses all the means to engage in 'playful seriousness' (Bourdieu 1984, 54), possessing an assured place in the world and a sense of distinction. Bourdieu (1984) also connects these aesthetics to particular bodies reflecting dietary and fashion markings of distinction.

For Bourdieu (1984, 309–10), the struggle over status is intricately tied to the habitus:

> The classification struggle that is waged initially within firms, a struggle for supremacy between production and publicity, between engineering and marketing […] and all the similar struggles that are fought out within the dominant fraction of the dominant class, are inseparable from conflicts of values that involve the participant's whole world views and arts of living, because they oppose not only different sectional interests but different scholastic and occupational careers and, through them, different social recruitment areas and therefore ultimate differences in habitus.

The habitus in Bourdieu's (1984, 1990b) schema is a 'structured and structuring structure', made up of a system of schemata generating classifiable practices and works.

The habitus also consists of a system of schemata of perceptions and tastes. The sum-total of these particular elements amounts to a lifestyle, which serves as a system of classifying and classified practices. Habitus and culture, here, always serve as 'an instrument of vision and di-vision, at once a product, a weapon, and a stake of struggles for symbolic life and death – and for this reason it cannot be the means to resolve the running battle for access to recognized social existence that everywhere defines and ranks humanity' (Wacquant 2005b, 21).

In relation to sport, Bourdieu (1978) asserted the importance of understanding sport as a site of struggle over the social definition of a given sport. This is part and parcel of a larger field of struggles over the definition of the legitimate body and the legitimate use of the body. These are struggles which 'in addition to the agents engaged in the struggle over the definition of sporting uses of the body, also involve moralists and especially the clergy, doctors (especially health specialists), educators in the broadest sense (marriage guidance counsellors, etc.), pacemakers in matters of fashion and taste (couturiers, etc.)' (Bourdieu 1978, 827). In the subsequent analysis I use Bourdieu's discussion of culture and habitus to analyse characteristics of Thai culture but also to show the ways in which the muay thai habitus reflects and challenges Thai culture: that is, it is a primary site of struggle. I show how muay thai as a cultural product reinforces Thai nationalism and serves as one way in which notions regarding the West are constituted. I use the concept of habitus as a tool for understanding 'the authentic' muay thai experience and the manifold meanings attached to being a muay thai fighter and possessing the legitimate muay thai body. I also show how the interaction with the individual habitus and the much broader classifying practices serve as the space for emergence, where an individual habitus can challenge doxa.

'Authentic' Thai Culture

When a 'felang' or 'ferang' (the Thai terms for foreigners) travels throughout Thailand, there is a sense, to the critical eye, that there is a contrived authenticity of what it means to be Thai, or the 'authentic' Thai experience. Segments of the tourism industry operate on the basis of presenting Thai or Thailand as a brand (Jory 1999). This is the selling of Thai products, as quintessentially Thai, in contradistinction to Western products. Since its escape from colonial rule, the Thai state has used culture as a basis of national integration (Reynolds 1991). Military regimes have tied the maintenance of Thai cultural identity to issues of national security (Reynolds 1991; Barme 1993). As such, a cultural bureaucracy – the National Identity Board within the Office of the Prime Minister – was set up to formulate and popularize notions of national identity. In the 1970s and 1980s, the Interior Ministry of the Monarchy's Village Scouts movement engaged in strategic activities of indoctrinating Thai villages with conservative ideologies regarding Thai culture in the struggle against communist insurgency (Bowie 1997). This movement sought to spread the foundations of Thai culture, including monarchy, Buddhism and aristocratic artistic forms.

The monarchy continues to play a key role in the political basis of the Thai nation. As I made my way through Bangkok, Chiang Mai, San Kampang and along the many roads in between, the picture of the king or the king and the queen (Sirikit), are found on billboards almost everywhere. The monarchy's existence is kept alive in and through a complex ideological apparatus that relies on the media and the army to maintain its hegemony. Furthermore, Thais are mandated by law to support national culture. The Constitution contains clauses that state that it is the duty of citizens and the state to support national culture and maintain the arts of the nation.

'Modernizing' Thailand often treats anything 'street' as undeveloped, lowbrow or kitsch (see Cornwel-Smith 2005). Public and official comments tend to gloss over the reality of local lifestyles, especially when they touch on taboos such as sex, gambling or magic. Yet while different classes in the rigid hierarchy socialize in separate worlds, most Thais live in mixed neighbourhoods, and display more tastes in common than they would probably admit (Corwel-Smith 2005).

Individuals of higher rank may also delight in ordinary activities such as markets, street food or soap operas. Even in the case of upper-class Thais, they regularly purchase food from street vendors (see Cornwel-Smith 2005). Nevertheless, society in Thailand is highly hierarchical (see Jory 1999). People in Thailand are aware of their social status, and use their age, skin colour, clothes, jewellery and location to make status judgements. Much like in Western countries, in visiting malls and markets in Chiang Mai I found that brand names bring distinction to the bearer. Handbags (Louis Vuitton, Fendi, Gucci), watches (Rolex) and luxury cars (Mercedes and BMW) are highly prized and are tools for instant distinction. Also, for those who can afford it, bleaching lotions are frequently used to make the skin whiter.

While walking around various Thai streets, both in Chiang Mai and San Kampang, the smell of many different types of food fill the air. Most of this 'street food' is served on a stick or is consumed by using a stick. Food vendors gather at markets day or night serving various types of morsels. In Chiang Mai, the infamous night market is filled with a cornucopia of different types of food appealing to manifold tastes. Some vendors display prepared dishes. Others cook on the spot, whether it is boiled, stir-fried, deep-fried, barbecued, marinated or pounded with a pestle and mortar. Morsels are displayed in glazed cabinets or arrayed in patterns on trays, racks, grills and griddles: every imaginable *khong knob khio* (thing to bite or chew) sits skewered on bamboo. The Thai habitus can be seen as a contrivance of 'Thai-ness'. Due in part to the consumption of morsels, the Thai body is lean. Whereas obesity is one of the most serious threats to public health in Western, late modern societies (see Crossley 2004a; Barness, Opitz and Gilbert-Barness 2007), less than 5 per cent of Thailand's population is obese.

While this only tells part of the story, Thai people view 'fat' Westerners with a level of contempt that is unmistakable. When I first arrived in San Kampang, the muay thai trainers and shop owners in town kept referring to me as '*pompoui*' and pinching the fat on the sides of my waist. I found out later that *pompoui* means fat man in Thai and is the object of ridicule and is often applied to overweight Westerners visiting Thailand. After I lost 12 kg, the title of *pompoui* was no longer applied to me and I noticed that the muay thai trainers applied the title to one of the incoming Western boxers. The other way in which Thais reveal what it means to be Thai, to have a Thai body qua habitus, is through its national sport, muay thai.

Muay Thai, The Science of Eight Limbs

Muay thai is one of Thailand's significant cultural exports. The film *Ong-Bak: The Thai Warrior* (2003) tells the story of a villager trained in the ancient art who travels to big-city Bangkok to retrieve a stolen Buddha head. Displaying the marvels of muay thai, the film shot Thai cinema into international recognition. It became a worldwide hit and achieved a cult following (Hunt 2005), with Tony Jaa exhibiting the flashier side of muay thai while highlighting the use of traditional, authentic Thai boxing.

Muay thai, translated as 'Thai boxing', is the national sport of Thailand. In many ways, muay thai stands in stark contrast to mainstream Thai culture. Specifically, muay thai is in contradistinction to the vision of the gentle, polite and passive Thai. Known as the science of eight limbs, muay thai is a stand-up style that involves the use of punches, elbows, (shin) kicks and knee strikes. Whereas the use of the foot is frowned upon in mainstream Thai culture, in Thai boxing the fighter uses the foot and the shin with great regularity.

Muay thai is what Chinese martial arts would call a 'hard' fighting style, as opposed to the 'soft' styles that cultivate 'internal' power (Rebac 1987). It is the most forceful and aggressive of the Eastern fighting styles (which is why it is favoured as a style in cage fighting), with its distinctive use of knees and elbows (see Spencer 2011).[2] Different from Japanese and Korean kicks that snap out from the knee, muay thai kicks generate power in much the same way as Western boxing, through keeping the leg straight and rotating

Figure 12.1. The head and feet in Thailand.

A sign warning of the 'Do's and Don'ts of Thailand' intended for foreigners in the Wat Phrathat Doi Suthep, a Theravada Buddhist temple in the Chaing Mai province of Thailand. The sign indicates that it is ill mannered to touch the head of another person or to use the foot for pointing. Photo courtesy of the author.

the hips in order to put the whole body's weight behind the kick. Knees, elbows and kicks generate power in this fashion, driving through the body of the opponent, rather than the snap at the point of the target as practised in many forms of karate and kung fu.

As a style of fighting, muay thai's formative period can be traced back 700 years. It was translated into a sport and developed from *muay boran* ('ancient boxing'), a more traditional combat style that also included the use of the head for strikes. Debate continues regarding the relationship between krabi krabong, a Siamese weapon-based art, and muay boran, with one side contending that muay boran was derived from krabi krabong and the other asserting that it developed alongside the weapon system (Moore 2004). Nevertheless, krabi krabong influence can be seen in the practice of the wai kru (see below). While muay boran and muay thai were initially a bare-knuckle style, practitioners of this style bound their forearms and hands with hemp. Myths abound of boxers dipping their hands in glass shards or broken shells to increase the goriness of the fight. The actual prevalence of this practice is not confirmed.

In many ways, muay thai serves as the means by which Thais have seen themselves as an independent nation and in distinction to their Burmese neighbours. One myth in particular forms the basis of the Thais' assertion of muay thai's supremacy over other striking arts. This story dates back to a sixteenth-century manuscript. The Burmese army was fast approaching and was about to invade Siam. The King of Burma, Bayinnaung, agreed to let his son fight the Prince of Siam, Narusun, also known as the Black Prince (see Karter and Mezger 2000). A fight was set up between the two princes and after hours of gruelling fighting, the Black Prince won by killing the king's son. The match stopped the Burmese army from invading Siam. To this day, an annual fight entitled the 'King's Tournament' is held in his memory.

The king has played a pivotal role in the salience and development of muay thai. King Chulalongkorn Rama V (r. 1868–1910) was integral to the increased popularity of the art across Thailand. The country was in a state of peace and muay thai was utilized for physical exercise and self-defence. This period is considered the golden age in muay thai. The king took special interest in the sport and regularly had scouts find fighters and set up matches at his palace. Within this period, training camps were established across Thailand, providing food and shelter to practitioners. Here, the practice of taking on the last name of the camp became commonplace; the fighter is then part of the family of the camp. When I fought in Taepae stadium, I took on the name of my camp.

It was not until King Rama VII (r. 1925–1935) that the official rules of muay thai were codified and the first ring was built at Suan Kalarp, in the Royal Palace. As part of this 'modernization', referees were initiated and the rounds were timed. The use of gloves over hemp rope became the common practice for protecting the hands of fighters. In addition, Lumpinee stadium served as the site of high-profile championship fights and display fights of Thai practitioners against foreign fighters. At this point, muay boran faded into the background as an antiquated style and muay thai ascended and was concretized as the Thai national sport.

Training methods of muay thai are often characterized as esoteric. This includes fighters lifting weights with their teeth to strengthen their necks, and kicking banana trees to condition or callus (Spencer 2009, 2011) their shins. Different from traditional

Figure 12.2. Thai training equipment.

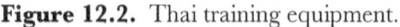

Clockwise from left: Banana heavy bag in Muay Thai camp in San Kampang; Traditional boxing bags in Muay Thai camp in San Kampang; Fourteen-ounce boxing gloves, bag gloves, and Muay Thai pads; Fighter wearing a Mongkol before his fight in the outskirts of Bao Sang Thailand. Photo courtesy of the author.

Western boxing, 'Thai pads' are used to include punches, elbows, kicks and knee strikes in training pad-holding sessions. In addition, while Western boxing utilizes heavy bags that are hung at a height for the purposes of punching, Thai boxing utilizes banana bags that are approximately 6 ft in length and do not rock back and forth as much as the traditional boxing heavy bag.[3]

Fighters adorn the *prajioud* and *mongkol* when they enter the ring. The prajioud are monocoloured or multicoloured armbands worn between the shoulder and the forearm. The mongkol is a headband with tassels on the end. Both of these items are used to ward off evil spirits, a tradition that harkens back to earlier muay styles and is related to the Buddhist culture to which muay thai is embedded. Prajioud and the mongkol both must be blessed by a Buddhist monk prior to usage and a prayer is said upon the practitioner by the coach upon putting on and after the mongkol is removed. Both the mongkol and the prajioud used to be worn during the fight, but the mongkol is no longer worn during the fight. In this same vein, fighters have their bodies tattooed by Buddhist monks to ward off evil spirits.

I have evinced above that Thai culture is characterized by a taste for the morsel and that Thais value a small, fit body. This is coupled with an adherence to Theravada Buddhist practices. As I experienced, northern Thailand is saturated with Buddhist temples. With its emphasis on the hardened body and the centrality of Buddhism, the muay thai habitus reflects the spirit of Thai culture. While muay thai serves as a mainstay of entertainment for Thai people in urban and rural areas, it concomitantly serves as a reflection of national pride and buttresses the position of the king and Buddhism in Thai culture. In the next sections, I will discuss how, in the translation of Western practitioners into a muay thai habitus, there is a transmogrification of the Westerner signified in his or her body but also in the way in which one views muay thai.

Ritual, Habitus and Becoming a Muay Thai Fighter

Ritual theory establishes ritual as a site of performance that enacts and manifests meaning for a system of symbols (Bell 1992, 32). A structured ritual is a means of reaffirmation, preservation and seeks to express a series of sacred logics (de Coppet 1992). Durkheim's (1961) claim is that religious rituals are an organized attempt to bring together the known and the unknown in a shared system of beliefs and practices. Ritual is contingent on social spaces, because it contains practices that can be transformed or modified in a way that posits the ritual as 'flexible and continuous' (Rappaport 1999, 271). It should be noted that ritual does something to practitioners and concomitantly agents are capable of doing something to the ritual. The ritual is determined by the social relationships of the individuals who are performing it and relies on the relationships between these individuals to make it what it is.

My impression of muay thai prior to my training trip to San Kampang was limited to the customary muay thai training regimes that are found in most martial arts clubs. That is, the sessions begin with the customary ritual of bowing in (hands pressed together in front of one's chest as you bow) with a '*Sa-wat-dee-Kraup*' (hello) and bowing out with '*khob-kun-Krub*' (thank you). The training session also takes on a rather structured character beginning with a warm-up, then an instruction of three or four techniques and then a summation with either plumb work (clinch work) or sparring for three or four 3-minute rounds. This usually takes about an hour.

In Thailand it is customary to train twice a day, once in the morning before the sun comes up and one more, longer session as the sun goes down. The morning session was approximately two hours long beginning at 7 a.m. and finishing at 9 a.m. and the evening session was three hours in length, beginning at 4 p.m. and ending at 7 p.m. Both sessions began with a 5 km run in the local area, past fields and through residential areas. Skipping for two or three rounds then follows this segment. Then the fighters would all line up in front of a bag and practise technique until they were called up to do techniques with the trainers on the pads. The last formal element of the training session was plumb work amongst the fighters in the ring. In itself, this format of muay thai training can be considered as merely an intensification of the kind of training that takes place across North American muay thai schools.

While many of the Thai fighters would do sit-ups and stretch after training sessions, many of the ferangs would opt for learning the *wai kru ram muay*, the ritual dance.[4] This is a ritual that is not practised or learned in many Western schools. The wai kru (for short)

Figure 12.3. The daily ritual of eating after the evening training session.

Photo courtesy of the author.

in style signifies the respective club that the fighter emanates from; that is, each school has their own style of wai kru that they practise. It takes place at the beginning of the match, prior to squaring off with one's opponent and is an offering to a fighter's trainers, and serves as a symbol of respect. This is the seen and known element of the ritual. The unknown element is magical, which is intended to ward off evil spirits. This is one of the experiences of the 'authentic'. When the ferangs in the camp I trained took up the wai kru, each habitus intersected with the dance in particular ways. One of the trainers, Kru Doe, would chuckle as he taught us the dance, with some of us (including myself) performing the movements in a robotic fashion. He would continuously urge us to relax, saying '*Sabai Sabai*'[5] as we made our way around the ring and dipped into the almost bird-like poses. *Sabai Sabai* is a call to relax, to flow through movements and to embrace the aesthetics of the dance.

The 'authentic' muay thai experience can also be found in a more mundane form, an often overlooked part of accounts of the sport. Here I am referring to the communal meal after every training session. After every training session, the cook would bring out rice and a local Thai dish (most of which were very spicy) and fighters would scurry to get the utensils and mat in place for the meal. In line with Simmel's (1997) assertion regarding the importance of the meal, this ritual serves as the basis of group cohesion. This ritualistic practice also serves to neutralize tensions that arise over the course of sparring and clinch work (cf. Collins 2004, 2008).

Authenticity, Beauty and Muay Thai

While in Chiang Mai, I was approached by the owner of a local muay thai gym, asking if I wanted to train traditional 'authentic' muay thai, implying that the club I was training at in San Kampang was not quite 'authentic' enough. Another gym out of Chiang Mai – Lanna muay thai – advertises the Lanna Doi Modt Hill camp, which takes place on the eastern face of Doi Modt (ant mountain). This camp promises the experience of traditional Thai boxing training, matched with the experience of training in the remote mountainside without the vanities of electricity and the distractions of the city.

Lanna muay thai taps into one motivation (amongst many) of Western fighters sojourning in Thailand: the quest for authentic Thai boxing, the way in which it was practised prior to its conversion into an international product, consumed on the big screen and practised in McDojo's (see Spencer 2011).[6] In relation to the big screen, *Kickboxer* (1989), starring Jean-Claude Van Damme, did much to distort Western visions of muay thai. The film featured the brutal Thai adversary Tong Po paralyzing an American kickboxing champion.[7]

Many of these Western accounts of muay thai are undergirded by racial and masculine notions that emphasize the smaller size of Thai men and their extreme power (see Hunt 2005). What I found in the course of my trip to Thailand was a constant assertion by Thai fighters that authentic muay thai is full of grace and beauty. This assertion was coupled with a dismissal of muay thai as pure brutality. The following field note illustrates one such assertion:

> We are standing around the stone picnic tables waiting in line for water. The sun is going down so it is starting to get a little cooler. Sweat is dropping off my body and I am exhausted. It is my turn to do 5 rounds on the pads with Kru Phon. I get some water from the cooler and sip it down quickly before the bell rings for the next round. I jog over to the ring pulling on my gloves. I step on to the side of the ring with both feet and weave my legs and body through the ropes. I step in front of Kru Phon and bow to him as the bell rings. He puts up his right arm, I drive my jab into the pad. Just as it hits he transitions to placing the pads in front of his ribs on the left side; I adjust my weight transferring over into a kick to the pads. This rhythm and movement keeps going for another two minutes, jab-kick, jab-kick. I am starting to feel the burn in my lungs. It is just the first round, geeze. Kru Phon then transitions to just having me throwing kicks. Left kick–right kick, left kick–right kick. I am lumbering about the ring and breathing heavy. I am flat footed. The bell rings and not a second too soon. I bend over and I am resting on the turnbuckle in the corner of the ring. Kru Phon walks over to me and says 'you need balana' [he means balance], I turn to look over at him. He is bouncing on his toes. He is a man in his mid- to late 30s but he is graceful and exact in his movements as he pirouettes

his way around the ring throwing kicks with ease and finesse. He adds 'muay thai is beau-ti-ful'. I continue to watch him as he throws head-level kicks, covering the distance of the ring with his footwork. It is a dance to him. (Field notes, May 2008)

When I arrived in Thailand, I was of the impression that what I would be learning is the 'deadly art' of muay thai. What I was exposed to is the beauty of the art. Kru Phon was a former Lumpinee boxing stadium champion (one of the top muay thai stadiums in Bangkok) and at one point was considered one of, if not the, top fighters in Thailand. Now he spends his time training and managing fighters in a relatively remote camp in northern Thailand. Oddly, unlike some of the other trainers in the camp, his body did not bear the typical signs of wear and tear associated with a fighter with 200 fights to his credit. He lacks the scars across his face and the brow of his head. He does not limp, moves gracefully, and when he is bare-chested, he looks like a muscular fighter twenty years his junior. Kru Phon's body tells the story; nothing he says will fully convey his story. Throughout my time in Thailand training, he tried to continually correct my movement and footwork, placing less emphasis on the Thai plumb (clinch). Evading and striking rather than engaging and striking. Prior to visiting Thailand, I had very Western visions of muay thai, of its brutality, and thought that my time would be spent learning to hit pads and bags as hard as I can. In this rural camp, my technique and balance became the prime focus, as the trainers were vigilant in their correction. Muay thai practice, here, is oriented towards the production of not only an ostensibly 'beautiful' body (svelte and muscular) but also a body that moves with nimbleness.

Nationalism, Bodies and Muay Thai

Beyond the assertion of the beauty of Thai boxing, both fighters and trainers and the common Thai assert that muay thai is their national sport and is used as a source of national pride. Undergirding films such as the aforementioned *Ong-Bak* (2003), *Tom Yum Goong* (2005)[8] and *Chaiya* (2007)[9] is the counter position of Thai fighters and muay thai to foreign fighters and other standing fighting styles – capoeira, kung fu and street fighting, respectively. This form of nationalism is replicated at the local level, as in Chiang Mai and in the rural areas of northern Thailand that I visited, where fight promoters pitted foreign and Thai fighters against each other in the main events. This was the case when I fought in Taepae stadium, as it was taken as self-evident that I would fight a Thai fighter (rather than another ferang). This cultural disposition is matched by a conceptualization of ferang fighters as giants who lack the technical habitus of the Thai fighter. This is particularly evident in *Somtum* (or *Muay Thai Giant*) (2008), the story of a large Australian named Barney who gets his passport stolen and is left penniless in Pattaya, Thailand. After being bullied by the local Thai men, he is taken in by two young Thai girls, who learn that when they give Barney som tam, a spicy Thai soup, he turns into a raging hulk. Barney is taught muay thai and then the girls and Barney use this reaction in the ring, where Barney is an unstoppable force. What is particular about this movie – the admixture of Thai food, muay thai and a Westerner – is that Thai food has the effect of vitalizing the otherwise tractable Westerner. The occident is signified as passive.

After living for a short period of time in Thailand, ferangs are all too aware of this Thai perception of foreigners. In some cases, ferang fighters wilfully embody this stereotype. While I was at a fight event in a rural area near Bao Sang, a rather large French fighter was pitted against a considerably smaller Thai fighter out of a popular muay thai gym in Chiang Mai.[10] The difference in size was unmistakable. Following an all-too-familiar narrative, the French fighter was less technical and much slower than the Thai fighter and the Thai fighter won a decisive victory over his 'giant' adversary.

A 'Beautiful' Boxer

One of the most internationally renowned Thai martial arts films that has not been mentioned so far is *Beautiful Boxer* (2004). It is the story of *khathoey* (transgender) muay thai fighter Nong Tum (aka Parinya Charoenphol) and her experiences in the world of muay thai boxing. In Thailand, khathoey signifies a male-to-male transgender person or effeminate gay male (Costa and Matzner 2007). Another related signifier is *phet thi sam*, which loosely translates as the third gender. The term khathoey generally means ladyboy and is said to have Khmer origins (Jackson 1999). I was made aware of Nong Tum the first day I arrived at the muay thai gym in San Kampang, where a film poster of *Beautiful Boxer* hung in the gym. The gym owner informed me that some of the trainers had trained the actor, Asanee Suwan, for his role as Nong Tum.

Nong Tum started boxing for self-defence, upon facing continuous ridicule and violence at the hands of bullies for being different. When Tum found that she was gifted at muay thai and that she could make a living out of the sport, she eventually used her earnings for a sex-change operation.[11] Nong Tum habitus in many ways signifies Thai culture, as she inhabits Thailand's third gender and possesses a proficient muay thai habitus. This mixture has brought her national and international media attention. She is an adept fighter who defeated ferang fighters (namely, Craig O'Flynn, a high-calibre Irish muay thai fighter), serving the nationalism that pervades so much of Thai culture. On the other hand, her habitus, while a product of her culture, challenges the notion of the 'authentic' muay thai fighter. While women have historically and generally been excluded and thereby erased from the reserved space of the muay thai contest (cf. Wacquant 2005), Nong Tum breaks through and challenges the very basis of this exclusion. She shows the fluidity of what the authentic is and could be. She reveals the authentic for what it is, a fluid object, open to endless resignifcations.

Conclusion

At the epicentre of the preceding analysis is, in Bourdieuian fashion, a questioning of the relationship between the aesthetic and the authentic; that is, the doxic acceptance of the reality of the 'authentic' muay thai experience. Beauty and authenticity is not just a matter of perspective but rather is enacted through various practices that work to signify and resignify what is muay thai. In this way, martial arts and combat sports should not be seen as static entities. Rather, martial arts and combat sports should be seen as fluid objects having their own developments that are the product of the bodies that take up these practices.

Focus on the concept of habitus as a tool and topic can move us closer to sensing the changes that occur at the micro-level and continually show us that agents are not merely the receptacles of forces beyond their control. They are, alongside the cultures to which they are embedded, continuously agents of change that modify and challenge doxa. In this chapter, I have shown how the habitus of Thai fighters challenges Western notions of muay thai and, in and through the immersion in the sport, notions regarding the sport are reformed anew. Thai nationalism is infused in muay thai and serves as the basis to push back against processes of Westernization.

Across Western media sources, elite-level, South African middle-distance runner Caster Semenya was the subject of considerable attention after it was found that she was born a hermaphrodite. This was another citation of how the Occident finds it difficult to deal with gender difference. Variations from the norm serve as fundamental challenges to the heterosexual matrix (see Butler 1990, 1993). As discussed, Thai history is filled with the figure of the khathoey, a third gender, and the case of Nong Tum challenges both Western and Thai conceptions of gender and combat sports. The focus on the habitus of Tum allows for a consideration of emergence that challenges doxa of authentic muay thai on another scale.

Notes

1 Bourdieu (1984) takes aim precisely at Immanuel Kant. The basis of this critique is beyond the scope of this chapter. In *Distinction* one can see how Bourdieu utilizes his technical corpus as a martial art, dismantling any grounds for the 'innate' nature of taste and by extension, the arbitrary basis of social distinctions. This is, in my humble view, the greatest gift of Bourdieu's legacy.
2 Western boxing and muay thai remain the two dominant stand-up styles.
3 Muay thai practitioners also utilize traditional heavy bags.
4 Thai fighters learn the wai kru as part of their livelihood.
5 *Sabai Sabai* also means that everything is relaxed and as it should be.
6 A McDojo is a school that teaches adulterated or ineffective martial art techniques and packages their programmes in the sole pursuit of making money.
7 Tong Po was played by Michel Qissi, a Moroccan-born actor.
8 *Tom Yum Goong* is a film that features Tony Jaa (the same actor that is in *On-Bak*) travelling to Australia to recover poached war elephants from a Vietnamese restaurant owner and gangster.
9 *Chaiya* or *Muay Thai Chaiya* is the story of brothers' muay thai pursuits, which ends with one of the brothers fighting a fierce 'ferang' fighter, Diamond Sullivan. Po is victorious over Diamond after being knocked down by the foreign fighter.
10 Oddly enough, my Thai opponent was 2 lb heavier than me when we squared off.
11 I am using 'she', recognizing the limits of the English language to convey people of an alternative sex or gender.

Chapter 13

CONCLUSION: PRESENT AND FUTURE LINES OF RESEARCH

Raúl Sánchez García and Dale C. Spencer

The many and divergent ways in which *Fighting Scholars* has engaged with the concept of habitus provides a solid ground to develop further research. In this concluding chapter, we first deal with the boundaries or possible limitations of the volume. Afterwards, we advance some present and future lines of research in order to encourage further research and debate regarding habitus within the field of ethnographic research on martial arts and combat sports.

Dealing with the boundaries or possible limitations of the volume we must state that while there is not a common discipline shared amongst the contributors, we believe that one of the main strengths of the volume is its interdisciplinary orientation. We concede that the by-product of this is that there is not a common lexicon that all the contributors share. The contributors offer different ways to approach habitus and ethnography that is initially proposed by Wacquant. However, the emphasis on habitus and ethnography closes the gap between the various disciplines. Other possible limitation is that all of them are committed to studying martial arts and combat sports through qualitative research. Nonetheless, this is so for epistemological reasons. One main reason lies in the fact that the Archimedean point that is proffered through quantitative approaches fails to afford the flesh-and-blood experience of martial arts and combat sports that is allowed through qualitative research (specifically through ethnography) and that is the key essence of a carnal sociology.

Continuing with the present and future lines of research, we engage with two main lines where, we believe, debate can be generated. First, debate can take place around the strengths and limitations of the concept of habitus from two different traditions of social analysis, specifically phenomenology and ethnomethodology. Second, a line of interdisciplinary debate can take place between the social and cognitive sciences, guided by neuroanthropology and the enactive paradigm.

Habitus Within Martial Arts and Combat Sports

Bourdieu's habitus has received considerable attention in the social sciences and both praises and critiques abound. This controversial concept and its relation to field and capital has been pivotal in the building of what he dubbed 'structuralist constructivism'. Bourdieu's proposal represents one of the 'big theories' that has promised a solution to the old macro–micro debate, generating bridges with the middle range or meso analysis. In critiques of his work, several claims have been lodged against Bourdieu's habitus. First, his version of habitus is seen as incompatible with the strategically rational choice accorded to his agents. Second, his habitus is viewed as overly deterministic, serving as a kind of microstructure within the individual. Third, Bourdieu's habitus is accused of being enmeshed and substituting the actual agent, neglecting the generative role of action and the part played by reflexivity in people's actions (see Jenkins 1982).

Wacquant's use of the concept of Bourdieu's version of habitus in his ethnography of boxing has been extensively discussed within the present volume, and in special issues of *Qualitative Sociology* (2005) and *Theory & Psychology* (2009). All of these collections are devoted to the epistemological and methodological issues generated by Wacquant's ethnographic work. Here, we present two alternative conceptualizations of the habitus that can enhance this concept in the ethnographic study of martial arts and combat sports. First, we explore the phenomenological concept of habitus offered by Nick Crossley and his concept 'reflexive body techniques' and then an ethnomethodological reading of habitus.

In the phenomenological tradition, habitus is a lived-through structure-in-process, continuously developing as an effect of the interactions of agent or group with others and their physical environment. In this tradition, it is the product of the power and pre-reflective tendency of the body–subject to habituate and, as such, maintain structures of comportment *and* experience that has proven valuable or useful (Merleau-Ponty [1962] 2002; Crossley 2001a, 39–40; Ostrow 1990). Habitus varies across groups, cultures and societies, reflecting the accordant membership (Durkheim [1913] 1995). They materialize into techniques that are the work of 'collective and individual practical reason rather than, in the ordinary way, merely the soul and its repetitive faculties' (Mauss [1934] 1973, 73). These corporeal schemata are *body techniques* (Mauss [1934] 1973) that are learned in and through imitation and repetition passed down through tradition.

Perhaps the most developed utilization of the concept of body techniques is in the work of Crossley (2004a, 2004c, 2005). Crossley (2005, 9) defines reflexive body techniques (RBTs) as '*those body techniques whose primary purpose is to work back upon the body, so as to modify, maintain or thematize it in some way*' (original emphasis). RBTs may involve more than one embodied agent where the body is worked on by another or by a team of embodied agents. RBTs are both techniques *of* the body and *for* the body. In the former sense, they are those techniques that are performed by the body and involving a type of knowledge and comprehension that consists completely in embodied competence, below the threshold of language and consciousness. In the latter sense, RBTs are techniques that transform and sustain the body in specific ways (Crossley 2004a; 2005, 10). RBTs are organized in ensembles, that is, they are collections of body techniques that are practised together for a common purpose or goal. They are purposive in the sense that RBTs can be transmogrified for varying reasons (Crossley 2005).

While Crossley refers to the relationship between martial arts and RBTs, he does not offer a sustained analysis of habitus and the ways in which people use RBTs to create martial bodies. This type of analysis can be found in the work of Dale Spencer (2009, 2011). Drawing on a phenomenological conception of habitus, Spencer explores how mixed martial arts fighters engage in 'body callusing' through the use of reflexive body techniques thereby allowing them to withstand the rigours of the sport. Used in this context, the phenomenological conception of habitus as a lived-through-structure in process, along with the concept of reflexive body techniques, allows for an understanding of moments of emergence at the individual and group level of novel practices as the human organism adapts to new situations that inevitably arise in martial arts and combat sports. The reflexive element that is built into this conception of habitus moves towards an understanding of the sometimes small differences in the habitus of each singularity, which often goes unnoticed in Bourdieu's approach to habitus.

Bourdieu's habitus has received several critiques about the diminished role of agency in social subjects. If considered as a kind of 'ministructure' inside the agent, it reproduces the social conditions of its production in every choice the agent may choose. Social change might be seen as compromised by this closed and circular social process. How could this sense of agency be expanded without having to discard the concept of habitus altogether? The contention put forth here is an ethnomethodological reading of habitus. (see Sánchez García 2008a; Wilson 2009).

Bourdieu's habitus *sociologizes* the 'natural attitude' of phenomenology, an attitude by which we find a world at hand in an unproblematic way. According to Bourdieu, the habitus acts as an internal operator that put in relation specific social conditions with specific kinds of natural attitudes, practical senses of acting and being in the world. Nonetheless, an ethnomethodological reading of the habitus precludes 'something inside the subject', dismissing some kind of inner personal belonging embedded in our bodies and brains.[1] Ethnomethodology helps to collapse the concepts of habitus and natural attitude by avoiding the strict separation between the personal and the social, always defining the habitus in social interactions, and related to 'what is a normal pattern of activity' in a given situation. An ethnomethodological approach shows that what is 'normal' is a legitimate natural attitude in a given situation and is inherently a political element of intersubjective social reality. That is why even when there is no gap between habitus and 'natural attitude', we cannot forget that there are different habitus that are socially acquired, not universally given. In addition, this is why some people feel at ease in certain situations – there is a match between habitus or natural attitude and what is normal in the social situation – and others just feel out of place, their habitus clashing with the normal, expected ways of behaving in this social situation.

The second advantage of an ethnomethodological reading of habitus is the introduction of a greater degree of dynamism. As habitus is acquired in dynamic social interactions, this practical sense of what is normal in a given situation is acquired/refined/re-elaborated along different circumstances, giving birth to specific 'personal styles'. Nonetheless, this is not to say that agents can personally change it for as long and as much as they desire. Social interactions have strong routinized (habitual) ways that put limits on continuous improvisation and change of the social pattern that would end up destroying any kind of communication between agents. An application of this approach to the field of martial arts and combat sports can be found in the contribution of Chapter 11, where Raúl Sánchez García examines the dynamic acquisition of a practical sense of violence (as part of the habitus) within boxing and aikido. Observed from a praxeological stance, the acquisition of different habitus of martial arts and combat sports (a boxing habitus, a capoeira habitus, a kyudo habitus, etc.) implies different embodied backgrounds that generates different ways of acting and behaving when confronted with supposed 'same stimulus' (e.g. a punch or a front kick). This is to say, an action of an opponent does not reach a passive subject but a subject already used to specific normal ways of dealing with these actions, something that they have acquired thorough several training interactions with partners.

A word of caution is called for here. As Wacquant's epilogue 'Homines in Extremis' reminds us, a distortion of the concept of habitus is likely when one loses sight, first of the varied internal constitution of habitus and, second, of the equally wide-ranging yet ever present relation between dispositions and positions. Thus, both further elaborations of habitus proposed by RBT and ethnomethodological readings should beware not to fall prey to the seductions of what Wacquant calls the 'enigmatic category of agency' to capture the dynamism of habitus (see the Epilogue to this volume, 192). In other words, dynamism is built into the very constitution of habitus as well as affected by its diverse, power-laden relation to the structures of social world in which it is plunged. Similarly, an overly narrow focus on the "interaction order" of the encounters of agents can make us lose sight of the struggles within the social fields that constrain the possibilities of such interaction orders.[2]

Habitus Meets the Cognitive Sciences

> An effective bodymind is hyperconscious, rather than unconscious. Developing this extrasensitive somatic consciousness is evidence of a growing martial identity. (Samudra 2008, 678n5)

In short order, Jaida Kim Samudra's statement highlights the potential pitfalls of using the Bourdieuian version of habitus as a kind of unconscious mechanism of agency when studying bodily practices such as martial arts and combat sports. By identifying consciousness with discourse, the 'practical sense' attached to the habitus must be of a non-conscious nature. Again, as Samudra reminds us in relation to martial arts: 'Those involved in kinaesthetic practices discover, instead, that one can be a fully conscious actor in the body without necessarily encoding the meaning of one's actions in words' (Samudra 2008, 666). In order to tackle the conscious versus unconscious debate around habitus in martial arts and combat sports, we consider it particularly fecund to establish a dialogue between social and cognitive sciences.

The interdisciplinary debate between social and cognitive sciences is one of the most promising lines of research in martial arts and combat sports. Skill acquisition in physical activities and sport has received a strong interest from sciences such as physiology, biomechanics and psychology. Other disciplines such as sociology or anthropology have given only sporadic attention to skill acquisition. Nevertheless, within these fields, two promising attempts have emerged to analyse skill acquisition in relation to martial arts and combat sports. Here we are referring to the relatively recent emergence of neuroanthropology and the enactive paradigm.

CONCLUSION

Greg Downey's 'neuroanthropology' (Downey 2010) presents an attempt to put cognitive sciences in conversation with the social sciences in relation to martial arts and combat sports. In his seminal research on capoeira (Downey 2005a), he was already influenced by an interdisciplinary approach.[3] From the ecological psychology of J. J. Gibson (1979) to Tim Ingold's (2000) anthropological analysis of skill acquisition and perception, Downey's research on capoeira tries to deal with the issue of how cultural patterns of training and behaviour may influence the structure of the body/brain of the participants. In a subsequent study on the special kind of handstand used in capoeira, the *bananeira* (Downey 2005b), he analyses how diverse forms of physical education form their participants' skills, perceptual abilities and physiological adaptations that distinguish them from practitioners of other activities. Elsewhere, he analyses the changes in visual perception (for example, a more refined 'sideways glance') due to the learning process of capoeira, suggesting that the participant acquires the specific 'sensorimotor knowing' as he or she progresses in the activity (Downey 2007b). He also analyses the role of imitation in the skill acquisition of capoeira (Downey 2008). Imitation must be considered not only as a psychological activity, but also as a social interactional relationship that has neural and perceptual consequences. The 'scaffolding technique' exemplifies a progressive pedagogy. It evolves from adapted exercises that restrict participants' degrees of freedom and perceptual uncertainty towards more complex and realistic movements. More recently, Downey has expanded his range of inquiry to other disciplines such as no-holds-barred fighting, aquatic sports, foraging, gymnastics and circus, and extreme endurance sports, showing the plasticity of the human nervous system and the ability to guide the development of our own bodies and those of others. Interesting as the proposal may be, nonetheless 'neuroanthropology' would need some key concepts in order to anchor the interdisciplinary debate in solid ground. We saw already (see Introduction) how Downey discarded altogether the possible use of the *habitus* as a tool of inquiry. However, we suggest that the enactive paradigm can act as a response to Downey's misgivings regarding the habitus and, as a guiding concept, habitus remains a solid ground to anchor debates across disciplinary boundaries.

The enactive paradigm is principally due to the path-breaking work of Francisco Varela.[4] Heavily influenced by the phenomenology of Maurice Merleau-Ponty, Varela was a biologist studying brain processes and interested in the relation between life and cognition. His entire research programme is characterized by the abandonment of the presuppositions of cognitivism, emergentism and a distancing from the ecological paradigm. His already classic work *The Embodied Mind* (Varela, Thomson and Rosch 1991) outlined the principal tenets of the enactive paradigm, where he argues that cognition is indissolubly linked to life and it is unfolded as the subject dynamically couples with the environment (physical and social). The subjects bring forward (enacts) a world from a background as he or she acts upon their surroundings. There is no 'external world out there' independently of the subject-knower. Varela criticizes approaches that are based on the image of a 'knowing mind' that apprehends an outer world. For Varela, the whole subject is embodied (mind as well) and cognition unfolds in this embodied sensorimotor coupling with the environment, a continuous process that constitutes life.

The question then is: how can the habitus be embedded into the enactive approach, allowing a fruitful debate between the social sciences and cognitive sciences? We suggest that this could be achieved by conceiving habitus as a kind of 'embodied background'. Looking back to the previous section, we had proposed an ethnomethodological reading of the habitus that precluded the possibility of 'something inside the subject', some kind of inner person embedded in our bodies and brains. There is no sense to talk about habitus unless the subject is interacting with the physical and social surroundings. Thus, from the enactive view, the habitus is precisely the natural, normal, unproblematic way of coupling between subject and the physical–social environment. The habitus constitutes the 'embodied background', the natural way of being in these surroundings, the normal pattern of activity from which a world and a subject co-emerges in this specific interaction.[5]

In relation to martial arts and combat sport, what does it mean when we say that a boxer has acquired a 'boxing habitus'? No more and no less than when this subject goes into the ring or is training or doing sparring he unfolds in his activity with the environment a recognizable 'world of boxing' and 'figure of a boxer'. World and subject co-emerge in the action from an embodied background qua boxing habitus. None of the fights and none of the sparring sessions seem exactly the same, insofar as we perceive slightly different actions each time. However, the boxing habitus constitutes the embodied background from which these specific actions emerge. This is to say that the habitus is not something static, but malleable. Precisely the process of learning the craft, of practising and exercising within the intersubjective activity of boxing, helps to acquire and refine the habitus. The boxer acquires a more sensitized attunement in the natural coupling with the world of boxing. There is a double direction of influence between habitus and praxis and it is in this dynamic that a boxer and their world of boxing (their personal style) co-emerge progressively. Some enactive-based research in martial arts has been conducted so far in the work of Sánchez García (2011) in aikido and Sánchez García and González (2013) in judo. Nonetheless, a lot of work has still to be done, expanding the research to several different disciplines in order to compare and find general and specific traits of the different martial arts' and combat sports' habituses.

Notes

1 Precisely, this kind of essentialist view of 'a thing inside a subject' has been subjected to a strong critique from dynamic system theory, which always takes into account the tight coupling of subject and environment through an activity. As Thelen and Smith state: 'The core assumption here is that knowledge or abilities are stored "things" that are timeless and exist outside their here-and-now performance. An experimental task is good only as it reflects a "true" reading of the underlying mental structure. This common viewpoint has run into serious difficulties, however, both empirically and theoretically. First, literally thousands of studies have demonstrated that children's knowledge or their ability to use certain procedures is extremely fluid and highly dependent on the entire context of the experimental situation, including the place of the experiment, the instructions and clues, their motivation and attention, and very subtle variations in the task.' (2006, 278)
2 See Sánchez García (2008b) for an analysis of the dynamic constitution of habitus without losing sight of social fields. This paper proposes an empirical analysis of the trajectory in the positions and habituses of some practitioners within the field of combat sports in Spain. The main argument is that even though they habituses and positions are not static, the changes are not random. Such dynamic trajectories are understood by putting them in relation with the

primary habituses formed in the social space previously to the entrance of the participants into the field of combat sports.
3 Downey's research on 'neuroanthropology' can be traced on the website http://blogs.plos.org/neuroanthropology/ where he collaborates with Daniel Lende, and associate professor in anthropology at the University of South Florida, who trained in medical, psychological and biological anthropology. Downey recalls how the year-long faculty seminar on 'embodiment' conducted by Anne Fausto-Sterling at Brown University during 2002–2003 was crucial to open the possibility of a hybrid discipline such as 'neuroanthropology'.
4 For an excellent introduction to the enactive paradigm see John Stewart, Oliver Gapenne and Ezequiel A. Di Paolo (eds) 2010.
5 The same kind of caution already mentioned before about alternative readings of habitus from ethnomethodology and reflexive body techniques applies here: a too narrow focus on the interaction order to analyse the acquisition of habitus (habitual couplings with the environment) could make us lose sight of the power relations established in the social fields.

Epilogue

HOMINES IN EXTREMIS: WHAT FIGHTING SCHOLARS TEACH US ABOUT HABITUS

Loïc Wacquant

The function of habitus is, precisely, to restore to the agent a generative and unifying power, a constructive and classifying potency, while at the same time reminding us that this capacity to construct social reality, itself socially constructed, is not that of a transcendental subject but that of a socialized body, which engages in practice organizing principles that are socially constructed and acquired in the course of a social experience at once situated and dated.

—Pierre Bourdieu, *Pascalian Meditations*[1]

I am gratified that *Body and Soul* served as stimulus and inspiration for the studies gathered in *Fighting Scholars*, since it was always my intention to make a case for, and to attract others to, the *incarnate study of incarnation* by practical example – rather than by theoretical expostulation or methodological supplication, which would have contradicted that very case. I am doubly pleased that its contributors have extended the reach and refined the arguments of my book in manifold new directions, connecting them with theoretical perspectives and empirical agendas beyond the one I pursued in my ethnography of the social springs and lived magnetism of prizefighting as plebeian bodily craft in the black American ghetto (Wacquant 2004a).

Fighting Scholars gathers lush materials and precise analyses of interest not only to sociologists of practice and embodiment within the narrow province of sport, but also to generalist students of discipline, violence, gender, religion, emotions, reflexivity, field methodology and social epistemology insofar as inquiring into martial arts and combat sports via apprenticeship inevitably raises these issues.[2] It also demonstrates the fruitfulness of deploying habitus as both empirical object (*explanandum*) and as method of inquiry (*modus cognitionis*) by providing collective support for five key propositions that, together, bolster and enrich Bourdieu's dispositional theory of action.

1. Habitus Is Fully Amenable to Empirical Inquiry

Fighting Scholars convincingly rebuts the oft repeated but seldom elaborated criticism that habitus is a 'black box' that muddles the analysis of social conduct, erases history and freezes practice in the endless replication of structure. This complaint has been recited now over three decades (see, for a sample, Connell 1983, 151; Elster 1983, 106; Boudon 1998, 176; King 2000; Liechty 2002, 22; Boltanski 2003; Mouzelis 2004, 109; Harris 2007, 237; Akram 2013, 57–9) in rote fashion by scholars who seem not to have noticed three stubbornly contrary facts. First, Bourdieu introduced habitus in his youthful cross-Mediterranean ethnographies of honor, kinship and power in Algeria and Béarn in order to account for cultural disjuncture and social transformation, not cultural congruence and social reproduction (Wacquant 2004c). Second, habitus alone never spawns a definite practice: it takes the *conjunction of disposition and position*, subjective capacity and objective possibility, habitus and social space (or field) to produce a given conduct or expression.[3] And this meeting between skilled agent and pregnant world spans the gamut from felicitous to strained, smooth to rough, fertile to futile. Third and relatedly, because they are acquired over time in diverse circumstances that can entail extended and abrupt travel across social space, and because they encounter a cosmos that may itself undergo swift and sweeping change as well as subject them to heterogeneous pressures and possibilities (as did the colonial society wracked by a nationalist war of liberation in which Bourdieu incubated his model of action), the dispositions of agents display varying degrees of internal integration. This is why Bourdieu ([1997] 2000: 160, 162) insists that 'habitus is neither necessarily adapted [to the situation], nor necessarily coherent'; it can be 'riven by internal contradiction and division'; and 'it can have its failings, critical moments of perplexity and discordance' when it produces unforeseen and nonconforming practices. All of which implies that it must be studied in its actual formation and extant manifestations, and not stipulated by analytic fiat.

Indeed, far from being a 'theoretical *deus ex machina*' (DiMaggio 1979, 1464) that keeps us locked in conceptual obscurity, habitus is a standing invitation to investigate the *social constitution of the agent*. It is not an answer to the conundrum of action – lately rephrased by invoking the equally enigmatic category of 'agency' – but a question or, better yet, an *empirical prompt*: an arrow pointing to the need to methodically *historicize the concrete agent* embedded in a concrete situation by reconstituting the set of durable and transposable dispositions that sculpt and steer her thoughts, feelings and conduct.

There are three ways to detect the architecture of the stratified system of schemata that compose habitus. The first, *synchronic and inductive*, is to trace out connections between patterns of preferences, expressions, and social strategies within and across realms of activity so as to infer their shared matrix. This is the approach followed by Bourdieu, for instance, in his early study of 'The Sentiment of Honor' among the Kabyles (Bourdieu 1966) and in his mature inquiry into the internal makeup of the French ruling class in *The State Nobility* (Bourdieu [1989] 1996). The second, *diachronic and deductive*, is to map out the social trajectories of agents so as so reconstitute the sequencing and sedimentation of layers of dispositions across time, for which the paradigmatic case is the sociography of the petty bourgeoisie offered in *Distinction* (Bourdieu 1984, 318–71). The third, *experimental*, is taken up in *Body and Soul* and by the contributors to this volume: it consists of studying the dedicated institutions and focused pedagogical programs that forge a specific habitus by submitting to them in the first person.[4]

2. Primary and Secondary Habitus

The 'fighting scholars' clear up another common misconception about habitus: that it is rigid, frozen, unchanging and unchangeable. By deliberately acquiring specialized dispositions they did not have, dispositions that are constitutive of a bodily trade and philosophy, they spotlight the *malleability* of habitus, in keeping with Bourdieu's ([1997] 2000, 161, my translation) late specification of the concept:

> Habitus change constantly as a function of new experiences. Dispositions are subject to a sort of permanent revision, but one that is never radical, given that it operates on the basis of premises instituted in the previous state. They are characterized by a combination of constancy and variation that fluctuates according to the individual and her degree of rigidity or flexibility.

This suggests the need to return to, and elaborate, Bourdieu's distinction between *primary* and *secondary* habitus, introduced in his work on education and underlying his analysis of the nexus of class and taste in *Distinction*. The primary habitus is the set of dispositions one acquires in early childhood, slowly and imperceptibly, through familial osmosis and familiar immersion; it is fashioned by tacit and diffuse 'pedagogical labor with no precedent'; it constitutes our baseline social personality as well as 'the basis for the ulterior constitution of any other habitus' (Bourdieu and Passeron [1970] 1977, 42–6). The secondary habitus is any system of transposable schemata that becomes grafted subsequently, through specialized pedagogical labour that is typically shortened in duration, accelerated in pace, and explicit in organization. This distinction echoes the contrast established by Bourdieu between 'the two modes of acquisition of culture', the familial and the academic, the experiential and the didactic, which indelibly stamp one's relation to culture and the character of one's cultural capital, of which habitus is the embodied form (Bourdieu 1984, 65–8): the first spawns the ease and insouciance that define excellence; the second bears the mark of effort and tension born of ascesis.

Every agent has a primary (generic) habitus, which is both springboard and matrix for the subsequent acquisition of a multiplicity of (specific) habitus. In the case of the fighting scholars, their martial or sporting habitus is a *tertiary formation*, grounded in their primary (gender, national, class, etc.) habitus and mediated by their scholastic habitus – which constitutes both a motivative resource and a built-in hindrance to gaining the practical mastery of a corporeal craft, insofar as it inclines the apprentice to a reflexive attitude. The casting of a secondary (tertiary, quaternary, quinary, etc.) habitus will thus be inflected by the distance separating it from the systems of dispositions that serve as scaffolding for its construction because they precede it. The greater that distance, the more difficult the traineeship, the greater the gaps and frictions between the successive layers of schemata, and the less integrated the resulting dispositional formation is likely to be. We can discern this prismatic and compositional logic at work in the differential manner in which the various authors of *Fighting Scholars* respond, depending on their class and academic inclinations, to the challenges of mastering a combative craft and in the degree to which they feel 'at home' in it, in the existential sense of being one with the social and symbolic microcosm it anchors (Jackson 1995).

3. The Cognitive, Conative and Affective Components of Habitus

By digging deep across types of martial and fighting arts, the field studies gathered in the present book suggest that one may analytically differentiate and empirically document three 'components' to habitus.[5] The first is *cognitive*: it consists in the categories of perception through which agents cut up the world, make out its constituents, and give them pattern and meaning. As the boxing gym adage goes, you will not become a prizefighter if you cannot 'tell a fish hook from a left hook', that is, without mastering the classificatory system that both separates and relates things, persons and activities into a distinctive semantic tapestry.

But habitus is not constituted merely of 'cognitive structures', as Bourdieu's own language sometimes seems to imply. A second, crucial, module spotlighted by the initiatory study of corporeal crafts is *conative*: it consists of proprioceptic capacities, sensorimotor skills, and kinesthetic dexterities that are honed in and for purposeful action. Because they are propelled by the first-person learning of the practical competencies that constitute boxing, taekwondo, capoeira, aikido, etc., in the real time and spaces where these are cultivated, the accounts composing *Fighting Scholars* illumine the pivotal role of the 'habitual body' (Merleau-Ponty [1948] 2004) as seat of trained proficiencies and spring of intentional conduct in the world.

Yet, to grow into a full-fledged member of a given microcosm, it still does not suffice to be able to interpret it and to act in it in conforming fashion; one must also aspire to be in it and of it; one must be motivated or moved by it over time. The third component of habitus is *affective* or, to speak more generally, cathectic (in the idiom of Talcott Parsons) or libidinal (in the vocabulary of Sigmund Freud). It entails the vesting of one's life energies into the objects, undertakings, and agents that populate the world under consideration. In other words, to make an adept pugilist (pianist, politician or professor) takes acquiring in practice the distinctive cognitive constructs and the skilled moves as well as developing the proper appetite for the stakes of the corresponding social game.[6] By documenting this lustful dimension of habitus formation, *Fighting Scholars* brings out the inescapable fact, highlighted by Marx ([1927] 1988) in his *Economic and Philosophic Manuscript of 1844* but studiously suppressed by social science ever since, that the incarnate social agent is a *suffering and desiring animal*.

4. Carnality Is Not a Problem but a Resource for Sociological Inquiry

That proposition applies to the social analyst, who engages in her research sociological categories, skills and desires – in short, her sociological habitus as a secondary (specific) system of dispositions mounted on her primary (generic) habitus. As every human being, she is a feeling and desiring animal who knows the world *by body in practice*, which practice encompasses but is not limited to the deliberate discursive deployment of instruments of objectivation in accordance with the standards of her discipline. This means that she can deepen and broaden her anthropological grasp by attending to her own fleshly understanding and sentient comprehension, and sifting them through her analytic filters, instead of ignoring them or denying their fecundity. Better yet, the sociologist can use initiatory immersion and practical entanglement in the world under study, *in conjunction with the classical tools of the social scientific method*, to convert her intelligent organism into a fleet vehicle for social detection and analysis.

This is what the 'fighting scholars' accomplish as they go about acquiring and dissecting the practical mastery that fighters gain of their art so as to transform themselves and actualize the potentialities it harbours. They do so in a spiraling and self-propelling movement: acquiring to dissect, dissecting to acquire, and so on. In the process, they demonstrate in action, and not just on paper, the methodological viability, theoretical fruitfulness, and empirical productivity of *carnal sociology* as a distinctive mode of inquiry. Put briefly, this approach takes seriously the embarrassing fact that social agents are motile, sensuous and suffering creatures of flesh, blood, nerves and sinews doomed to death, who know it and make their world through and with their enskilled and exposed 'mindful bodies' (Scheper-Hughes and Lock 1987). And it insists that this proposition applies to the sociologist no less than to the people she studies, be they Thai boxers, lathe operators, school teachers or corporate lawyers.

Carnal sociology is based on a bet (or a dare): that we can *turn carnality from problem to resource* for the production of sociological knowledge. It asks that we revoke the dominant dualistic paradigm of embodiment, canonized by Descartes at the start of the rationalist revolution[7] and percolating through multiple lineages to permeate most strands of social thought, from utilitarianism and structuralism to critical theory and hermeneutics, which share in the 'dogma of the ghost in the machine' (Ryle [1949] 2000). Doing a Bourdieu on Bourdieu, it proposes that we use habitus as a methodological pathway, through the technique of apprenticeship, to pry into the forging and functioning of habitus as spring of social action. The aim here is to fashion a sociology *from* the body that does justice to the *active side of embodiment* and captures adept and sensuous organisms, not just as socially construct-*ed*, but as socially construct-*ing*. This is not a call to hurl ourselves into the abyss of subjectivity (as the slippery genre of 'auto-ethnography' does) but, on the contrary, a demand that we deepen objectivity by acknowledging that embodied knowledge and competency are productive constituents of objective reality. For carnal sociology, gaining a visceral grasp of the *vis viva* of the social world is not a distraction from, or a rejection of, the Durkheimian agenda of sociological reason but an indispensable means for its realization (Wacquant 2009b, 121–2).

5. We Are All Martial Artists

We now come to the most critical yet most prickly of all questions: does any of this matter beyond the martial arts and combat sports, symbolically rich but socially marginal activities after all? Beyond the restricted perimeter of athletic avocations or performance crafts, including among them not only music, theater, and dance, but also preaching and politics? The greatest challenge that the fighting scholars leave untackled in this book is that of extending the teachings of their carnal investigations of corporeal trades to practice in general. Is such an extension warranted and, if so, is it possible? The title of this essay is intended to indicate that it is both possible and warranted, indeed needed if we are to produce full-colour accounts of social life conveying the 'taste and ache of action' instead of erasing them as conventional social science routinely does (Wacquant 2004a, vi–xii): sociologists and anthropologists hard at work learning an agonistic bodily art in order to disclose its inner workings are social beings, plural, collectively engaged (*homines*) in embodied activities staged inside circles of shared commitments that make them but extreme instances (*in extremis*) of what every social agent is and does as she navigates the world.

I bring up this proposition because it drove me to study boxers in the first place: I was not motivated to spend three years in a boxing gym just to plumb the idiosyncratic features of the Manly Art. Aside from the sheer pleasure of being enwrapped in a gripping sensual and moral universe, I ploughed ahead in my journey among pugs because I held – and I still hold – that the ring offers an especially propitious experimental setting to show how social competency is fabricated and membership bestowed (Wacquant 2005a). I am keenly aware of the objection that practices vary in their 'physicality', or in their reliance on discursive reason, such that a prizefighter would seem to differ radically on that count from, say, a philosophy professor. For this objection was raised forcefully and rather intimidatingly by none other than John Searle after I presented the theoretical implications of *Body and Soul* to his Workshop on Social Ontology at Berkeley in April of 2010. While Searle agrees that some notion much like habitus, which he calls 'the Background', is needed to account for social action,[8] he considers that there is a 'dramatic difference' (his words) between an athletic and an intellectual craft, one that renders transferring knowledge gained about the one to the other too risky if not invalid. He would advise to study 'intermediate cases', such as that of the soldier (in his response to my argument, he drew on the experiences of his son as a tank officer in a US Army battalion stationed in Germany).[9]

I am not convinced. I take the difference between pugilists and philosophers to be one of *degree and not one of kind*. The existential situation of the generic, run-of-the-mill agent is not ontologically different from that of the fighter and of the fighting scholar: like them, she is a sentient being of flesh and blood, bound to a particular point in physical space and tied to a given moment in time by virtue of her incarnation in a fragile organism. This porous, mortal organism exposes her to the world and thus to the risk of pain (emotional as well as physical) and injury (symbolic as well as material); but it also propels her onto the stage of social life, where she evolves in practice the visceral know-how and prediscursive skills that form the bedrock of social competency. Though carnal sociology is particular apt for studying social extremes, its principles and techniques apply across all social institutions, for carnality is not a specific domain of practices but a fundamental constituent of the human condition and thus a necessary ingredient of all action.[10] For this reason, and until this methodological strategy is practically invalidated, I would urge social analysts to start from the assumption that, *pace* Searle, we are all martial artists of one sort or another.

Notes

1 All translations of Pierre Bourdieu in the Epilogue are made by L. Wacquant from the French original, though English-language editions have been cited for ease of reference.
2 Proof is that the same roster of themes is tackled, frontally or sideways, by the more discursivist collection of Farrer and Whalen-Bridge (2012) on *Martial Arts as Embodied Knowledge* and by the articles gathered in the thematic issue of *Actes de la recherche en sciences sociales* on 'Martial Practices and Combat Sports' (no. 179, September 2009), on the commercialization of cage fighting, the adaptation of Brazilian *vale tudo* in Bolivia, the codification of duel sports across Asia, the gender effects of the entry of women into boxing, and the social uses of *pencak silat* in the Indonesian military.
3 Bourdieu ([1997] 2000, 149) writes, 'Dispositions do not lead in a determinate manner to a determinate action: they reveal and accomplish themselves only in appropriate circumstances and in relation to a situation.' They may 'remain always in the state of virtualities' or 'manifest themselves in different, and even opposite, practices depending on the situation'. For the 'principle of action' resides 'neither in a subject… nor in a "milieu"' but 'in the ontological complicity between two states of the social, history made body and history made thing'.
4 See Desmond (2007) on wildland firefighters and Mears (2012) on runway models, for two methodologically germane studies of the production of the stereotypic forms of masculine and feminine bodily capital respectively (namely, physical prowess and sexualized parading). Two further variants of the observational approach are to study habitus-forming pedagogies in action through close-up interviews, as in Herzfeld's (2003) account of small-town artisans in Crete, and through archival documentation, as Charles Suaud (1978) does in his historical reconstitution of the production of the sacerdotal habitus in rural Brittany.
5 I regret having left this distinction implicit in *Body and Soul*, as I did most theoretical arguments, in keeping with a stylistic design geared to conveying the aisthesis of pugilism. Clarifying it would have bolstered the thesis that *pugilistic desire* intervenes as a crucial mediation between the structures of class marginality, racial subordination and masculine hubris and the extant practices of boxers in and out of the ring.
6 In *Pascalian Meditations*, Bourdieu ([1997] 2000, 164) proposes that producing the dispositions required by a particular field (in the sense of *champ*) entails a 'work of specific socialization [which] tends to foster the transformation of the originary libido, that is, the socialized affects constituted in the domestic sphere', through 'the transference of this libido onto the agents and institutions belonging to that field'. In his acid critique of Sartre's projection of his intellectual unconscious onto his famous phenomenological vignette on the café waiter, Bourdieu ([1997] 2000, 153–5) reiterates that one 'enters into the persona of the waiter not as an actor playing a role but, rather, like a child identifying with his father'. He suggests that the conversion of generic (narcissistic, sexual) libido into specific *libidines* operates via the redirection of desire toward, and the quest for recognition from, cathected persons beyond the familial circle.
7 Cartesian dualism presents itself as the inescapable corollary of the application of rationalism in social inquiry. But this claim is refuted by the emergence, out of the same intellectual movement spanning in the seventeenth century, of the monism of Spinoza and the pluralism of Leibniz (Phemister 2006). Indeed, both Spinoza and Leibniz are, along with Ernst Cassirer, major sources of Bourdieu's philosophical anthropology and social epistemology (more so, I would contend, than Pascal, in spite of Bourdieu's own self-professed affiliation).
8 'The thesis of the Background is simply this: intentional phenomena such as meanings, understandings, interpretations, beliefs, desires, and experiences only function within a set of Background capacities that are not themselves intentional' (Searle 1992, 175). A few pages later, Searle notes that the Background is 'closely related' to Bourdieu's habitus (177).

9 This points to a deeper difference in philosophical anthropology: for Searle (2009), humans are, first and foremost, 'language-speaking animals' and language is the grand creator of social institutions and glue of human civilizations across history. I see humans as visceral creatures impelled by socialized drives and desires for which language provides a second-order means of social construction.
10 Academics live under the comforting illusion that 'physicality' is a property of a restricted class of practices that does not concern them because the specificity of *scholarly embodiment* resides in the radical effacement of the body proper from the phenomenological foreground: the scholastic condition as withdrawal from practical urgency intensifies the modal experience of 'bodily absence' (Leder 1990). But the most 'mental' of actors, such as the mathematician or the philosopher, are incarnate beings; and thinking itself is a deeply corporeal activity, as the 'embodied cognition' movement is now showing from within cognitive science (Shapiro 2011).

REFERENCES

Abramson, Corey M. and Darren Modzelewski. 2011. 'Caged Morality: Moral Worlds, Subculture, and Stratification Among Middle-Class Cage-Fighters'. *Qualitative Sociology* 34: 143–75.
Akram, Sadiya. 2013. 'Fully Unconscious and Prone to Habit: The Characteristics of Agency in the Structure and Agency Dialectic'. *Journal for the Theory of Social Behaviour* 43 (1): 45–65.
Alexander, Jeffrey C. 1995. *Fin de Siècle Social Theory*. London: Verso.
_____. 2003. *The Meanings of Social Life: A Cultural Sociology*. Oxford and New York: Oxford University Press.
Alexias, George and Elina Dimitropoulou. 2011. 'The Body as a Tool: Professional Classical Ballet Dancers' Embodiment'. *Research in Dance Education* 12 (2): 87–104.
Almeida, Bira. 1986. *Capoeira: A Brazilian Art Form*. Berkeley, CA: North Atlantic Books.
Alonso, Marcelo. 2005. 'Quebra Silêncio'. *Tatame*. June.
Alter, Joseph S. 1992. *The Wrestler's Body: Identity and Ideology in North India*. Berkeley, CA: University of California Press.
Amado, Jorge. 1993. *The War of the Saints*. Translated by Gregory Rabassa. New York: Bantam Books.
Anasi, Robert. 2002. *The Gloves: A Boxing Chronicle*. New York: North Point Press.
Anderson, Eric. 2008. '"I Used To Think Women Were Weak": Orthodox Masculinity, Gender Segregation, and Sport'. *Sociological Forum* 23: 257–80.
Angleman, Amy, Yoshihiko Shinzato, Vincent van Hasselt and Stephen Russo. 2009. 'Traditional Martial Arts Versus Modern Self-Defense Training For Women: Some Comments'. *Aggression and Violent Behavior* 14: 89–93.
Anon. 1942. 'Jiu Jitsu Now Being Stressed at Yale as Part of Compulsory War Training'. *New York Times*, 13 September, D5.
Anti-Defamation League. 2003. *Unraveling Anti-Semitic 9/11 Conspiracy Theories*. New York: Gorowitz Institute. Online: www.adl.org/anti_semitism/9-11conspiracytheories.pdf (accessed 20 April 2010).
Ashkenazi, Michael. 2002. 'Ritual and the Ideal of Society in Karate'. In D. E. Jones (ed.), *Combat, Ritual and Performance*, 99–118. Westport, CT: Praeger.
Assunção, Matthias R. 2005. *Capoeira: The History of an Afro-Brazilian Martial Art*. London: Routledge.
_____. 2007. 'History and Memory in *Capoeira* Lyrics from Bahia, Brazil'. In N. P Naro, R. Sansi-Roca and D. H. Treece (eds), *Cultures of the Lusophone Black Atlantic*, 199–218. London: Palgrave.
Atkinson, Paul. 2006. *Everyday Arias*. Walnut Creek, CA: Alta Mira Press.
Bachelard, Gaston. 1971. *Epistémologie*. Paris: Presses Universitaires de France.
Barme, Scot. 1993. *Luang Wichit Wathakan and the Creation of a Thai Identity*. Singapore: Institute of Southeast Asian Studies.
Barness, Lewis, John Opitz and Gilbert-Barness Enid. 2007. 'Obesity: Genetic, Molecular, and Environmental Aspects'. *American Journal of Medical Genetics* 143 (24): 3016–34.
Bar-On Cohen, Einat. 2006. 'Kime and the Moving Body: Somatic Codes in Japanese Martial Arts', *Body & Society* 12 (4): 73–93.
_____. 2007. 'Timing in Karate and the Body in its Own Right'. *Social Analysis*. 51 (3): 1–22.
_____. 2009a. 'Kibadachi – Pain and Crossing Boundaries Within the Lived-In-Body and Within Sociality'. *Journal of the Royal Anthropological Institute (incorporating Man)* 15: 610–29.

———. 2009b. 'Opening and Closing Ritual in Japanese Martial Arts and the Dismantling of Violence'. *Journal of Ritual Studies* 23 (1): 29–44.

———. 2009c. 'Survival, An Israeli Ju Jutsu School of Martial Arts: Violence, Body, Practice and the National'. *Ethnography* 10 (2): 153–83.

———. 2011. 'Once We Put Our Helmets On There Are No More Friends: The "Fights" Session in the Israeli Army Course for Close-Combat Instructors'. *Armed Forces and Society* 37 (3): 512–33.

———. 2012. 'The Forces of Homology: The 1928 Rites of Succession to the Throne of Hirohito, Emperor of Japan'. *History and Anthropology* 23 (4): 425–45.

———. Forthcoming. 'Perfect Praxis in *Aikidō* – a Reflexive Body-Self'. In Terry Evens, Don Handelman and Christopher Roberts (eds), *Reflecting on Reflexivity*, a special issue of *Social Analysis*.

Bateson, Gregory. 1972. *Steps in the Ecology of the Mind*, New York: Ballentine.

Behar, Ruth. 1996. *The Vulnerable Observer: Anthropology That Breaks Your Heart*. Boston: Beacon Press.

Bell, Catherine. 1992. *Ritual Theory, Ritual Practice*. Oxford: Oxford University Press.

Ben-Ari, Eyal. 1991. 'Transformation in Ritual, Transformation Of Ritual: Audiences and Rites in a Japanese Commuter Village'. *Ethnology* 30 (2): 135–47.

Bensa, Alban. 1995. *Chroniques Kanak. L'ethnologie en marche*. Paris: Ethnies.

Bishop, John. 2002. 'Alan Lomax and Choreometrics'. In Judy Mitoma (ed.), *Envisioning Dance on Film and Video*. Online: http://www.media-generation.com/Articles/Lomax/lomax2.pdf (accessed 12 March 2012).

Blacker, Carmen. 1975. *The Catalpa Bow – A Study of Shamanistic Practices in Japan*. London: George Allen & Unwin.

Blumer, Herbert. 1966. *Symbolic Interaction*. Englewood Cliffs: Prentice-Hall.

Boltanski, Luc. 2003. 'Usages faibles, usages forts de l'habitus'. In Pierre Encrevé and Rose-Marie Lagrave (eds), *Travailler avec Bourdieu*, 153–61. Paris: Flammarion.

Boudon, Raymond. 1998. 'Social Mechanisms without Black Boxes'. In Peter Hedström and Richard Swedberg (eds), *Social Mechanisms: An Analytical Approach to Social Theory*, 172–203. Cambridge: Cambridge University Press.

Boundas, Constantin. 2004. 'Virtual/Virtuality'. In A. Parr (ed.), *The Deleuze Dictionary*, 296–8. Edinburgh: Edinburgh University Press.

Bourdieu, Pierre. 1962. 'Célibat et condition paysanne'. *Etudes Rurales* 5, 6: 32–136.

———. 1966. 'The Sentiment of Honour in Kabyle Society'. In John Peristiany (ed.), *Honour and Shame*, 193–24. Chicago: University of Chicago Press. Reprinted in *Algeria 1960* (Cambridge: Cambridge University Press, 1979).

———. 1977. *Outline of a Theory of Practice*. Cambridge: Polity Press.

———. 1978. 'Sport and Social Class'. *Social Science Information* 17 (6): 819–40.

———. 1984. *Distinction. A Social Critique of Judgement of Taste*. Cambridge, MA: Harvard University Press.

———. 1990a. *In Other Words*. Cambridge: Polity Press.

———. 1990b. *The Logic of Practice*. Cambridge: Polity Press.

———. (1989) 1996. *The State Nobility: Elite Schools in the Field of Power*. Cambridge: Polity Press.

———. 1998. *Practical Reason: On The Theory of Action*. Stanford, California: Stanford.

———. (1997) 2000. *Pascalian Meditations*. Cambridge: Polity Press.

———. 2001. *Masculine Domination*. Stanford: Stanford University Press.

———. 2002. 'Participant Objectivation: The Huxley Medal Lecture'. *Journal of the Royal Anthropological Institute* 9 (2): 281–94.

———. 2003. *Distinction: A Social Critique of the Judgement of Taste*. London: Routledge.

———. 2005. 'Habitus'. In J. Hillier and E. Rooksby (eds), *Habitus: A Sense of Place*, 43–52. Aldershot: Ashgate.

Bourdieu, Pierre and Alban Bensa. 1985. 'Quand les Canaques prennent la parole'. *Actes de la recherche en sciences sociales* 56: 69–85.

Bourdieu, Pierre, L. Boltanski, R. Castel, J.-C. Chamboredon. 1965. *Photographie: un art moyen*. Paris: Les Editions de Minuit.
Bourdieu, Pierre, Alain Darbel, Jean-Pierre Rivet and Claude Seibel. 1963. *Travail et travailleurs en Algérie*. Paris and The Hague: Mouton.
Bourdieu, Pierre and Jean-Claude Passeron. (1970) 1977. *Reproduction in Education, Society and Culture*. London: Sage.
Bourdieu, Pierre and Loïc Wacquant. 1992. *An Invitation to Reflexive Sociology*. Cambridge: Polity Press.
Bowie, Katherine. 1997. *Rituals of National Loyalty: An Anthropology of the State and the Village Scout Movement in Thailand*. New York: Columbia University Press.
Brown, David. H. K. and Aspasi Leledaki. 2010. 'Eastern Movement Forms as Body-Selftransforming Cultural Practices in the West: Towards A Sociological Perspective'. *Cultural Sociology* 4, 1: 123–54.
Brown, David H. K., George Jennings and Andrea Molle. 2009. 'Exploring Relationships Between Asian Martial Arts and Religion'. *Stadion* 35: 47–66.
Brown, David H. K., George Jennings and Aspasi Leledaki. 2008. 'The Changing Charismatic Status of the Performing Male Body in Asian Martial Arts Films'. *Sport in Society* 11 (2/3): 174–94.
Brown-Saracino, Japonica, Jessica Thurk and Gary A. Fine. 2008. 'Beyond Groups'. *Qualitative Research* 8 (5): 547–66.
Browning, Barbara. 1995. *Samba*. Bloomington, IN: Indiana University Press.
_____. 1998. *Infectious Rhythm*. New York: Routledge.
Bruster, R. 1982. 'Testa: A Brutally Beautiful African Martial Art'. *Inside Kungfu* 9 (10): 49–52.
Burke, D. T., S. Al-Adawi, Y. T. Lee and J. Audette. 2007. 'Martial Arts as Sport and Therapy'. *Journal of Sports Medicine and Physical Fitness* 47: 96–102.
Burke, Peter and María Pallares-Burke. 2008. *Gilberto Freyre: Social Theory in the Tropics*. Oxford: Peter Lang.
Burrow, Sylvia. 2007. 'Body Limits to Autonomy: Emotion, Attitude, and Self-Defence'. In S. Sherwin, S. Campbell and L. Meynell (eds), *Agency and Embodiment*, 126–44. Philadelphia: University of Pennsylvania Press.
Butler, Judith. 1990. *Gender Trouble*. Abingdon: Routledge.
_____. 1993. *Bodies That Matter: On the Discursive Limits of Sex*. New York: Routledge.
Butler, Kim D. 1998. 'Afterword: Ginga Baiana'. In H. Kray (ed.), *Afro-Brazilian Culture and Politics*, 158–75. Armonk, NY: ME Sharpe.
Butryn, Ted M. and Larry deGaris. 2008. 'Johnny Rodz and the Jade Ring: Larry and Ted's Excellent Adventure in Pro Wrestling'. In Michael Atkinson and Kevin Young (eds), *Tribal Play: Subcultural Journeys Through Sport*, 337–51. Bingley: Emerald Group Publishing.
Capoeira, N. 1995. *The Little Book of Capoeira*. Berkeley, CA: North Atlantic Books.
_____. 2002. *Capoeira: Roots of the Dance – Fight – Game*. Berkeley, CA: North Atlantic Books.
_____. 2006. *A Street-Smart Song*. Berkeley, CA: Blue Snake Books.
Casalis, Matthieu, 1983a. 'The Semiotics of Gesturality in Japanese Archery'. *Semiotica* 43 (3/4): 321–36.
_____. 1983b. 'The Semiotics of Japanese Rock Gardens'. *Semiotica* 44 (3/4): 349–62.
Casati, Roberto and Achille C. Varzi. 1994. *Holes and Other Superficialities*. Cambridge, MA: MIT Press.
Century, Douglas. 2000. *Street Kingdom: Five Years Inside the Franklin Avenue Posse*. New York: Warner Books.
_____. 2001. 'Ghetto Blasters: Born in Prison, Raised in the 'Hood, The Deadly Art of 52 Blocks is Brooklyn's Baddest Secret'. *Details* 19 (9): 77–9.
Chami-Sather, Grece. 2004. 'Focus, Self-Confidence and Self-Control, Transfer of Teaching Techniques from a Taekwondo Den into the Regular Classroom'. *The Sport Journal* 7 (2). Online: http://www.thesportjournal.org/tags/volume-7-number-2 (accessed 20 February 2004).

Chan, Stephen. 2000. 'The Construction and Export of Culture as Artefact: The Case of Japanese Martial Arts'. *Body & Society* 6 (1): 69–74.

Channon, Alex. 2010. '"Hit Me!": Mixed-Sex Martial Arts and the Subversion of Gender'. Paper presented at the 6th Meeting of the Transnational Working Group for the Study of Gender and Sport, University of Bath, UK, November 26–7.

———. 2012. 'Way of the Discourse: Mixed-Sex Martial Arts and the Subversion of Gender'. PhD diss., Loughborough University.

Chiang, Linda H. 1994. 'Beyond the Language: Native Americans' Nonverbal Communication' Paper presented at the Annual Meeting of the Midwest Association of Teachers of Educational Psychology (23rd, Anderson, IN, October 1–2, 1993), ERIC Document Reproduction Service No. ED 368540.

Choi, Hong Hi. 2008. *Encyclopedia of Taekwon-Do*. International Taekwon-do Federation Publishers.

Churchill, Caryl. 1968. *The Marriage of Toby's Idea of Angela and Toby's Idea of Angela's Idea of Toby*. Unpublished play.

Classen, Constance. 1993. *Worlds of Sense: Exploring the Senses in History and Across Cultures*. New York: Routledge.

Claudio de Campos, Rosario, Neil Stephens and Sara Delamont. 2010. '"I'm Your Teacher, I'm Brazilian!" Authenticity and Authority in European *Capoeira*'. *Sport, Education and Society* 15 (1): 103–20.

Colebrook, Claire. 2004. 'Actuallity'. In A. Parr (ed.), *The Deleuze Dictionary*, 9–11. Edinburgh: Edinburgh University Press.

Collins, Randall. 2004. *Interaction Ritual Chains*. Princeton, NJ: Princeton University Press.

———. 2008. *Violence: A Microsociological Theory*. Princeton, NJ: Princeton University Press.

Connell, Robert [Raewyn] W. 1983. *Which Way is Up? Essays on Sex, Class and Culture*. Sydney: George Allen & Unwin.

———. 1995. *Masculinities*. Cambridge: Polity Press.

———. 2002. *Gender*. Cambridge: Polity Press.

Connerton, Paul. 1989. *How Societies Remember*. Cambridge: Cambridge University Press.

Cooks, Leda. M. and Katie LeBesco. 2006. 'Introduction: The Pedagogy of the Teacher's Body'. *The Review of Education, Pedagogy, and Cultural Studies* 28: 233–38.

Cornwel-Smith, Philip. 2005. *Very Thai: Everyday Popular Culture*. Bangkok and London: River Books.

Costa, Lee R. and Andrew Matzner. 2007. *Male Bodies, Women's Souls: Personal Narratives of Thailand's Transgendered Youth*. London and New York: Routledge.

Crossley, Nick. 1995. 'Merleau-Ponty, the Elusive Body and Carnal Sociology'. *Body & Society* 1 (1): 43–63.

———. 2001a. 'The Phenomenological Habitus and Its Construction'. *Theory & Society* 30: 81–120.

———. 2001b. *The Social Body: Habit, Identity and Desire*. London: Sage Publications.

———. 2004a. 'Fat is a Sociological Issue: Obesity Rates in Late Modern, "Body Conscious" Societies'. *Social Theory and Health* 2 (3): 222–53.

———. 2004b. Ritual, Body Technique and (Inter)subjectivity'. In K. Schilbrack (ed.), *Thinking Through Ritual: Philosophical Perspectives*, 31–51. London: Routledge.

———. 2004c. 'The Circuit Trainer's Habitus'. *Body & Society* 10 (1): 37–69.

———. 2005. 'Mapping Reflexive Body Techniques: On Body Modification and Maintenance'. *Body & Society* 11 (1): 1–35.

———. 2006a. 'The Networked Body and the Question of Reflexivity'. In D. Waskul and P. Vannini (eds), *Body/Embodiment*, 21–34. Aldershot: Ashgate.

———. 2006b. 'In The Gym'. *Body & Society* 12 (3): 23–50.

———. 2007. 'Researching Embodiment by Way of "Body Techniques"'. In C. Shilling (ed.), *Embodying Sociology*, 80–94. Oxford: Blackwell.

Crump, Thomas. 1991. *The Death of the Emperor – Japan at the Crossroads*. Oxford: Oxford University Press.

Da Matta, Roberto. 1991. *Carnivals, Rogues and Heroes*. Notre Dame, IN: University of Notre Dame Press.
Darling, A. and J. Perryman. 1974. Karate Behind Bars: Menace or Means of Spiritual Survival. *Black Belt* (July): 16–21.
De Coppet, Daniel. 1992. *Understanding Rituals*. London: Routledge.
De Garis, Laurence. 1999. 'Experiments in Pro Wrestling: Toward a Performative and Sensuous Sport Ethnography'. *Sociology of Sport Journal* 16: 65–74.
De Grave, Jean-Marc. 2011. 'The Training of Perception in Javanese Martial Arts'. In D. S. Farrer and J. Whalen-Bridge (eds), *Martial Arts as Embodied Knowledge*, 123–44. New York: State University of New York Press.
Delamont, Sara. 2005a. 'Four Great Gates: Directions, Dilemmas and Distractions in Educational Research'. *Research Papers in Education* 20 (1): 85–100.
———. 2005b. 'No Place For Women Among Them?' *Sport, Education and Society* 10 (3): 305–20.
———. 2005c. 'Where the Boys Are'. *Waikato Journal of Education* 11 (1): 7–26.
———. 2006. 'The Smell of Sweat and Rum: Teacher Authenticity in Capoeira Classes'. *Ethnography and Education* 1 (2): 161–76.
———. 2009. 'The Only Honest Thing'. *Ethnography and Education* 4 (1): 51–64.
Delamont, Sara and Neil Stephens. 2006. 'Balancing the *Berimbau*. Embodied Ethnographic Understanding'. *Qualitative Inquiry* 12 (2): 316–39.
———. 2007. 'Excruciating Elegance: Representing the Embodied Habitus of *Capoeira*'. *Qualiti Working Paper*, presented in August 2007 at the School of Social Sciences, Cardiff University.
———. 2008. 'Up On the Roof: The Embodied Habitus of Diasporic Capoeira'. *Cultural Sociology* 2: 57–74.
Deleuze, Gilles. 1994. *Difference and Repetition*. New York: Columbia University Press.
Deleuze, Gilles and Félix Guattari. (1987) 2005. *A Thousand Plateaus – Capitalism a Schizophrenia*. Minneapolis, MN: University of Minnesota Press.
De Prycker, Valérie. 2011. 'Self-Conscious Control: Broadening the Notion of Control Through Experience Flow and Wu-Wei'. *Zygon*, 46 (1).
De Welde, Kristine. 2003. 'Getting Physical: Subverting Gender Through Self-Defense'. *Journal of Contemporary Ethnography* 32: 247–78
Desmond, Matthew. 2007. *On the Fireline: Living and Dying with Wildland Firefighters*. Chicago: University of Chicago Press.
DiMaggio, Paul. 1979. 'Review Essay: On Pierre Bourdieu'. *American Journal of Sociology* 84 (6): 1460–74.
Donohue, John J. 2002. 'Wave People: The Martial Arts and the American Imagination'. In D. E. Jones (ed.), *Combat, Ritual and Performance: Anthropology of the Martial Arts*, 65–80. Westport, CT: Praeger.
Dowling, Collette. 2000. *The Frailty Myth: Redefining the Physical Potential of Women and Girls*. New York: Random House.
Downey, Greg. 2005a. *Learning Capoeira*. Oxford: Oxford University Press.
———. 2005b. 'Educating the Eyes: Biocultural Anthropology and Physical Education'. *Anthropology in Action* 12 (2): 56–71.
———. 2007a. 'Producing Pain: Techniques and Technologies in No-Holds-Barred Fighting'. *Social Studies of Science* 37 (2): 201–26.
———. 2007b. 'Seeing With a "Sideways Glance": Visuomotor "Knowing" and the Plasticity of Perception'. In Mark Harris (ed.), *Ways of Knowing: Anthropological Approaches to Crafting Experience and Knowledge*, 222–24. New York: Berghahn.
———. 2008. 'Scaffolding Imitation in Capoeira: Physical Education and Enculturation in an Afro-Brazilian Art'. *American Anthropologist* 110 (2): 204–13.
———. 2010. 'Practice Without Theory'. *Journal of the Royal Anthropological Institute*. 16 (1): 22–40.
Draeger, Donn F. 1979. 'An Introduction to Hoplology', *Hoplos*, 1 (1): 3–4.

Dreyfus, Hubert and Stuart Dreyfus. 1986. *Mind Over Machine: The Power of Human Intuition and Expertise in the Era of the Computer*. Oxford: Blackwell.

Dunlop, Marcelo. 2009. 'The Guard' *Gracie Magazine*, 143 (February): 20–30.

Dunning, Eric. 2011. '"Testing" Elias: Aspects of Violence Viewed in Long Term Perspective'. *Papers* 96 (2): 309–39.

Durkheim, Emile. (1912) 1995. *Elementary Forms of Religious Life*. New York: Free Press.

———. (1913) 1975. 'Le problème religieux et la dualité de la nature humaine.' In Victor Karady (ed.) *Textes Vol. 2: Religion, morale, anomie*, 23–59. Paris: Editions de Minuit.

———. 1961. *The Elementary Forms of Religious Life*. Translated by J. Swain. New York: Collier Books.

Duyvenak J. J. L. 1947. 'The Philosophy of Wu Wei'. *Asiatische Studien* 1: 81–102.

Dykhuizen, Jeffrey C. 2000. 'Training in Culture: The Case of Aikido Education and Meaning-Making Outcomes in Japan and the United States'. *International Journal of Intercultural Relations* 24 (6): 741–61.

Eldershaw, Lynn P., Maria Mayan and Anne Winkler. 2007. 'Through a Painted Window: On Narrative, Medicine, and Method Interview with Arthur W. Frank Conducted ny the International Institute for Qualitative Methodology EQUIPP Students November 16, 2005'. *International Journal of Qualitative Methods* 6 (3): 121–39.

Elias, Norbert. 1978. *What is Sociology?* New York: Columbia University Press.

———. 1986. 'Introduction'. In Norbert Elias and Eric Dunning (eds), *Quest for Excitement: Sport and Leisure in the Civilizing Process*. London: Blackwell.

———. 1987. *Involvement and Detachment*. Oxford: Blackwell.

———. 1991. *The Symbol Theory*. London: Sage.

———. 2000. *The Civilizing Process*. London: Blackwell.

———. 2001. *The Society of Individuals*. New York: Continuum.

———. 2006. *The Court Society*. Dublin: University College Dublin Press.

———. 2007. *Involvement and Detachment*. Dublin: University College Dublin Press.

Elias, Norbert and Eric Dunning. 1966. 'Dynamics of Group Sports with Special Reference to Football'. *British Journal of Sociology* 17 (4): 388–402.

———. 1986. *Quest for Excitement: Sport and Leisure in the Civilizing Process*. London: Blackwell.

Elias, Norbert and John Scotson. 1994. *The Established and the Outsiders*. London: Sage.

Eliasoph, Nina. 2005. 'Theorizing from the Neck Down: Capturing Bodies Acting in Real Space and Time. *Qualitative Sociology* 28 (2) (Summer): 159–69.

Elster, Jon. 1983. *Sour Grapes: Studies in the Subversion of Rationality*. Cambridge: Cambridge University Press.

Emerson, Robert M., Rachel Fretz and Linda Shaw. 1995. *Writing Ethnographic Fieldnotes*. Chicago: University of Chicago Press.

Endresen, I. and D. Olweus. 2005. 'Participation in Power Sports and Antisocial Involvement in Preadolescent and Adolescent Boys'. *Journal of Child Psychology and Psychiatry*, 46 (5): 468–78.

Ericsson K. Anders, Michael A. Prietula and Edward T. Cokely. 2007. 'The Making of an Expert'. *Harvard Business Review*. Online: http://www.ncbi.nlm.nih.gov/pubmed/17642130 (accessed 8 December 2011).

Eriksen, Jorgen. 2010. 'Mindless Coping in Competitive Sport: Some Implications and Consequences'. *Sport, Ethics and Philosophy* 4 (1): 66–86.

Evens, Terrance M. S. 1999. 'Bourdieu and the Logic of Practice: Is All Giving India Giving or is "Generalized Materialism" Not Enough'. *Sociological Theory* 17 (1): 3–31.

Farquhar, Judith. 2005. 'Whose Bodies?' *Qualitative Sociology* 28 (2): 191–96.

Farrer, Douglas. 2007. 'The Perils and Pitfalls of Performance Ethnography'. *International Sociological Association* 6: 17–26.

Farrer Douglas S. and John Whalen-Bridge. 2012. *Martial Arts as Embodied Knowledge: Asian Traditions in a Transnational World*. Albany, NY: State University of New York Press.

Favret-Saada, Jeanne. (1978) 1980. *Deadly Words: Witchcraft in the Bocage*. Cambridge: Cambridge University Press.

Fincham, Ben, Mark McGuinness and Lesley Murray (eds). 2010. *Mobile Methodologies*. London: Palgrave.
Fine, Gary A. 2003. 'Towards a Peopled Ethnography'. *Ethnography* 4 (1): 41–60.
———. 2004. 'Review of Loïc Wacquant, *Body and Soul: Notebooks of An Apprentice Boxer*'. *American Journal of Sociology* 110–12 (September): 505–7.
Frank, Adam D. 2003. 'Taijiquan and the Search for the Little Old Chinese Man: Ritualizing Race Through Martial Arts.' PhD diss. (unpublished). The University of Texas at Austin.
Freedman, Diane P. and Martha S. Holmes (eds). 2003. *The Teacher's Body: Embodiment, Authority, and Identity in the Academy*. Albany, NY: State University of New York Press.
Gans, Herbert. 1995. *The War Against the Poor*. New York: Pantheon.
Geertz, Clifford. 1973. *The Interpretation of Cultures*. New York: Basic Books.
Geurts, Kathryn L. 2002. *Culture and the Senses: Bodily Ways of Knowing in an African Community*. Berkeley, CA: University of California Press.
Gibson, James J. 1979. *The Ecological Approach to Visual Perception*. Boston: Houghton Mifflin.
Gillis, Alex. 2008. *A Killing Art: The Untold Story of Tae Kwon Do*. Toronto: ECW Press.
Girton, George D. 1986. 'Kung Fu. Towards a Praxiological Hermeneutic of the Martial Arts'. In Harold Garfinkel (ed.), *Ethnomethodological Studies of Work*. 59–88. London: Routledge.
Gladwell, Malcolm. 2005. *Blink: The Power of Thinking without Thinking*. New York: Back Bay Books.
Goffman, Erving. 1989. 'On Fieldwork'. *Journal of Contemporary Ethnography* 18 (2): 123–32.
Goodridge, Janet. 1999. *Rhythm and Timing of Movement and Performance: Drama, Dance and Performance*. London: Jessica Kingsley.
Gracie, Reila. 2006. *Carlos Gracie: O Criados de Uma Dinastia*.
Gracie, Renzo and Royler Gracie. 2001. *Brazilian Jiu Jitsu: Theory and Technique*. Montpelier: Invisible Cities Press.
Gracie, Rickson. 1999. *Choke*. Polygram Motion Pictures.
Graham, Elizabeth. 2009. 'Beginning Martial Arts as an Adult: Preliminary Analysis'. Presented at the 26th Annual Qualitative Analysis Conference, Ontario, May.
———. 2010. 'Being a Black Belt'. Presented at the 27th Annual Qualitative Analysis Conference, Ontario, May.
Green, Kyle. 2011. 'It Hurts So It Is Real: Sensing the Seduction of Mixed Martial Arts'. *Social and Cultural Geography* 12 (4): 377–96.
Green, Thomas A. 2003a. 'Surviving the Middle Passage'. In Thomas A. Green and Joseph R. Svinth (eds), *Martial Arts in the Modern World*: 129–48, Westport, CT: Praeger.
———. 2003b. 'Freeing the Afrikan Mind'. In Thomas A. Green and Joseph R. Svinth (eds), *Martial Arts in the Modern World*: 229–48. Westport, CT: Praeger.
———. 2012. 'Sick Hands and Sweet Moves: Aesthetic Dimensions of a Vernacular Martial Art'. *Journal of American Folklore* 125 (497): 286–303 .
Green, Thomas A. and Joseph Svinth. 2003. 'The Circle and the Octagon: Maeda's Judo and Gracie's Jiu-Jitsu'. In T. Green and J. Svinth (eds), *Martial Arts in the Modern World*. Westport, CT: Praeger.
Gross, G. Ki-Rin. *Taekwon-Do Manual: Be a Black Belt*.
Guérandel, Carine and Christine Mennesson. 2007. 'Gender Construction in Judo Interaction'. *International Review for the Sociology of Sport* 42 (2): 167–86.
Gutiérrez García, Carlos. 2004. 'Introducción y desarrollo del judo en España (de principios del S. XX a 1965): el proceso de implantación de un método educativo y de combate importado de Japón'. León. Universidad de León.
Guthrie, Sharon R. 1995. 'Liberating the Amazon: Feminism and the Martial Arts'. In Judith Ochshorn and Ellen Cole (eds), *Women's Spirituality, Women's Lives*: 107–19. New York: The Haworth Press.
Halberstam, J. 1998. *Female Masculinity*. London: Duke University Press.
Hamilton, Greg. 1994. *An Ethnography of Aikido*. Colorado College.

Hammersley, Martyn and Paul Atkinson. 2007. *Ethnography: Principles in Practice*. London: Routledge.
Handelman, Don. 1998. 'The Transformation of Symbolic Structures through History and the Rhythms of Time'. *Semiotica* 119 (3/4): 403–25.
Handelman, Don and Galina Lindquist. 2011. 'Religion, Politics and Globalization: The Long Past Foregrounding the Short Present, Prologue and Introduction'. In *Religion, Politics, and Globalization - Anthropological Approaches*. New York: Berghahn.
Hanley, B. 2011. 'The Rashguard Rasputin: How an Unassuming Kiwi Became the World's Premier BJJ Instructor'. *Fighter's Only* 27 (5): 62–3.
Hargreaves, Jennifer. 1994. *Sporting Females: Critical Issues in the History and Sociology of Women's Sports*. London: Routledge.
———. 1997. 'Women's Boxing and Related Activities: Introducing Images and Meanings'. *Body & Society* 3: 33–49.
Harris, Mark. 2007. *Ways of Knowing: Anthropological Approaches to Crafting Experience and Knowledge*. New York: Berghahn.
Hastrup, Kirsten. 1995. *A Passage to Anthropology: Between Experience and Theory*. London: Routledge.
Heidegger, Martin. 1962. *Being and Time*. San Francisco: Harper and Row.
Henderikus J. Stam. 2009. 'Habitus, Psychology, and Ethnography: Introduction to the Special Section'. *Theory & Psychology* 2009 (19): 707–11.
Henry, Jacques M. and Howard P. Comeaux. 1999. 'Gender Egalitarianism in Coed Sport: A Case Study of American Soccer'. *International Review for the Sociology of Sport* 34: 277–90.
Herzfeld, Michael. 1985. *The Poetics of Manhood*. Princeton, NJ: Princeton University Press.
———. 2003. *The Body Impolitic: Artisans and Artifice in the Global Hierarchy of Value*. Chicago: University of Chicago Press.
———. 2009. 'The Cultural Politics of Gesture: Reflections on the Embodiment of Ethnographic Practice'. *Ethnography* 10 (2): 131–52.
Heywood, Leslie and Shari L. Dworkin. 2003. *Built to Win: The Female Athlete as Cultural Icon*. Minneapolis: University of Minnesota Press.
Hilgers, Mathieu. 2009. 'Habitus, Freedom, and Reflexivity'. *Theory & Psychology*. 19 (6): 728–55.
Himmelsbach, Vawn. 2007. Muay Thai. In CBC News In Depth: Exercise and Fitness. Online: http://www.cbc.ca/news/background/exercise_fitness/muay-thai.html (accessed 15 March 2007).
Hockey, John and Jacqueyn Allen-Collinson. 2009. 'The Sensorium at Work: The Sensory Phenomenology of the Body'. *The Sociological Review* 57 (2): 217–39.
Hogeveen, Bryan. 2011. 'Skilled Coping and Sport: Promises of Phenomenology'. *Sport, Ethics and Philosophy* 5 (3): 245–56.
Holcombe, Charles. 2002. 'Theater of Combat'. In D. E. Jones (ed.), *Combat, Ritual and Performance: Anthropology of the Martial Arts*: 153–74. Westport, CT: Praeger.
Hollander, Jocelyn. 2004. 'I Can Take Care of Myself: The Impact of Self-Defense Training on Women's Lives'. *Violence Against* Women 10: 205–35.
Holloway, Joseph E. (ed.), *Africanisms in American culture*: 283–325. Bloomington: Indiana University Press.
Holloway, Thomas, H. 1989. 'A Kind of Healthy Terror'. *The Hispanic American Historical Review* 69 (4): 637–76.
Hubert, Henri and Marcel Mauss. 1964. *Sacrifice*. Chicago: University of Chicago Press.
Hugues, Everett C. 1994. *On Work, Race, and the Sociological Imagination*. Edited by Lewis A. Coser. Chicago: University of Chicago Press.
Hunt, Leon. 2005. '*Ong-Bak*: New Thai Cinema, Hong Kong and the Cult of the "Real"'. *New Cinemas: Journal of Contemporary Film* 3 (2): 69–84.
Hurst, George C. 1998. *Armed Martial Arts, Swordsmanship and Archery*. Yale: Yale University Press.
Hyers, Conrad M. 1974. *Zen and the Comic Spirit*. London: Rider and Company.
Ingold, Tim. 2000. *The Perception of the Environment: Essays in Livelhood, Dwelling and Skill*. London: Routledge.

REFERENCES

Inness, Sherrie A., ed. 2004. *Action Chicks: New Images of Tough Women in Popular Culture*. New York: Palgrave MacMillan.
Inside BJJ. 'Andre Galvao'. 26 June 2011. Online: http://www.insidebjj.com/2011/06/26/andre-galvao-2/ (accessed 20 July 2011).
Jackson, Michael. 1995. *At Home in the World*. Durham: Duke University Press.
Jackson, Peter. 1999. *Lady Boys, Tom Boys, Rent Boys: Male and Female Homosexualities in Contemporary Thailand*. New York and London: Routledge.
Jamous, Haroun and Bernard Peloille. 1970. 'Professions or Self-Perpetuating System?' In John A. Jackson (ed.), *Professions and Professionalisation*: 109–52. Cambridge: Cambridge University Press.
Jenkins, Richard. 1982. 'Pierre Bourdieu and the Reproduction of Determinism'. *Sociology* 31: 270–81.
——. 1991. *Pierre Bourdieu*. London: Routledge.
——. 2002. *Pierre Bourdieu* (second edition). London: Routledge.
Jennings, George B. 2010. 'Fighters, Thinkers and Shared Cultivation: Experiencing Transformation Through the Long-Term Practice of Traditionalist Chinese Martial Arts'. PhD diss. (unpublished). University of Exeter.
Jennings, George, David H. K. Brown and Andrew C. Sparkes. 2010. '"It Can Be a Religion If You Want": Wing Chun Kung Fu as a Secular Religion'. *Ethnography* 11 (4): 533–57.
Johnson, Tara. S. 2006. 'Performing A/Sexual Teacher: Cartesian Duality in Education'. *The Review of Education, Pedagogy, and Cultural Studies* 28: 253–66.
Jones, David E. 2002. *Combat, Ritual, and Performance: Anthropology of the Martial Arts*. Westport, CT: Praeger.
Jory, Patrick. 1999. 'Thai Identity, Globalisation and Advertising Culture'. *Asian Studies Review* 23 (4): 461–87.
Joseph, Janelle. 2008a. 'Going to Brazil: Transnational and Corporeal Movements of a Canadian-Brazilian Martial Arts Community'. *Global Networks* 8 (2): 194–213.
——. 2008b. The Logical Paradox of the Cultural Commodity. *Sociology of Sport Journal* 25 (4): 498–515.
Kale, Pratima. 1970. 'The Guru and the Professional: The Dilemma of the Secondary School Teacher in Poona, India'. *Comparative Education Review* 14 (3): 371–76.
Kantorowicz, Ernst H. (1957) 1997. *The King's Two Bodies: a Study in Mediaeval Political Theology*. New Jersey: Princeton University Press.
Karter, Karon and Guy Mezger. 2000. *The Complete Idiot's Guide to Kickboxing*. US: Alpha Books.
Kasper, Deborah. 2009. 'Ecological Habitus: Toward a Better Understanding of Socioecological Relations'. *Organization Environment* 22: 311.
Katz, Jack. 2001. 'From How to Why (Part 1)'. *Ethnography* 2 (4): 443–77.
——. 2002. 'From How to Why (Part 2)'. *Ethnography* 3 (1): 63–90.
Katz, Michael B., ed. 1993. *The 'Underclass' Debate: Views from History*. Princeton, NJ: Princeton University Press.
Kawamura, Eiko. 1994. 'Chaos and Cosmos in Zen'. *Diogenes* 165, 42 (1): 67–83.
Kerr, John. 2005. *Rethinking Aggression and Violence in Sport*. London: Routledge.
King, Anthony. 2000. 'Thinking with Bourdieu Against Bourdieu: A "Practical" Critique of Habitus'. *Sociological Theory* 18 (3): 417–33.
Kontos, Pia. 2006. 'Habitus: An Incomplete Account of Human Agency'. *The American Journal of Semiotics* 21 (1–4): 69–85.
Krug, Gary J. 2001. 'At the Feet of the Master: Three Stages in the Appropriation of Okinawan Karate into Anglo-American Culture'. *Cultural Studies - Critical Methodologies* 1 (4): 395–410.
Lafferty, Yvonne and Jim McKay. 2004. '"Suffragettes in Satin Shorts"? Gender and Competitive Boxing'. *Qualitative Sociology* 27: 249–76.
Lake Norman Tang Soo Do Academy. 2001. 'History of Tang Soo Do'. Online: http://www.angelfire.com/nc3/tangsoodo/tangsoodohistory.htm (accessed 20 September 2012).

Lakes, Kimberley and William Hoyt. 2004. 'Promoting Self-Regulation Through School-Based Martial Arts Training'. *Applied Developmental Psychology* 25: 283–302.
Lave, Jean. 1977. Cognitive Consequences of Traditional Apprenticeship Training in West Africa. *Anthropology and Education Quarterly* 8 (3): 177–80.
Lave, Jean and Etienne Wenger. 1991. *Situated Learning*. Cambridge: Cambridge University Press.
Law, Mark. 2008. *The Pyjama Game: A Journey into Judo*. London: Aurum Press.
Lawler, Jennifer. 2002. *Punch: Why Women Participate in Violent Sports*. Terra Haute, IN: Wish Publishing.
Leder, Drew. 1990. *The Absent Body*. Chicago: University of Chicago Press.
Lenskyj, Helen. 1986. *Out of Bounds: Women, Sport and Sexuality*. Toronto: The Women's Press.
Lévi-Strauss, Claude. 1968. *The Savage Mind*. Chicago: University of Chicago Press.
Lewis, John L. 1992. *Ring of Liberation*. Chicago: University of Chicago Press.
Liang, Liu-Chia, 1978. *36th Chamber of Shaolin* (also released as *The Master Killer*). Hong Kong: Shaw Brothers.
Liechty, Mark. 2002. *Suitably Modern: Making Middle-class Culture in a New Consumer Society*. Princeton, NJ: Princeton University Press.
Light, Richard. 2001. 'The Body in the Social World and the Social World in the Body: Applying Bourdieu's Work to Analyses of Physical Activity in Schools'. Online: http://www.aare.edu.au/01pap/lig01450.htm (accessed 15 July 2009).
Lizardo, Omar. 2009. 'Is a "Special Psychology" of Practice Possible? From Values and Attitudes to Embodied Dispositions'. *Theory & Psychology* 19: 713–27.
Lökman, Paula. 2011. 'Becoming Aware of Gendered Embodiment: Female Beginners Learning Aikido'. In Eileen Kennedy and Pirkko Markula (eds), *Women and Exercise: The Body, Health and Consumerism*: 266–79. London: Routledge.
London, Jack. 1905. *The Game*. New York: McMillan.
———. 1909. 'A Piece of Steak'. *Saturday Evening Post* 182, November 20.
———. 1911a. 'The Mexican'. *Saturday Evening Post*, August 19.
———. 1911b. 'The Abysmal Brute'. *Popular Magazine*.
Looser, D. 2011. 'Radical Bodies and Dangerous Ladies: Martial Arts and Women's Performance, 1900–1918'. *Theatre Research International* 36 (1): 3–19.
Lorraine, Tamsin. 2005. 'Lines of Flight'. In A. Parr (ed.), *The Deleuze Dictionary*: 144–46. Edinburgh: Edinburgh University Press.
Lowry, David. 1995. *Autumn Lightning: The Education of an American Samurai*. Virginia: Shambala.
———. 2005. *Persimmon Wind: A Martial Artist's Journey in Japan*. New Jersey: Koryu Books.
Loy, David. 1985. 'Wei-Wu-Wei: Nondual Action'. *Philosophy East and West* 35 (1): 73–86.
Luna, Edward. 2005. 'Secret Histories and Bodily Practices in Capoeira Angola: The Game-Dance-Fight from Bahia, Brazil'. Master's diss. (unpublished). Ohio State University.
Machado, R. 2002. *The Essence of Brazilian Jiu Jitsu*. New Delhi: Unique Publications.
Manning, Philip. 2009. 'Three Models of Ethnographic Research: Wacquant as Risk-Taker'. *Theory & Psychology* 19: 756–77.
———. 2005. *Freud and American Sociology*. Cambridge: Polity Press.
Marcoulatos, Iordanis. 2001. 'Merleau-Ponty and Bourdieu on Embodied Significance'. *Journal of the Theory of Social Behaviour* 31 (1): 1–27.
Marcus, George. 1998. *Ethnography through Thick and Thin*. Princeton, NJ: Princeton University Press.
Martínez Guirao, Javier E. 2011. 'Una aproximación antropológica al cuerpo como arma en las artes marciales'. *Revista de Antropología Experimental* 11: 113–25.
Marx, Karl. (1927) 1988. *Economic and Philosophic Manuscript of 1844*. New York: Promotheus Books.
Matthews, David. 2002. *Looking For a Fight. How a Writer Took On the Boxing World From the Inside*. London: Headline.

Mauss, Marcel. (1934) 1979. 'Body Techniques'. In M. Mauss, *Sociology and Psychology: Essays*: 97–123. London: Routledge and Kegan Paul.
McCaughey, Martha. 1997. *Real Knockouts: The Physical Feminism of Women's Self Defense*. London: New York University Press.
———. 1998. 'The Fighting Spirit: Women's Self-Defense Training and the Discourse of Sexed Embodiment'. *Gender and Society* 12: 277–300.
McCaughey, Martha and Neal King (eds). 2001. *Reel Knockouts: Violent Women in the Movies*. Austin, TX: University of Texas Press.
McDonagh, Eileen and Laura Pappano. 2008. *Playing with the Boys: Why Separate is Not Equal in Sports*. New York: Oxford University Press.
McGovern, Sean. 2004. 'The Ryōan-ji Zen Garden: Textual Meaning in Topographical Form'. *Visual Communication* 3 (3): 344–59.
McGowan, C. and R. Pessanha. 1998. *The Brazilian Sound*. Philadelphia, PA: Temple University Press.
Mead, George H. 1934. *Mind, Self and Society*. Chicago: University of Chicago Press.
Mears, Ashley. 2011. *Pricing Beauty: The Making of a Fashion Model*. Berkeley, CA: University of California Press.
Mennesson, Christine. 2000. 'Hard Women and Soft Women'. *International Review for the Sociology of Sport* 35 (1): 21–33.
———. 2004. 'Être une femme dans un sport masculin'. *Sociétés Contemporaines* 55: 69–90.
Merleau-Ponty, Maurice. 1968. *The Visible and the Invisible*. Evanston: Northwestern University Press.
———. (1962) 2002. *The Phenomenology of Perception*. New York: Routledge.
———. (1948) 2004. *The World of Perception*. London: Routledge.
Messner, Michael. 1988. 'Sports and Male Domination: The Female Athlete as Contested Ideological Terrain'. *Sociology of Sport Journal* 5: 197–211.
———. 1990. 'When Bodies are Weapons: Masculinity and Violence in Sport'. *International Review for the Sociology of Sport* 25: 203–20.
Mills, C. Wright. 1959. *The Sociological Imagination*. Oxford: Oxford University Press.
Mishima, Yukio. (1968) 1970. *Sun and Steel*. New York: Kodansha International.
———. (1968) 1998. *Ken*. New York: Kodansha International.
Moore, Tony. 2004. *Muay Thai: The Essential Guide to Mastering the Art*. New Holland Publishing.
Mouzelis, Nicos. 2004. *Sociological Theory: What Went Wrong? Diagnosis and Remedies*. London: Routledge.
Murphy, John P. 2006. *Music in Brazil*. Oxford: Oxford University Press.
Myles, John F. 2004. 'From Doxa to Experience Issues in Bourdieu's Adoption of Husserlian Phenomenology Theory'. *Culture & Society* 21 (2): 91–107.
Ness, Sally A. 1992. *Body, Movement, and Culture: Kinesthetic and Visual Symbolism in a Philippine Community*. Philadelphia: University of Pennsylvania Press.
Neuman, Joshua. 2005. 'History of the World, Part 2: Jewish Conspiracy Theory: The Satire'. 21 October. *Slate*. Online: http://www.slate.com/id/2128525/ (accessed 20 April 2010).
Ohnuki-Tierney, Emiko. 1994. 'The Power of Absence: Zero Signifiers and their Transgressions'. *L'Homme* 130, 34 (2): 59–76.
O'Neill, E. 2011. 'Ed O'Neill Rolls with Rorion Gracie'. Online: http://www.youtube.com/watch?v=5wVlZX6Bw9E (accessed 11 December 2012).
O'Neill, Terry. 1987. 'Terry O'Neill Interviews Mel Gibson'. *Fighting Arts International* 8 (2): 10–14.
Onishi, Hiroshi. 1993. 'Chinese Lore for Japanese Spaces - Immortals and Sages: Paintings from Ryoanji Temple'. *The Metropolitan Museum of Art Bulletin, New Series* 51 (1): 3–47.
Osella, Caroline and Filippo Osella. 1998. 'Friendship and Flirting: Micropolitics in Kerala, South India. *Journal of the Royal Anthropological Institute* 4 (2): 189–206.

Ostrow, James. 1990. *Social Sensitivity: A Study of Habit and Experience*. New York: State University of New York Press.
Parmigiani, Stefano, Alessandro Bartolomucci, Paola Palanza, Paola Galli, Nicoletta Rizzi, Paul F. Brian and Riccardo Volpi. 2006. 'In Judo, *Randori* (Free Fight) and *Kata* (Highly Ritualized Fight) Differentially Change Plasma Cortisol, Testosterone, and Interleukin Levels in Male Participants'. *Aggressive Behavior* 32 (5): 481–89.
Pauka, Kirstin. 1998. *Theatre and Martial Arts in West Sumatra: Randai and Silek of the Minangkabau*. Athens, OH: Ohio University Press.
Peligro, Kid. 2003. *The Gracie Way: An Illustrated History of the World's Greatest Martial Arts Family*. Montpelier, VT: Invisible Cities Press.
Pitton, Debra, Frank D. Warring, and S. Hunter. 1994. Multicultural Messages: Nonverbal Behaviors in the Classroom (ERIC Document Reproduction Service No. ED362519).
Phemister, Pauline. 2006. *The Rationalists: Descartes, Spinoza and Leibniz*. Cambridge: Polity Press.
Plummer, Ken. 2001. *Documents of Life 2: An Invitation to a Critical Humanism*. London: Sage.
Polly, Matthew. 2007. *American Shaolin: One Man's Quest to Become a Kung Fu Master*. London: Abacus.
Powell, Goran. 2006. *Waking Dragons: A Martial Artist Faces His Ultimate Test*. Chichester: Summerdale.
Qualitative Sociology. 2005. 'Special Issue on Loïc Wacquant's *Body & Soul*'. 28 (2).
Radford, Julie. 2009. 'Word Searches: On the Use of Verbal and Non-Verbal Resources During Classroom Talk'. *Clinical Linguistics & Phonetics* 23 (8): 598–610.
Rappaport, Roy. 1999. *Ritual and Religion in the Making of Humanity*. Cambridge: Cambridge University Press.
Read, Paul. 2010. *The Manual of Bean Curd Boxing: Tai Chi and the Noble Art of Leaving Things Undone*. e-book: Smashwords.com
Rebac, Zoran. 1987. *Thai Boxing Dynamite: The Explosive Art of Muay Thai*. Boulder, CO: Paladin.
Reed-Danahay, Deborah, ed. 1997. *Auto/Ethnography: Rewriting the Self and the Social*. New York: Berg.
_____. 2005. *Locating Bourdieu*. Bloomington: Indiana University Press.
Reis, Andre L. T. 2005. *Capoeira: Health and Social Well-Being*. Brasilia: Thesaurus Editor de Brasilia Ltd.
Rennesson, Stéphane. 2011. 'Thai Boxing: Networking of a Polymorphous Clinch'. In D. S. Farrer and J. Whalen-Bridge (eds), *Martial Arts as Embodied Knowledge*, 145–60. New York: State University of New York Press.
Reynolds, Craig J., ed. 1991. *National Identity and its Defenders: Thailand, 1939–1989*. Chiang Mai: Silkworm Books.
Ribeiro, Saulo. 2008. *Jiu Jitsu University*. California: Victory Belt.
Rivero Herraiz, Antonio and Raúl Sánchez -García. 2011. 'The British Influence in the Birth of Spanish Sport'. *The International Journal of the History of Sport* 28 (13): 1788–1809.
Robbins, Derek. 2007. 'Sociology as Reflexive Science: On Bourdieu's Project'. *Theory, Culture and Society* 24 (5): 77–98.
Rosario, Claudio de Campos, Neil Stephens and Sara Delamont. 2010. 'I'm Your Teacher! I'm Brazilian!' *Sport, Education and Society* 15 (1): 103–20.
Roth, Amanda and Susan A. Basow. 2004. 'Femininity, Sports and Feminism: Developing a Theory of Physical Liberation'. *Journal of Sport and Social Issues* 28: 245–65.
Ryan, Michael, J. 2011. 'I Did Not Return a Master, But Well Cudgeled Was I: The Role of "Body Techniques" in the Transmission of Venezuelan Stick and Machete Fighting'. *Journal of Latin American and Caribbean Anthropology* 16 (1): 1–23.
Ryle, Gilbert. (1949) 2000. *The Concept of Mind*. Chicago: University of Chicago Press.
Said, Edward W. 1978. *Orientalism*. New York: Vintage.
Samudra, Jaida Kim. 2006. 'Body and Belonging in a Transnational Indonesian Silat Community'. PhD diss., Department of Anthropology, University of Hawai at Manoa.
_____. 2008. 'Memory in Our Body: Thick Participation and the Translation of Kinesthetic Experience'. *American Ethnologist* 35 (4): 665–81.

Sánchez García, Raúl. 2006. 'Paradigma cultural y violencia en la sociedad española: el caso de los deporte de combate en la CAM'. Diss. (unpublished). UPM.
———. 2008. 'Análisis etnometodológico sobre el dinamismo del habitus en Bourdieu y Elias dentro del desarrollo de actividades corporales'. *REIS* 124: 209–31.
———. 2009. 'Boxeo y proceso de civilización en la sociedad española'. *Apunts* 96: 5–13.
———. 2011. 'Tactical Dimensions of Kata: Developing Motor Intelligence in Aikido'. Paper presented at the Scientific Congress on Martial Arts and Combat Sports at the Instituto Politécnico de Viseu (Portugal), 13–15 May.
———. 2012. 'Kano's Unintended Consequences: Judo and the Transformation of Japanese Martial Traditions'. Paper presented at the Scientific Congress on Martial Arts and Combat Sports, Genoa, 8–10 June.
Sánchez García, Raúl and Amador González. 2013. 'Cadenas hápticas y metáforas motrices como estrategias didácticas para la enseñanza de habilidades motrices'. *Educación XXI* (under review).
Sánchez García, Raúl and Dominic Malcolm. 2010. 'Decivilizing, Civilizing or Informalizing? The International Development of Mixed Martial Arts'. *International Review for the Sociology of Sport* 45: 39–58.
Sapon-Shevin, Mara. 2009. 'To Touch and Be Touched: The Missing Discourse of Bodies in Education'. In H. S. Shapiro (ed.), *Education and Hope in Troubled Times: Bold Visions of Change For Our Children's World*: 168–83. New York: Routledge.
Sasaki, Ken-ichi. 2011. '"Mind" in Ancient Japanese: The Primitive Perception of its Existence'. *Diogenes* 57 (3): 3–19.
Scambler, Graham and Maggie Jennings. 1998. 'On the Periphery of the Sex Industry: Female Combat, Male Punters, and Feminist Discourse'. *Journal of Sport and Social Issues* 22: 416–30.
Schneider, Sara K. 2010. 'Learning India's Martial Art of Kalarippayattu'. *Journal of Asian Martial Arts* 19 (3): 46–63.
Scheper-Hughes, Nancy and Margaret M. Lock. 1987. 'The Mindful Body: A Prolegomenon to Future Work in Medical Anthropology'. *Medical Anthropology Quarterly* 1 (1): 6–41.
Searle, John R. 1992. *The Rediscovery of the Mind*. Cambridge, MA: MIT Press.
———. 2009. *Making the Social World: The Structure of Human Civilization*. New York: Oxford University Press.
Shapiro, Lawrence. 2011. *Embodied Cognition*. New York: Routledge.
Sheard, Kenneth. G. 1992. 'Boxing in the Civilizing Process'. PhD diss. (unpublished). Cambridge: Anglia Polytechnic University.
———. 1997. 'Aspects of Boxing in the Western "Civilizing Process"'. *International Review for the Sociology of Sport* 32 (1): 31–57.
Sheard, Kenneth G. and Patrick Murphy. 2006. 'Boxing Blind. Unplanned Process in the Development of Modern Boxing'. *Sport in Society* 9 (4): 542–58.
Sheridan, Sam. 2007. *A Fighter's Heart: One Man's Journey Through the World of Fighting*. New York: Grove Press.
Shilling, Chris. 2004. 'Physical Capital and Situated Action: A New Direction for Corporeal Sociology'. *British Journal of Sociology of Education* 25 (4): 473–87.
———. 2008. *Changing Bodies: Habit, Crisis, and Creativity*. Los Angeles: Sage.
Silk, Michael. 2005. 'Sporting Ethnography: Philosophy, Methodology and Reflection'. In David Andrews, Daniel Mason and Michael Silk (eds), *Qualitative Methods in Sports Studies*: 65–103. Oxford: Berg.
Simmel, Georg. 1997. 'Sociology of the Meal'. In D. Frisby (ed.), *Simmel on Culture*. London: Sage.
Skoss, Diane, ed. 1997. *Koryu Bujutsu: Classical Warrior Traditions of Japan (Vol 1)*. New Jersey: Koryu Books.
———. 1999. *Sword and Spirit: Classical Warrior Traditions of Japan (Vol 2)*. New Jersey: Koryu Books.
———. 2002. *Keiko Shokon: Classical Warrior Traditions of Japan (Vol 3)*. New Jersey: Koryu Books.

Slingerland, Edward. 2003. *Effortless Action: Wu-Wei as Conceptual Metaphor and the Spiritual Ideal in Early China*. New York: Oxford University Press.
Soet, John. 2001. *Martial Arts Around the World II*. Burbank, CA: Unique Publications.
Souza, R. 2008. *The Budo Challenge*. Online: http://www.budochallenge.com/ (accessed 7 January 2012).
Sparkes, Andrew C. 2009. 'Ethnography and the Senses: Challenges and Possibilities'. *Qualitative Research in Sport and Exercise* 1 (1): 21–35.
Spencer, Dale. 2009. 'Habit(us), Body Techniques and Body Callusing: An Ethnography of Mixed Martial Arts'. *Body & Society* 15 (4): 119–43.
———. 2011. *Ultimate Fighting and Embodiment: Violence, Gender and Mixed Martial Arts*. New York and London: Routledge.
———. 2012. 'Narratives of Despair and Loss: Pain, Injury and Masculinity in the Sport of Mixed Martial Arts' *Qualitative Research in Sport, Health and Exercise* 4 (1): 117–37.
Stahl, Robert J. 1994. 'Using "Think-Time" and "Wait-Time" Skillfully in the Classroom'. (Report 1994-05-00). In ERIC Clearinghouse for Social Studies/Social Science Education (ERIC Document Reproduction Service No. ED30885).
Standal, Oyvind and Moea Vegard. 2011. 'Merleau-Ponty Meets Kretchmar: Sweet Tensions of Embodied Learning'. *Sport, Ethics and Philosophy* 5 (3): 256–70.
Stephens, Neil. 2007. 'Collecting Data from Elites and Ultra Elites'. *Qualitative Research* 7 (2): 203–16.
Stephens, Neil and Sara Delamont. 2006a. 'Balancing the *Berimbau*'. *Qualitative Inquiry* 12 (2): 316–39.
———. 2006b. 'Samba no mar'. In D. Waskul and P. Vaninni (eds), *Body/Embodiment*, 109–22. Aldershot: Ashgate.
———. 2009. 'They Start to Get *Malicia*'. *British Journal of Sociology of Education* 30 (5): 537–48.
———. 2010a. '"Roda Boa! Roda Boa!" Legitimate Peripheral Participation in Diasporic *Capoeira*'. *Teaching and Teaching Education* 20 (1): 113–18.
———. 2010b. 'Vin de Bahia pra lhe ver'. In B. Fincham, M. McGuiness and L. Murray (eds), *Mobile Methodologies*, 85–102. London: Palgrave.
———. 2013. 'I Can See It in the Nightclub'. *Sociological Review* (forthcoming).
Stevens, John. 2001. *The Sword of No Sword: Life of the Master Warrior Tesshu*. Boston, MA: Shambala Press.
Stewart, John, Oliver Gapenne and Ezequiel A. Di Paolo (eds). 2010. *Enaction: Toward a New Paradigm for Cognitive Science*. Cambridge, MA: MIT Press.
Stoller, Paul. 2005. 'The Presence of the Ethnographic Present: Comments on Loïc Wacquant's Body and Soul'. *Qualitative Sociology* 28 (2): 197–99.
Stones, Rob. 2005. *Structuration Theory*. London: Palgrave MacMillan.
Suaud, Charles. 1978. *La vocation: Conversion et reconversion des prêtres ruraux*. Paris: Minuit.
Sudnow, David. 2001. *Ways of the Hand: A Rewritten Approach*. Cambridge, MA: MIT Press.
Sugden, John. 1996. *Boxing and Society: An International Analysis*. Manchester: Manchester University Press.
Swedenburg, Ted. 1997. 'Islam in the Mix: Lessons of the Five Percent'. Paper presented at the Anthropology Colloquium. University of Arkansas. Online: http://comp.uark.edu/~tsweden/5per.html (accessed 12 March 2012).
Tan, Kevin. 2008. 'Peaceful Warriors: Bodies of Culture, History and Power in the Practice of Aikido in Canada'. PhD diss. (unpublished). University of Alberta.
Teixeira Reis and L. André. 2005. *Capoeira: Health and Social Well-being*. Brasilia: Thesaurus.
Theberge, Nancy. 2000. 'Gender and Sport'. In Jay Coakley and Eric Dunning (eds), *Handbook of Sports Studies*: 322–33. London: Sage.
Thelen, Esther and Linda Smith. 2006. 'Dynamic Systems Theory'. In William Damon and Richard M. Lerner (eds), *Handbook of Child Psychology, Volume: Theoretical Models of Human Development*, 258–312. Oxford: Wiley.
Theory & Psychology. 2009. 'Special Section on Habitus in the Work of Loïc Wacquant'. 19 (6).

Thompson, Robert F. 1990. 'Kongo Influences on African American Artistic Culture'. In Joseph E. Holloway (ed.), *Africanisms in American Culture*, 283–325. Bloomington: Indiana University Press.
Throop, Jason and Keith M. Murphy. 2002. 'Bourdieu and Phenomenology'. *Anthropological Theory* 2 (2): 185–201.
Tincani, Matt and Shannon Crozier. 2007. 'Comparing Brief and Extended Wait-Time During Small Group Instruction for Children with Challenging Behavior'. *Journal of Behavioral Education* 16: 355–67.
Travassos, S. 1999. Mandinga. *Estudos Afro-Asiaticos* 35: 67–79.
Turner, Bryan S. 1988. *Status*. Milton Keynes: Open University Press.
———. 1992. *Regulating Bodies*. London: Routledge.
———. 1995. *Medical Power and Social Knowledge*. London: Sage.
Twigger, Robert. 1999. *Angry White Pyjamas*. London: Orion.
Urry, John. 2007. *Mobilities*. Cambridge: Polity Press.
Varela, Francisco, Evan Thompson and Eleanor Rosch 1991. *The Embodied Mind*. Cambridge, MA: MIT Press.
Verter, Bradford. 2003. 'Spiritual Capital: Theorizing Religion with Bourdieu against Bourdieu'. *Sociological Theory* 21 (2): 150–74.
Vianna, Hermano. 1999. *The Mystery of Samba*. Chapel Hill, NC: University of North Carolina Press.
Vieira, A. L. B. M. 2004. 'Capoeira and the Game of Life'. Lisbon: privately printed pamphlet.
Villamon, Miguel, David Brown, Julián Espartero and Carlos Gutiérrez. 2004. 'Reflexive Modernization and the Disembedding of Judo from 1946 to the 2000 Sydney Olympics'. *International Review for the Sociology of Sport* 39 (2): 139–56.
Wachs, Faye L. 2002. 'Levelling the Playing Field: Negotiating Gendered Rules in Coed Softball'. *Journal of Sport and Social Issues* 26: 300–16.
Wacquant, Loïc. 1985. *L'École inégale. Éléments de sociologie de l'enseignement en Nouvelle-Calédonie*. Paris and Nouméa: Editions de l'ORSTOM with the Institut Culturel Mélanésien.
———. 1989. 'Corps et âme: notes ethnographiques d'un apprenti-boxeur'. *Actes de la recherche en sciences sociales* 80: 33–67.
———. 1992. 'The Social Logic of Boxing in Black Chicago: Towards a Sociology of Pugilism'. *Sociology of Sport Journal* 9: 221–54.
———. 1995a. 'The Pugilistic Point of View: How Boxers Think and Feel About Their Trade'. *Theory & Society* 24 (4): 489–535.
———. 1995b. 'Pugs at Work: Bodily Capital and Bodily Labor Among Professional Boxers'. *Body & Society* 1 (1): 65–94.
———. 1995c. 'Protection, discipline et honneur: une salle de boxe dans le ghetto américain'. *Sociologie et sociétés* 27 (1): 75–89.
———. 1996a. 'L' "underclass" urbaine dans l'imaginaire social et scientifique américain'. In Serge Paugam (ed.), *L'Exclusion: l'état des savoirs*, 248–62. Paris: Editions La Découverte.
———. 1996b 'From Charisma to Persona: On Boxing and Social Being'. In *The Charisma of Sport and Race*, 21–37. Berkeley: Doreen B. Townsend Center for the Humanities, Occasional Papers, n. 8 (including a debate with Gerald Early).
———. 1997. 'Three Pernicious Premises in the Study of the American Ghetto'. *International Journal of Urban and Regional Research* 21 (2): 341–53.
———. (1992) 1998a. 'Inside the Zone: The Social Art of the Hustler in the Black American Ghetto'. *Theory, Culture & Society* 15 (2): 1–36.
———. 1998b. 'The Prizefighter's Three Bodies'. *Ethnos: Journal of Anthropology* 63 (3): 325–52.
———. 1998c. 'A Fleshpeddler at Work: Power, Pain, and Profit in the Prizefighting Economy'. *Theory & Society* 27 (1): 1–42.
———. 1998d. 'Sacrifice.' In Gerald Early (ed.), *Body Language: Graywolf Forum Two*, 47–59. St Paul, MN: Graywolf Press.
———. 2001. 'Whores, Slaves, and Stallions: Languages of Exploitation and Accomodation Among Professional Fighters'. *Body & Society* 7 (2/3) (special issue on 'Commodifying Bodies'): 181–94.

———. 2002a. 'Taking Bourdieu into the Field'. *Berkeley Journal of Sociology* 46: 180–86.
———. 2002b. 'Scrutinizing the Street: Poverty, Morality, and the Pitfalls of Urban Ethnography'. *American Journal of Sociology* 107 (6): 1468–1532.
———. 2004a. *Body and Soul: Notebooks of an Apprentice Boxer*. New York: Oxford University Press.
———. 2004b. 'Decivilizing and Demonizing: The Remaking of the Black American Ghetto'. In *The Sociology of Norbert Elias*, edited by S. Loyal and S. Quilley. Cambridge: Cambridge University Press. 95–121.
———. 2004c. 'Following Pierre Bourdieu into the Field'. *Ethnography* 5 (4): 387–414.
———. 2004d. 'Habitus'. In J. Beckert and M. Zafirovski (eds), *International Encyclopedia of Economic Sociology*, 315–19. London: Routledge.
———. 2005a. 'Carnal Connections: On Embodiment, Membership and Apprenticeship'. *Qualitative Sociology* 28 (4): 445–74.
———. 2005b. 'Pointers on Pierre Bourdieu and Democratic Politics'. In Loïc Wacquant (ed.), *Pierre Bourdieu and Democratic Politics*, 10–28. Cambridge: Polity Press.
———. 2005c. 'Shadowboxing with Ethnographic Ghosts: A Rejoinder,' *Symbolic Interaction* 28 (3): 441–47.
———. 2007a. 'Busy Louie in the Ring: A Sociologist Among Prizefighters.' In Michael Berkowitz and Ruti Ungar (eds), *Fighting Back? Jewish and Black Boxers in Britain*, 106–13. London: University College of London.
———. 2007b. 'Decivilizing the Penal State'. Keynote address to the International Conference on Civilizing and Decivilizing Processes, Institut für England- und Amerikastudien, Johann Wolfgang Goethe-Universität, Frankfurt am Main, 22 November.
———. 2008. *Urban Outcasts: A Comparative Sociology of Advanced Marginality*. Cambridge: Polity Press.
———. 2009a. 'Chicago Fade: Putting the Researcher's Body Back into Play'. *City* 13–14: 510–16.
———. 2009b. 'The Body, the Ghetto and the Penal State'. With a prefatory article by Black Hawk Hancock, 'Following Loïc Wacquant into the Field'. *Qualitative Sociology* 32 (1): 101–29.
———. 2010. 'Jack London en ethnologue amateur du pugilisme'. Preface to Jack London, *Un Steak*. Paris: Libertalia.
———. 2011. 'Habitus as Topic and Tool: Reflections on Becoming a Prizefighter'. *Qualitative Research in Psychology* 8: 81–92.
———. 2013. 'Marginalité, ethnicité, pénalité dans la ville néolibérale: une cartographie analytique'. *Revue de l'Institut de sociologie*, forthcoming.
Wade, Lisa. 2011. 'The Emancipator Promise of the Habitus: Lindy Hop, the Body, and Social Change'. *Ethnography* 12 (2): 224–46.
Wainwright, Steven, Clare Williams and Bryan Turner. 2006. 'Varieties of Habitus and the Embodiment of Ballet'. *Qualitative Research* 6 (4): 535–58.
Walford, Geoffrey. 2009. 'The Practice of Writing Ethnographic Fieldnotes'. *Ethnography and Education* 4 (2): 117–30.
Warde, Alan. 2005. 'Consumption and Theories of Practice'. *Journal of Consumer Culture* 5 (2): 131–53.
Waskul, Dennis and Vannini, Philip (eds). 2006. *Body/Embodiment*. Aldershot: Ashgate.
Weiner, B. 1990. 'History of Motivational Research in Education'. *Journal of Educational Psychology* 82 (4): 616–22.
Williams, Mark A. and David Elliot. 1999. 'Anxiety, Expertise and Visual Search Strategy in Karate'. *Journal of Sport & Exercise Psychology* 21: 362–75.
Willson, Margaret. 2010. *Dance Lest We All Fall Down*. Seattle: University of Washington Press.
Wilson, Lee. 2009. 'Jurus, Jazz Riffs and the Constitution of a National Martial Art in Indonesia'. *Body & Society* 15 (3): 93–119.
Wilson, William Julius. 1978. *The Declining Significance of Race: Blacks and Changing American Institutions*. Chicago: University of Chicago Press.

———. 1987. *The Truly Disadvantaged: The Inner City, the Underclass, and Public Policy*. Chicago: University of Chicago Press.

Wolf, T. 2005. *The Bartitsu Compendium, Volume I: History and Canonical Syllabus*. Raleigh, NC: Lulu.

Woodward, Kath. 2008. 'Hanging out and Hanging About: Insider/Outsider Research in the Sport of Boxing'. *Ethnography* 9: 536–56.

Woo-Ping, Yuen. 1978. *Drunk Monkey in the Tiger's Eye* (also released as *Drunken Master*). Hong Kong: Seasonal Film Corporation.

Wright, Tom and Katsuhiko Mizuno. 2008. *Zen Gardens – Kyoto's Nature Enclosed*. Suiko Books.

Wulff, Helena. 2008. 'Ethereal Expression'. *Ethnography* 9 (4): 518–36.

Wyrod, Robert (1999/2000) 'Warriors of the South Side: Race and the Body in the Martial Arts of Black Chicago'. *Berkeley Journal of Sociology* 44: 126–50.

Yuasa, Yasuo. 1987. *The Body – Towards a Mind-Body Theory*, edited by T. P. Kasulis and translated by Nagatomo Shigenori and T. P. Kasulis. Albany, NY: State University of New York Press.

Zarrilli, Philip. 2000. *When the Body Becomes All Eyes: Paradigms, Practices, and Discourses of Power in Kalarippayattu, a South Indian Martial Art*. New Dheli: Oxford University Press.

———. 2005. '"*Kalarippayattu* is Eighty Percent Mental and Only the Remainder is Physical": Power, Agency and Self in a South Asian Martial Art'. In James H. Mills (ed.), *Subaltern Sports: Politics and Sport in South Asia*, 19–46. London: Anthem Press.

Zetaruk, M. N., M. A. Violan, D. Zurakowski and L. J. Micheli. 2005. 'Injuries in Martial Arts: A Comparison of Five Styles'. *British Journal of Sports Medicine* 39: 29–33.

Zivin, G., N. Hassan, G. DePaula, D. Monti, C. Harlan, K. Hossain and K. Patterson. 2001. 'An Effective Approach to Violence Prevention: Traditional Martial Arts in Middle School'. *Adolescence* 36 (143): 443–59.

www.ingramcontent.com/pod-product-compliance
Lightning Source LLC
Chambersburg PA
CBHW021825300426
44114CB00009BA/333